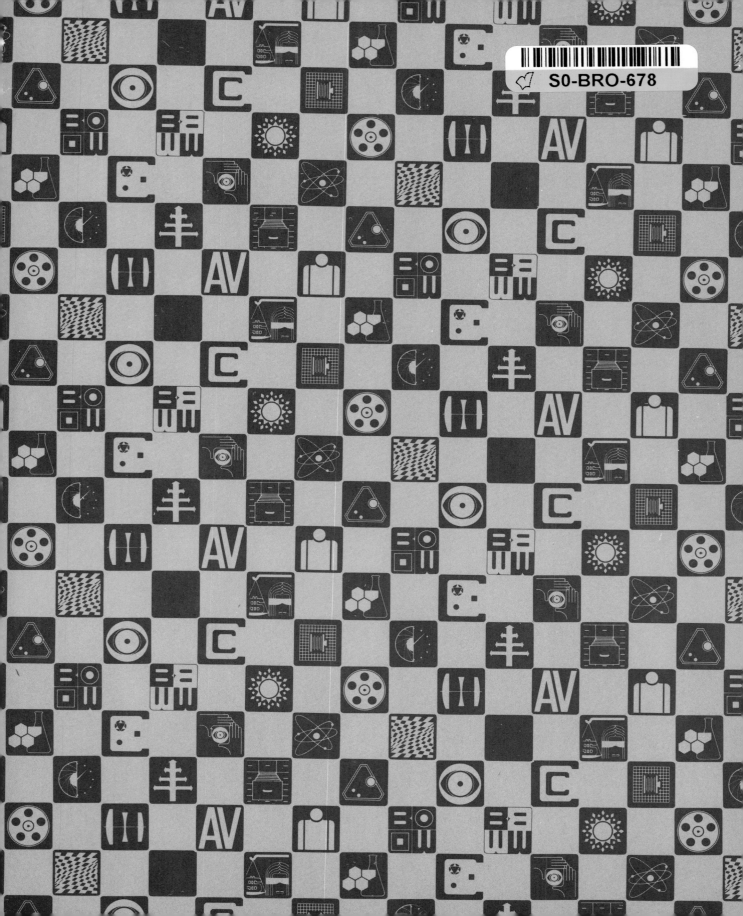

Encyclopedia
of **Practical**
Photography

Volume **11**

Pap-Proc

Edited by and published for
EASTMAN KODAK COMPANY

AMPHOTO
American Photographic Book Publishing Company
Garden City, New York

Note on Photography

The cover photos and the photos of letters that appear elsewhere in this encyclopedia were taken by Chris Maggio.

Library of Congress Cataloging in Publication Data

Amphoto, New York.
    Encyclopedia of practical photography.

    Includes bibliographical references and index.
    1. Photography—Dictionaries. I. Eastman
Kodak Company. II. Title.
TR9.T34   770'.3   77–22562

ISBN 0–8174–3050–4 Trade Edition—Whole Set
ISBN 0–8174–3200–0 Library Edition—Whole Set
ISBN 0–8174–3061–X Trade Edition—Volume 11
ISBN 0–8174–3211–6 Library Edition—Volume 11

Manufactured in the United States of America

Editorial Board

The *Encyclopedia of Practical Photography* was compiled and edited jointly by Eastman Kodak Company and American Photographic Book Publishing Co., Inc. (Amphoto). The comprehensive archives, vast resources, and technical staffs of both companies, as well as the published works of Kodak, were used as the basis for most of the information contained in this encyclopedia.

Symbol Identification

 Audiovisual

 Color Processing and Printing

 Picture-Making Techniques

 Biography

 Equipment and Facilities

 Scientific Photography

 Black-and-White Materials

 Exposure

 Special Effects and Techniques

 Black-and-White Processing and Printing

 History

Special Interests

 Business and Legal Aspects

 Lighting

 Storage and Care

 Chemicals

 Motion Picture

 Theory of Photography

 Color Materials

 Optics

 Vision

Guide for the Reader

Use this encyclopedia as you would any good encyclopedia or dictionary. Look for the subject desired as it first occurs to you—most often you will locate it immediately. The shorter articles begin with a dictionary-style definition, and the longer articles begin with a short paragraph that summarizes the article that follows. Either of these should tell you if the information you need is in the article. The longer articles are then broken down by series of headings and sub-headings to aid further in locating specific information.

Cross References

If you do not find the specific information you are seeking in the article first consulted, use the cross references (within the article and at the end of it) to lead you to more information. The cross references can lead you from a general article to the more detailed articles into which the subject is divided. Cross references are printed in capital letters so that you can easily recognize them.

Example: *See also:* ZONE SYSTEM.

Index

If the initial article you turn to does not supply you with the information you seek, and the cross references do not lead you to it, use the index in the last volume. The index contains thousands of entries to help you identify and locate any subject you seek.

Symbols

To further aid you in locating information, the articles throughout have been organized into major photographic categories. Each category is represented by a symbol displayed on the opposite page. By using only the symbols, you can scan each volume and locate all the information under any of the general categories. Thus, if you wish to read all about lighting, simply locate the lighting symbols and read the articles under them.

Reading Lists

Most of the longer articles are followed by reading lists citing useful sources for further information. Should you require additional sources, check the cross-referenced articles for additional reading lists.

Metric Measurement

Both the U.S. Customary System of measurement and the International System (SI) are used throughout this encyclopedia. In most cases, the metric measurement is given first with the U.S. customary equivalent following in parenthesis. When equivalent measurements are given, they will be rounded off to the nearest whole unit or a tenth of a unit, unless precise measurement is important. When a measurement is considered a "standard," equivalents will not be given. For example: 35 mm film, 200 mm lens, 4″ × 5″ negative, and 8″ × 10″ prints will not be given with their customary or metric equivalents.

How Articles are Alphabetized

Article titles are alphabetized by letter sequence, with word breaks and hyphens not considered. Example:

> Archer, Frederick Scott
> Architectural Photography
> Archival Processing
> Arc Lamps

Abbreviations are alphabetized according to the letters of the abbreviations, not by the words the letters stand for. Example:

> Artificial Light
> ASA Speed

Contents
Volume 11

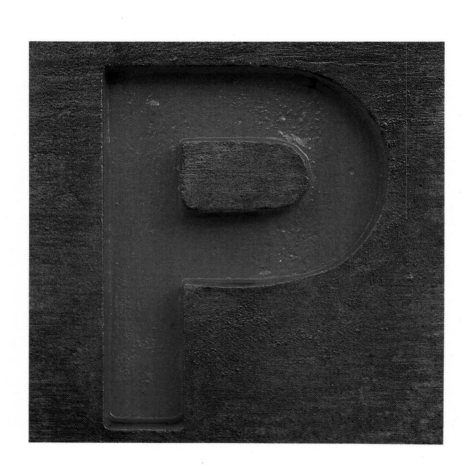

Paper Negative

In the early days of photography, before glass plates and films were invented, some photographers made their photographs on sensitized paper. When the photographs were processed, they had paper negatives that they contact-printed to obtain paper positive prints.

A characteristic of prints made from paper negatives is that the texture of the paper prints along with the image. To minimize this texture, early users would wax or oil the paper, a practice that was only partially successful. Paper-negative prints were most satisfactory when they were fairly large, so that the paper texture did not interfere too severely with the picture detail. Even so, they were best when the picture subject relied more on broad effects rather than fine detail.

Paper negatives and prints from them can be easily made today. Usually the paper negatives are not made in a camera, however. Rather, they are made in a darkroom from film negatives or from color transparencies.

One big advantage to paper negatives, in addition to the soft graphic effects resulting from the texture, is that they are fairly easy to retouch, so they are a good medium to use when objects have to be removed from the picture, or when other major retouching is required.

Paper for Paper Negatives

To keep the paper texture to a reasonable minimum, a thin-base paper is desirable. Furthermore, it should have a smooth surface that takes pencil easily, and should not have the paper manufacturer's name printed on the back of the paper base, lest it appear in the final print.

Three papers that are available at the time of this writing, and that meet the requirements for paper negatives, are Kodabromide paper, A surface, Kodak Polycontrast paper, A surface, and Kodak Azo paper, A surface. The first two are enlarging-speed papers, while the last one is a contact-speed paper. There are uses for both. Kodabromide and Azo papers are graded contrast papers, while Polycontrast paper is a selective-contrast paper.

The A surface is a smooth, lustre surface with some tooth in it so that it can be retouched easily with pencil.

If your originals are color slides, you will make your paper negatives by enlargement, so choose a paper of that speed. If you start with film negatives, make enlarged, final-size film diapositives (intermediate positives), and contact-print the positives to make the paper negatives, you can use a contact-speed paper or, with reduced illumination, an enlarging-speed paper.

Water-resistant papers are not very satisfactory for paper-negative work because the paper back does not take retouching easily.

Making Positives from Negatives

When your original is a negative, the first step is to make an intermediate positive, or diapositive. The diapositives can be made on film or on paper. Film has the advantage that it can be made relatively small or large, because it can be enlarged or contact-printed to make the paper negative. A paper positive must be contact-printed.

Final prints will show the additional texture of the positive if paper is used, while the final prints made with film diapositives will show only the paper texture of the paper negatives. If major retouching is required, a paper diapositive is likely to be easier to work with.

A common approach is to enlarge the negative up to an intermediate size on film—the largest size that will fit your enlarger. Dye and pencil retouching can be done on this diapositive, which is then enlarged to the final-size paper negative on which more retouching can be done.

Retouching in two stages is convenient. Adding density on the positive will result in darker tones in the print, while adding density on the negative results in lighter tones in the print. Thus, there is no need to reduce density by brief wash or reducers.

If the diapositive is to be paper, the same paper is used as for the paper negative. If film is to be used for the positive, almost any continuous-tone sheet film can be used. If the original is a black-and-white negative, moderate-speed blue-sensitive or orthochromatic film that can be handled under a red safelight is convenient. Kodak commercial film is a good choice. When the origi-

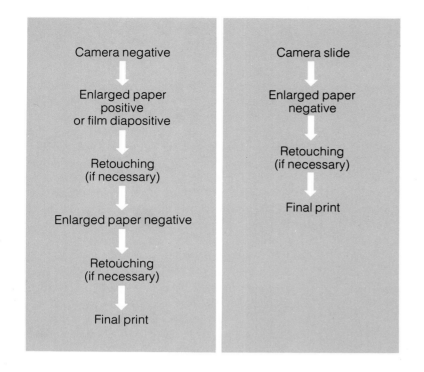

Camera negative

⬇

Enlarged paper positive
or film diapositive

⬇

Retouching
(if necessary)

⬇

Enlarged paper negative

⬇

Retouching
(if necessary)

⬇

Final print

Camera slide

⬇

Enlarged paper negative

⬇

Retouching
(if necessary)

⬇

Final print

When making a paper negative from a camera negative, an enlarged paper positive, or film diapositive, must be made first. With a camera slide, a paper negative can be made directly.

nal is a color negative, better tone reproduction of colors will result if a panchromatic film is used. Kodak Super-XX film has good reproduction characteristics for this use. Both commercial and Super-XX films come in sizes up to 11″ × 14″

Making a Film Diapositive

A diapositive can be made just like an enlargement. Cropping and dodging are both done when necessary.

Exposure and development should be such that the first positive looks dark, even in the highlights, and has low contrast. It should be judged by transmitted light. Every step in the process tends to pick up contrast, so it is important to keep the contrast low in the diapositive.

With an orthochromatic film, a red safelight can be used, but panchromatic film must be handled in complete darkness. Stopping, fixing, washing, and drying are the same as with any sheet film.

The film positive can be retouched with dyes and pencil. Red retouching dye shows where the dye is, but you must learn how much dye results in how much change in density in the later paper negative. The effect of neutral dyes is much easier to judge. Any pencil retouching must be done after the dye work is finished and thoroughly dry.

Making a Paper Diapositive from Negatives

Paper diapositives are made just like regular enlargements, except that they must have lower contrast and higher densities. Even the highlights should look fairly dark when the print is viewed by reflection. On an illuminator, there should be good separation in both highlight and shadow regions, but overall low contrast. The contrast of selective-contrast papers can be changed by using filters. If you have difficulty getting the contrast low enough even with a PC1 filter, you can try two PC1 filters, which will lower the contrast even more.

WARNING: Some batches of paper may show a mottling effect from the use of a double PC1 filter.

The paper is processed in the same manner as any enlargement.

Above: (Left) A straight print made from the original negative. The photographer enlarged the original negative onto a sheet of film that was the same size as the final print. Some film can be re-touched, using a pencil for fine detail and a chamois stamp (available from art-sup-ply stores), rubbed in black chalk, for the large areas. Or, a piece of matte acetate can be taped to the film to receive the retouching. (Center) The film positive was contact-printed onto a sheet of sin-gle-weight paper to produce the paper negative. (Right) Extensive retouching with black chalk and pencil was done on the back of the paper negative. Clouds were added to the sky, and density to the house and road. When the retouching was complete, the photographer made contact prints by using a printing frame. The finished print is shown at left.

Paper positives can be retouched using pencil and powdered charcoal dust, which is made by scraping a soft pencil lead with a knife or sandpaper. Balls of cotton, cotton swabs, and various sizes of artists' stumps can be used to apply the powdered charcoal dust. This is used to darken broad areas in the paper diapositives.

If the original is a color negative, the tonal reproduction of colors in the final print will show darkening of the warm colors and lightening of the cool colors, as compared to a panchromatic rendition. The contrast in various areas may vary somewhat, because the color negative acts like a variable Polycontrast filter. In general, it is better to use a panchromatic film for the diapositives of color negatives.

Making the Paper Negative

The paper negative should have the same tone contrast and density characteristics as the paper positive—low contrast and high density. It can be enlarged from similar-size film diapositives, or contact-printed from full-size film or paper diapositives. It is processed like a standard enlargement. When dry, the paper negative can be retouched using the same materials used to retouch paper positives.

To minimize the paper texture, flash the paper through the paper base just prior to the image exposure. You will have to experiment to find the amount of flashing that is enough to lower the texture effect, but not enough to affect the negative image. An adequate amount will have been achieved when the negative image (when processed) shows paper texture superimposed over the image, but without significantly affecting contrast or density of the image.

Paper negatives can be made directly from color transparencies. Transparencies have much brighter contrast than diapositives, so it is very difficult to keep the contrast low enough in paper negatives made directly from transparencies. Masking the transparencies is the best way to lower the contrast. However, if the lowest-contrast paper is used (such as Polycontrast paper with two PC1 filters), and if the highlights are held back and shadow areas printed in, successful paper negatives can be made without masking. An alternate route is to make an intermediate negative on a continuous-tone film, such as Super-XX film, and develop to a low-contrast index. This additional step has the advantage of giving better gray-tone rendering of colors, because the film is panchromatic while the paper is not.

Printing the Paper Negative

Nearly any photographic paper can be used to make the final prints from a paper negative. Glossy papers are rarely used. Smooth, lustre-surface papers emphasize the paper-negative texture, while rough or tapestry surfaces tend to minimize it.

When the negative is contact-printed with its emulsion side toward the emulsion of the paper, maximum detail is obtained in the print. If a softer image is desired to subdue detail, the paper negative can be printed with its paper-base side against the paper emulsion. This procedure emphasizes the paper texture. The prints from paper negatives are processed in the usual manner.

Contact-Printing Equipment

Because of the broad treatment of detail, the paper-negative procedure is usually used to make fairly large-size prints.

Large-size contact printers are made for graphic-arts and drawing-reproduction uses, but are quite costly for the home darkroom.

The enlarger can be used for a light source, and an improvised contact-printer can be made on the enlarger easel. Use a flat piece of ¾-inch plywood for the base, several inches larger each way than the print size. Cover this with a relatively thin (approximately 1 cm [½ inch] thick) piece of soft, plastic-foam material. Get a piece of heavy plate glass (½ inch thick) about an inch larger each way than the print size. The paper to be printed goes on the foam with the emulsion side up, and the paper negative goes on top of this, emulsion side either way (see the preceding section on printing the paper negative). Carefully place the plate glass on top of the paper negative to hold it in contact with the paper. Expose with the enlarger light. Reasonable printing times are obtained with this procedure when enlarging papers are being used.

• *See also:* CALOTYPE; CONTACT PRINTING; RETOUCHING.

Papers, Photographic

Photographic papers differ widely in their characteristics, but basically they consist of a light-sensitive coating on a paper support. The coating, called the emulsion, consists of a suspension of silver-halide salts in gelatin. The chemical composition of the silver salt, the method of its formation, and the addition of special agents determine such characteristics as speed, color sensitivity, contrast, and image tone. Modern papers are made in different surfaces, base tints, and base weights to suit various applications, as well as to enhance the artistic presentation of the photograph. In addition, emulsions are designed for various processing methods.

Photographic Characteristics

Emulsion Speed. Photographic papers vary widely in speed, or sensitivity to light, according to the particular use of the material. Papers for contact printing are slow and cannot be used for enlarging on ordinary equipment. Enlarging (or projection) papers vary considerably in speed. Fast enlarging papers are used when short exposures are needed in high-volume production. They are also useful in making big enlargements from small negatives or when negatives are so dense that exposure would be too long on a slower material.

The contrast of an emulsion also affects printing speed. For a given paper, the higher the contrast grade, the slower the speed. Single-contrast-grade papers have a single printing speed. These include some black-and-white portrait papers, those with panchromatic emulsions, and color printing papers.

ASAP Speeds. Some manufacturers determine black-and-white paper speeds in accordance with the latest procedure specified by the American National Standards Institute (ANSI), PH2.2. This standard method provides a simple way to express paper speed with just one number. Paper speeds determined by this method are preceded by the initials ASAP (American Standards Association Paper). Speeds of paper processed by activation or stabilization procedures are not ASAP speed, and are labeled "effective paper speeds."

The ASAP speed numbers indicate the relative speed of different papers. The series of ASAP speed numbers is as follows:

1, 1.2, 1.6, 2, 2.5, 3, 4, 5, 6, 8, 10, 12, 16, 20, 25, 32, 40, 50, 63, 80, 100, 125, 160, 200, 250, 320, 400, 500, 630, 800, and 1000.

In this series, the difference between any two consecutive numbers represents an exposure change of ⅓ f-number. Thus, if the speed difference between two papers is three intervals—for example, from 25 to 50—the exposure difference is one stop. (The speed numbers for films and papers are measured with reference to different points on the D-log H curves; consequently, there is no direct relationship between paper-speed numbers and film-speed numbers.)

Paper-speed numbers are useful in photographic printing for assessing approximate exposures when you change from one kind of paper to another, or from one contrast grade of paper to another. For example, if the exposure for a certain negative printed on Kodabromide paper, grade no. 3 is known, the approximate exposure for another grade can be calculated. Just multiply the known exposure by the speed number of the paper used, and then divide the result by the speed number for the paper you wish to use.

The speed numbers given in paper data sheets are for the average product. Exposures calculated by means of these numbers may not be exactly correct, because exposure in printing is critical, and because aging or adverse storage conditions may alter the speed of an emulsion. Further, the subjective nature of print density may require that more or less exposure be given to obtain a desired effect. Consequently, speed numbers are intended to provide a starting point in determining correct exposure, and a basis for comparing the relative speeds of different papers.

The ASAP speeds are determined with tray development in a specified developer very similar to Kodak Dektol developer. When prints are developed in other developers, a speed change can be expected. The speeds given for papers when machine processed are not ASAP speeds, but are calculated in the same manner and compare with the speeds given for papers when processed in the standard developer.

Once you have found the actual speed of a box of paper, the time determinations for the remaining sheets in the box should remain fairly constant if the paper is properly stored.

Exposure and Development Latitude

The degree of latitude possessed by a paper is the amount by which you can deviate from the ideal exposure and development without an appreciable loss of print quality. Since it is not possible to judge exposures accurately all the time, some latitude is necessary for the sake of economy.

Development Latitude. Papers that do not change appreciably in contrast and image tone with reasonable variations in development are said to have good development latitude. However, for best quality, the developing time should be as near as possible to that recommended for the paper.

Exposure Latitude. Photographic papers generally do not have wide exposure latitude. In fact, print exposure is critical. Even small errors readily affect print quality. This is particularly true of contrasty papers, such as No. 4 and No. 5. For this reason, always aim to make negatives that print well on a less contrasty paper, such as No. 2. Panchromatic black-and-white and color papers have essentially no exposure or processing latitude when normal, high-quality prints are desired.

Color Sensitivity

Black-and-white papers are usually coated with emulsions sensitive to the ultraviolet, violet, and blue parts of the spectrum. A number of modern papers, however, have some sensitivity to green. Selective-(multiple- or variable-) contrast papers have two emulsion components—a high-contrast, blue-sensitive component, and a low-contrast, green-sensitive component. Contrast is varied by printing through filters that control the amount of exposure affecting each layer.

The increasing use of color negatives has resulted in the production of black-and-white papers with panchromatic emulsions. These papers make it possible to obtain prints from a color negative that translate all colors into equivalent shades of gray with great fidelity. A print on a blue- (or blue-green) sensitive emulsion renders reds and some greens that are far darker than normal.

Color-printing papers have three emulsion layers that are individually sensitive to red, green, and blue light. The dyes in the color slide or negative being printed, and the color filtration used for the printing light, control the exposure of each layer.

Since the safelight that should be used with any photographic material depends on color sensitivity, as well as on emulsion speed, always use the safelight filter recommended in the data sheet for a particular paper. Improper safelighting leads to unwanted variations in print contrast caused by safelight fog. For an explanation of this effect, see the article SAFELIGHTS.

Contrast of Papers

In black-and-white printing it is often necessary to adjust the contrast of prints so that they yield a natural-seeming result from negatives that have a density range that is either too high or too low. Also, the photographer may wish to create special effects by increasing or decreasing the natural contrast of the subjects.

Consequently, photographic papers are made in different degrees of contrast. Some papers are available in several contrasts or grades. Others have built-in contrast control, which is effected by the use of filters over the enlarger lens or over the printing light source. These are known as selective-contrast papers. Still other papers are made in one contrast grade only; these are used primarily in applications, such as portraiture, where negative quality is readily controllable by setting up standard lighting and processing conditions.

Selective-Contrast Papers. The contrast of most modern photographic papers can be changed only within narrow limits by increasing or decreasing development, or by the use of various developers. Selective-contrast papers, however, are designed so that contrast can be varied by using suitable filters during enlarging.

The contrast range available with Kodak selective-contrast papers is equal to about four contrast grades of ordinary papers, that is, from grade no. 1 through grade no. 4. One advantage in using these papers is that they provide degrees of contrast halfway between the normal contrast spacings.

Thus, seven degrees of contrast in half-grade steps are available when most Kodak selective-contrast papers are used in conjunction with Kodak Polycontrast filters.

Selective-contrast papers are particularly useful in reducing the amount of paper that must be kept in stock. One box of paper provides all the different contrasts needed to print all but the most difficult negatives. Thus, the need for buying and storing several grades of paper is eliminated, and the possibility of seldom-used grades deteriorating with age does not arise.

Graded-Contrast Papers. Although selective-contrast papers offer many advantages, papers that come in different contrast grades are preferred by many photographers. There is a wider selection of surfaces, image tones, weights, and sizes available in graded-contrast papers.

Contrast grades may be specified by a name or by a number. A single manufacturer may use the name-contrast method for some products and the number-contrast method for others. In addition, there is no definite correlation between the contrast characteristics of the products of different manufacturers, even though the grade name or number may be the same. The accompanying table lists the names and numbers used for Kodak black-and-white papers. A method for matching the contrast responses of papers from different manufacturers is described in the article GRAY SCALES.

Physical Characteristics

Photographic papers consist of one or more emulsion layers on a paper base. As the accompanying diagrams show, the construction of a paper is related to the kind of processing for which it is designed. In order to provide a uniform white (or tint) background, conventional- (fiber) base papers have a baryta coating between the base and the emulsion. (*See:* BARIUM SULFATE.) Water-resistant or resin-coated papers have pigments included in the upper resin layer.

Paper Base. The paper base, or support, used in the manufacture of high-quality photographic paper must be free from substances that might affect the unprocessed emulsion or the silver image after processing. Also, the characteristics of the paper must be compatible with coatings placed upon it. The fibrous structure of the paper must be able to withstand immersion in the various processing solutions, as well as prolonged washing after processing. Clearly, these are stringent requirements for a material such as paper.

At one time, only paper made from cotton rags could meet the above specifications. Today, practically all photographic paper base is manufactured from a combination of different wood pulps that have the purity and strength necessary for high-grade paper bases.

Base Weights. The weight of a paper refers to its thickness. Kodak papers are classified as

CONTRAST GRADES BY NAME AND NUMBER

Contrast Categories of Name-Grade Papers	Contrast Categories of Number-Grade Papers	Description
Soft	1	Yields normal prints from high-contrast negatives where density scale is long or subject contrast is high.
Medium	2	Gives normal prints from normal-contrast negatives where density scale and subject contrast are average.
Hard	3	Produces normal prints from low-contrast negatives with short density scale, or subjects requiring slightly more tonal separation in the print.
Hard	4	Provides normal prints from very low-contrast negatives where extra contrast is needed for separation of tones.
Extra hard	5	Delivers normal prints from extremely low-contrast negatives where the negative density scale is very short.
Ultra hard	—	Delivers acceptable prints from ultra low-contrast negatives. Or, this grade can be used for line copy and special effects where compressed midtones are wanted.

Construction of Photographic Papers

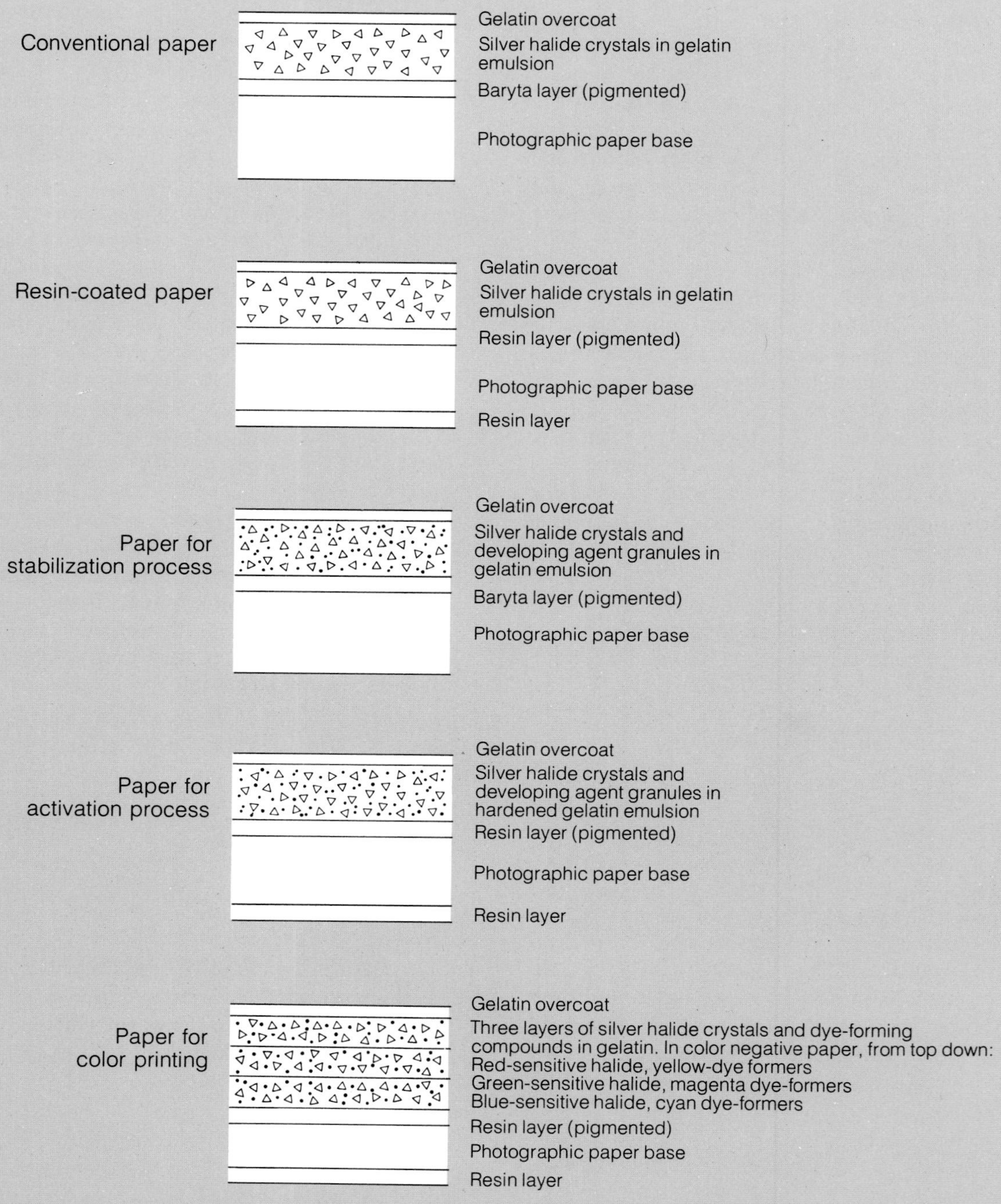

Conventional paper

- Gelatin overcoat
- Silver halide crystals in gelatin emulsion
- Baryta layer (pigmented)
- Photographic paper base

Resin-coated paper

- Gelatin overcoat
- Silver halide crystals in gelatin emulsion
- Resin layer (pigmented)
- Photographic paper base
- Resin layer

Paper for stabilization process

- Gelatin overcoat
- Silver halide crystals and developing agent granules in gelatin emulsion
- Baryta layer (pigmented)
- Photographic paper base

Paper for activation process

- Gelatin overcoat
- Silver halide crystals and developing agent granules in hardened gelatin emulsion
- Resin layer (pigmented)
- Photographic paper base
- Resin layer

Paper for color printing

- Gelatin overcoat
- Three layers of silver halide crystals and dye-forming compounds in gelatin. In color negative paper, from top down:
  Red-sensitive halide, yellow-dye formers
  Green-sensitive halide, magenta dye-formers
  Blue-sensitive halide, cyan dye-formers
- Resin layer (pigmented)
- Photographic paper base
- Resin layer

lightweight, single weight, medium weight, and double weight. Other manufacturers use similar designations.

Lightweight stock is a thin paper with characteristics that make it suitable for the illustrative pages in manuals or reports, or when weight is a prime consideration.

Single-weight papers are generally used for prints up to about 8″ × 10″. Prints on double-weight paper are easier to handle and process in sizes larger than 8″ × 10″, but this is often a question of preference, the use to which the prints are put, or whether or not they are mounted. An exception is Kodak mural paper, which is made with a tough single-weight base to withstand the handling and folding necessary in making big enlargements, as well as to facilitate making splices as nearly invisible as possible when large prints or photomurals are made in more than one piece.

Medium-weight stock is generally used for special-purpose papers, such as some of those made in rolls for continuous processing.

PHOTOGRAPHIC PAPER THICKNESS

Thickness	Code	Nominal (Unprocessed) ANSI Standard Thickness (Inches)
Lightweight	LW	.0043 to .0059
Single weight	SW	.0059 to .0083
Medium weight	MW	.0083 to .0111
Double weight	DW	.0111 to .0190

Water-Resistant Base: The use of a water-resistant (resin-coated) base provides good dimensional stability for applications where this characteristic is important. Also, processing times are shorter than usual because the base does not absorb water and chemical solutions to the same extent as ordinary paper does. Water-resistant papers are usually on a medium-weight paper base.

Dimensional Stability of Paper Base. In photographic work, the term "dimensional stability" means the change in size that materials such as paper and film undergo during processing, washing, and drying, as well as the changes that occur due to varying relative humidity and temperature.

Generally speaking, paper is the least dimensionally stable of all the sensitized materials used in photography. When paper is soaked with chemical solutions or water, it expands according to the amount of liquid absorbed. After drying, the paper may or may not return to its original size. Any increase in size that takes place is particularly noticeable with prints that have been ferrotyped; to a large extent, they then hold the wet size.

For most practical purposes, the changes in size that take place in photographic paper when it has been wetted or soaked are fairly constant. Paper is manufactured in rolls, and when the paper is wet, it expands considerably more across the width of the roll than along the length. As a broad guide, the paper base expands about 1 inch across the width of a 40-inch roll. The expansion along the length of the roll is less—about 1 inch in every 12 feet of paper.

In most photographic work where paper is used, dimensional changes are unimportant, but in some applications, such as making photomurals in several sections that are to be wet-mounted as one picture, the wet stretch should be calculated and the enlarged image made correspondingly smaller.

The water-resistant papers can be considered to have no wet stretch for all normal uses.

Paper Sizes. Photographic papers may be supplied in standard-size sheets, or in long rolls of various widths for automatic processors and bulk users. Sheet sizes are commonly supplied in packages of 10 to 500 sheets. The following table lists the standard sheet sizes; not all papers are available in all sizes.

Base Tints: The tint is the color of the paper stock or a composite of the color of the paper and the coating applied to it in manufacture. A white-base paper might vary from the cold white of Kodak Velox paper to the warm white of a portrait paper such as Kodak Ektalure paper (Y). Cream-white base is considerably warmer than any of the whites. It is most suitable for portraits and pictorial subjects where a feeling of warmth is desired.

"Cold" in reference to paper tint refers to white with a very slight blue cast, while "warm" and "cream" mean that the white has a slight yellow-brown hue.

STANDARD SHEET SIZES OF PHOTOGRAPHIC PAPERS

Inches	Centimetres
2½ X 2½	6.4 X 6.4
2½ X 3½	6.4 X 8.9
2¾ X 4½	7.0 X 11.4
3 X 4¾	7.6 X 12.1
3¼ X 4½	8.3 X 11.4
3⁷⁄₁₆ X 5⁷⁄₁₆ (postcard size)	8.7 X 13.8
3½ X 4½	8.9 X 11.4
3½ X 5	8.9 X 12.7
3½ X 5¾	8.9 X 14.6
4 X 5	10.2 X 12.7
5 X 7	12.7 X 17.8
6½ X 8½	16.5 X 21.6
8 X 10	20.3 X 25.4
8½ X 11	21.6 X 28
10 X 10	25.4 X 25.4
10 X 12	25.4 X 30.5
11 X 14	28 X 35.6
12 X 20	30.5 X 50.8
14 X 17	35.6 X 43.2
16 X 20	40.6 X 50.8
20 X 24	50.8 X 61

Fluorescent Brighteners: Fluorescent material is sometimes added to a paper to give extra brightness to the prints. Kodak Ektamatic papers used in stabilization processing are examples. However, the brightening effect varies with the amount of ultraviolet radiation in the light by which prints are viewed. Moreover, the effect of a brightener is not easily appreciated unless prints on a brightened and a nonbrightened paper are compared side by side.

Since brighteners tend to leach out of the paper during processing, prints that have been developed for considerably different times appear to have different degrees of brightness; and to the eye, this is equivalent to different degrees of grayness. Consequently, in manual processing of papers containing a brightening agent, developing time should be as uniform as possible.

Image Tone. The term "image tone" refers to the color of the silver image. The color varies from brown through warm black and neutral black to blue black. Image tone is largely a question of grain size, but its appearance is influenced by the tint of the paper base. Many factors, such as developing time, developing temperature, fixing time, and drying temperature, tend to alter the character of the silver grains, and consequently the image tone of the print. Variations in image tone caused by erratic processing are not as noticeable with cold-tone papers as they are with warm-tone materials. To maintain the characteristic image tone of a warm-tone paper, it is therefore necessary to pay attention to those factors in processing that change image tone.

Surface Characteristics

Photographic papers are made in a variety of surface textures and degrees of gloss or sheen. Some papers, however, have a smooth surface without noticeable texture. Sheen varies from the high gloss of a ferrotyped print to the almost complete absence of sheen in a matte paper. In general, smooth, high-gloss papers are used in commercial work where fine detail must be preserved in the prints, and for reproduction where a surface texture might be reproduced as an objectionable pattern in the reproduction.

The following text describes the combinations of surface characteristics of Kodak papers. Other manufacturers offer papers with some of the same characteristics, as well as a variety of others. As with contrast designations, the descriptive names and code designations do not have corresponding meanings among various manufacturers.

Surfaces of Kodak Papers. The Kodak line of papers for amateur and professional photography consists of nine combinations of surface texture and lustre. As further detailed, each combination is indicated by a letter of the alphabet.

With these textures and degrees of lustre, combined with the variations in image tone and base tint, you have a wide choice of paper to create mood and to suggest the lighting conditions that existed when the picture was taken. As in all manufactured materials, there are slight batch-to-batch variations in paper characteristics.

Smooth Glossy—F. All Kodak papers thus designated, except those on water-resistant paper base, can be ferrotyped. A ferrotyped print yields the densest blacks and, therefore, the longest density range possible in a photographic print. F-surface water-resistant papers produce the high gloss without ferrotyping.

Smooth High Lustre—J. This surface has no noticeable pattern, and it yields a density range somewhat lower than that of F-surface papers.

Smooth Lustre—A and N. Although this surface has no noticeable pattern, it has less sheen than the smooth high-lustre paper just described. The letter A indicates a lightweight base that may be folded, whereas N indicates a special surface with enough "tooth" for pencil retouching.

Fine-Grained Lustre—E and G. These letters indicate a slightly pebbled surface, which has little effect on fine detail. It is a good choice for most pictures when a smooth or a glossy surface is undesirable. E papers are made with a white or warm-white paper base while G papers have a cream-white tint.

Fine-Grained High Lustre—K. This surface has a slightly pebbled surface similar to the fine-grained lustre, but with a higher sheen. It yields a fairly high density range for strong, bright effects. The tint is a warm white.

Tweed Lustre—R. This surface has a fairly rough texture that tends to subdue fine detail and to emphasize the larger masses and planes in a subject. It is good for big enlargements and large head-and-shoulders portraits.

Silk High Lustre—Y. This surface has a cloth-like appearance and a high lustre. It is generally used for wedding and school photography, as well as for snow scenes and other brilliant pictorial subjects. Y-surface papers have a cream or warm-white tint.

Tapestry Lustre—X. This surface has a canvas-like texture suitable for large portraits and broad pictorial effects. A hand-colored print on this surface strongly resembles an original oil painting.

Processing Photographic Papers

As the diagrams of paper construction show, the emulsion design of a paper is determined by the intended processing. The greatest range of black-and-white papers is designed for conventional tray processing in developer, stop bath, and fixer solutions, followed by washing. Papers of this type are available in all weights and surfaces.

Two kinds of papers are designed for specialized machine processing. Papers for stabilization processing have developing-agent granules incorporated in the emulsion. They are intended for processing in a machine that roller-transports them through two solutions at an average rate of 1 inch per second. An activator solution causes the developer granules to develop the image; a stabilizer solution makes the image temporarily stable. These papers may also be tray-developed, and may be fixed and washed in the usual manner to obtain the same permanence as conventionally processed prints.

Papers for activation processing have halide-plus-developer emulsions like those of stabilization papers, but the gelatin is hardened to withstand high temperatures. Typically, the image is developed within 9 seconds in an activator solution, followed by a rapid-acting conventional stop bath, and a high-concentration, high-temperature fixer. A spray wash and forced drying deliver a dry print of conventional permanence in an average of 55 seconds.

Papers designed for activation processing usually have water-resistant bases to minimize absorption, and are on medium-weight stock so as to move through processing machines without cracking or buckling. Papers designed for stabilization processing usually have a conventional (fiber) base.

Color-printing papers have a three-layer emulsion coated on a water-resistant base. A paper must be specifically designed either for conventional processing for prints from negatives, or for reversal processing for prints from slides and transparencies. Either kind of processing can be carried out in trays, or in hand-activated or motor-driven processors.

Special-Purpose Papers

Printing-out papers produce images by the action of light alone; no development is required. The image may be fixed for permanence, but it has a characteristic purplish tone that is not widely accepted for ordinary images. These papers are most commonly used to provide temporary (unfixed) portrait proofs.

Direct-positive papers can be exposed in a camera and reversal-processed to yield a positive print. They are primarily used in automatic, coin-operated photo booths. They have the limitation of being orthochromatic, of providing only a single copy for each exposure, and of producing a reversed image unless a mirror or prism is incorporated in the camera system.

Various papers with panchromatic emulsions can be used to make full-scale black-and-white prints from color negatives, or to make black-and-white color-separation prints from color negatives for use in photomechanical reproduction.

There are a number of very high-contrast papers for use in the graphic arts and reprographic fields. They are primarily used for the production of screened prints for halftone reproduction, or to reproduce architectural drawings and similar originals. However, they are also used in illustrative and pictorial work for a wide variety of special effects. Other high-contrast papers are used for recording or printing the displays of instruments such as oscilloscopes.

Some so-called print papers are not, in fact, papers; they consist of conventional emulsions on a white, translucent plastic base. They are used to produce transparencies that are to be viewed or displayed by transmitted light.

• *See also:* BARIUM SULFATE; BLACK-AND-WHITE PRINTING; BLACK-AND-WHITE PRINTS FROM COLOR FILMS; COLOR PRINTING FROM NEGATIVES; COLOR PRINTING FROM TRANSPARENCIES; CONTACT PRINTING; CONTRAST; DIRECT POSITIVE PAPER PHOTOGRAPHY; GRAY SCALES; PRINTING-OUT PAPERS; SCREENED NEGATIVES AND PRINTS; STABILIZATION PROCESS; STORAGE OF SENSITIZED MATERIALS AND PROCESSING SOLUTIONS; VARIABLE CONTRAST.

Paraformaldehyde

Paraform, triformal, trioxymethylene, polyoxymethylene

Used as an accelerator for litho-film developers; also useful as a hardener in place of formaldehyde, especially where dry packaging is required.

Formula: $(CH_2O)_3$
Molecular Weight: 90.06

This white crystalline powder smells strongly of formaldehyde. It is slightly soluble in water and alkaline solutions, and insoluble in alcohol and ether.

Parallax

Parallax is a change in appearance and orientation of objects when seen from different viewpoints; the term parallax is also used to refer to the difference between the viewpoints themselves. This latter usage is the common one when referring to the parallax problem with camera viewfinders.

Human vision of depth depends on parallax. Each eye sees objects from two viewpoints about 65 mm (2½ inches) apart. The left and right eye images, on the retina, have parallax—that is, they are not identical. The spacing between various parts of the subject being viewed varies according to the angular differences. These differences are interpreted by the brain as differences in distance, and three-dimensional depth is perceived.

Cameras With Viewfinders

When a camera has a separate viewfinder, it must necessarily be placed at some distance from the lens of the camera, and the result is that it will see the subject from a different angle. With small cameras this difference is slight, and only presents problems when the camera is used for close-up photography. For instance, even press cameras, where the finder may be as much as 8 or 10 cm (3 or 4 inches) above or to one side of the lens, give no problems when used at distances of 2 m (6 feet) and beyond. On the other hand, small twin-lens reflexes, where the separation between lenses is seldom more than 6 cm (2½ inches), present problems when used for close-up and copy work.

The simplest way of overcoming this problem is to place one or two marks in the finder indicating the top of the frame at, for example, 0.9 and 0.6 m (3 and 2 feet, respectively). Then, when framing the picture, first compose it exactly as desired, then note some object that is at the top edge of the frame, and tilt the camera upward until that object is on the mark corresponding to its distance.

Approximate Framing

Some twin-lens reflex cameras have a simple mechanism by which the mask surrounding the ground-glass screen is shifted up and down by focusing the mechanism, so that the finder and the

These photos demonstrate the problem of viewfinder parallax. While the image in the viewfinder appears correctly framed, as at the left, the camera lens sees the image differently, as at the right, because it is at a slightly different angle. The problem can be overcome by marking the finder as described in this article.

camera both cover the same field at all focus distances. This compensation is limited, and in most cases, does not extend to very close ranges.

Some small rangefinder cameras also have parallax compensation; in these, the entire finder is tilted up and down by a cam connected to the focusing mount of the lens. This method, too, can only approximate the two fields and becomes less accurate at close ranges.

The reason neither method works adequately at close ranges is that while the axes of the lens and finder can be made to coincide at the subject point, they are no longer parallel. Thus, each sees a different aspect of the subject, and while the final image may be correctly centered, the picture will not exactly correspond to what is seen in the finder at the time it is taken if there are subjects at close and far distances.

Visualize, for instance, a small object that is to be photographed in a full frontal view. If the camera finder is above the lens, then it will see not only the front of the object but also its top surface; the final picture, however, will not show the top.

This problem was quite severe with certain professional motion-picture cameras that, because of the size of the sound-proofing enclosure, had finders placed as much as a foot to one side of the lens. In photographing a full-face close-up, the finder would see a slight profile and one ear only, while the camera would see the subject full-face and with both ears showing.

Such cameras gave difficulties even at moderately large distances; one would compose a shot so that the subject appeared centered on the background, only to find that the finished film showed background objects that had been thought to be safely out of the frame.

Single-Lens Reflex Cameras

In addition to view cameras, the only camera that is completely free of parallax problems is the single-lens reflex camera in which focusing, framing, and photography are all done through one lens. The image is shifted from ground glass to film by a movable mirror behind the lens. The modern single-lens reflex (SLR) camera is one example of

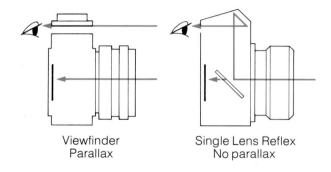

Viewfinder
Parallax

Single Lens Reflex
No parallax

A comparison of viewing systems. The error of parallax becomes more serious as the camera is moved closer to the subject.

this type, although the older reflexes, such as the Graflex camera, were also free from parallax problems. Most modern professional motion-picture cameras today also have reflex viewing, and the cameraman's job is greatly simplified by the use of cameras such as the Mitchell BNCR, the Arriflex, and the Eclair Camerette, among others.

Television Cameras

Parallax is likewise not a problem with television cameras; these do not have finders in the normal sense of the word. The so-called finder of the TV camera is actually a small cathode-ray tube, on which is displayed the image as it is actually seen by the picture tubes of the camera itself; it is, in fact, the transmitted picture, and so shows exactly what the camera sees.

• *See also:* PERSPECTIVE; STEREO PHOTOGRAPHY; VISION.

Paraphenylene-Diamine

1,4-diaminobenzene and 1,4-benzenediamine

A developing agent once very popular for producing extremely fine-grained negatives. It was often combined with other developing agents for this purpose, and a series of developers by Dr. Sease of Dupont, containing paraphenylene-di-

amine and glycin, was very popular during the 1930's. It was also used as the developing agent in a reversal-first developer with a caustic alkali and a silver solvent. Most color developing agents are derived from paraphenylene-diamine.

Formula: $NH_2C_6H_4NH_2$
Molecular Weight: 108.14

White to yellowish crystals, slightly soluble in cold water. Paraphenylene-diamine hydrochloride is also available; in this form it is much more soluble, but being somewhat acidic, cannot be used for preparing low-alkalinity developers. Therefore the hydrochloride must be used with an alkali.

CAUTION: It is toxic, and stains hands and clothing. It causes allergic reactions in some persons. Developers containing paraphenylene-diamine should not be handled with bare hands; if hands must be immersed, rubber gloves should be used.

Pathé, Charles

(1863–1958)
French industrialist

Charles Pathé and his two brothers formed the firm of Pathé Frères to market the Edison phonograph and Kinetoscope. They later worked with Lumière to develop other motion-picture systems and began to build cameras and projectors of their own. The Pathé motion-picture cameras were very popular in the early days of the cinema; Billy Bitzer photographed D. W. Griffith's *Birth of a Nation* with a hand-cranked Pathé camera.

Around 1912, Pathé Frères introduced a new system of home movies, using nonflammable films, 28 mm wide, under the trademark Kok.* The Pathé organization also showed early color motion pictures under the trade name Pathécolor; these films were made by coloring black-and-white films through hand-cut stencils. They introduced another home-movie system, Pathé-Baby (marketed in the United States as Pathex), using 9.5 mm films.

---

*Kok (pronounced "coke") is a play on the French word "coq," meaning rooster, which is the well-known Pathé trademark.

During the late 1930's, Pathé devised a system of small-film sound motion pictures for country theaters, known as Pathé-Rural; the film was 17.5 mm wide and had a sound track on one edge. This system was abandoned when France was occupied by the Germans in the early years of World War II; the occupying authorities ordered the projectors and films changed to 16 mm. After World War II, the Pathé organization was merged into the French Kodak organization and is currently known as Kodak-Pathé Ltd.

Paul, Robert W.

(1869–1943)
English motion-picture pioneer

In 1894, Paul began to manufacture Edison Kinetoscopes (evidently without any prior arrangement with Edison, since the machine had apparently not been patented in England). Later, when Edison refused to supply films for Paul's machines, Paul built his own camera, printer, and developing equipment.

About 1896, Paul built a motion-picture projector called the "Theatrograph." To keep up with the growth of the theatrical motion picture, Paul built (circa 1899) a studio where he produced a number of trick films. Later, with the late Professor Silvanus P. Thompson, he took up the making of animated films.

By 1910, Paul decided that the motion-picture business was of no further interest to him. He shut down his plants, destroyed all his negatives, and devoted his full time to the making of scientific instruments.

Perspective

Perspective is the way in which objects that exist in real three-dimensional space are imaged on a two-dimensional plane. The perspective in a photograph is, in a sense, an illusion—the sensations of depth and space are achieved automatically by a number of perspective principles that relate to vision, optics, geometry, and some of the physical realities of objects and of air.

When it makes photographs of three-dimensional subjects, the camera always creates a perspective. The perspective changes as the camera position, called the viewpoint, changes. From a given position, changing the focal length of the lens does not change the *actual* viewpoint, but it may change the *apparent* viewpoint in the final picture. Often, when the focal length of the lens is changed, the camera position is also changed, which does change the perspective.

An artist learns the principles of perspective to help him or her draw, on paper or canvas, scenes that exhibit believable perspective. Since the photographer's camera gives perspective automatically, it might be thought that there is no need to learn these principles. However, if the photographer knows the perspective principles, and applies them with skill, photographs will show good rendition of subject shapes and forms, and will provide the viewer with a good sensation of volume, space, depth, and distance when viewing the photographs. Further, the photographer will be able to expand or compress the sensation of space and distance to serve visual purposes, and he or she can provide a strong sense of scale in pictures.

Depth in Vision

Nearly all objects that are seen have three dimensions. Two dimensions, length and width, define a plane with area. The third dimension adds solidity or depth. *Shape* is a two-dimensional factor, while *form* is the three-dimensional equivalent of shape. Objects exist in air, usually with space or distance between them. The human visual mechanism is so made that shapes and forms and distances can be clearly perceived.

A large part of the sensation of depth occurs because there is parallax between the two eyes. Each eye sees the subject from a slightly different viewpoint. This causes the images on the retinas to be slightly different (the perspectives of the two images are not quite the same). The signals sent to the brain from the retinal images show up the differences, and the brain interprets them as a mental perception of depth. Of course, we are not consciously aware of this happening. The things we see just look like three-dimensional objects spread out in a world that is real to us.

From this small, flat image on paper, the enormous distances existing in the original subject can still be sensed. This is due to the ability of a normal focal-length lens to give natural looking perspective automatically.

Such vision is called stereoscopic vision, and it covers distances from the nearest point at which the eyes can fuse the two images, to as far away as *stereo infinity,* which in most cases is about 2000 feet. This varies from person to person, some having limited stereo vision, and with conditions of light and atmosphere. Stereo infinity is the distance at which the parallax differences between the two retinal images become less than the resolving power of the eyes.

Although true stereo vision extends only to stereo infinity, the sensation of distance does not stop there. Objects as far away as the eyes can see are still perceived to have form and distance separation. This is due to the many depth clues that aid the observer in determining the thickness of objects (their form) and their relative distances. These depth clues, of course, do not first start at stereo infinity. They are at work in helping the perception of depth at all distances. The principles of perspective are the explanations of the depth clues.

Depth in Pictures

True stereo pictures are often called 3-D, or three-dimensional pictures. They are usually taken as two photographs with the camera lenses spaced about 65 mm (2½ inches) apart, which is the average human interpupillary distance. Such pictures are viewed in a stereo viewer, in which each eye sees a separate picture. As in 3-D vision of the original subject, the two pictures are fused together in the mind, into perception of depth. Both parallax vision and the depth clues aid the viewer in seeing the picture in 3-D. (*See:* STEREO PHOTOGRAPHY.)

In all pictures taken with a single camera lens (2-D pictures), the sensation of depth cannot be due to parallax stereo vision. It is due only to the perspective of the picture, provided by the depth clues that work both in the vision of real objects and in the photographs of those objects.

Putting the depth clues to work in the making of photographs for the purpose of strengthening the illusion of the third dimension is the application of the principles of perspective. The principles of perspective can be divided into the following categories:

1. Geometric perspective.
2. Light and cast-shadow perspective.
3. Aerial perspective.

Geometric Perspective

The viewer of a scene has a viewpoint when a picture is taken. The camera lens is the viewpoint;

With stereo pictures, the centers of the two images are the same distance apart as are the pupils of average human eyes. By focusing one eye on each picture and fusing the images, a single, three-dimensional image will appear.

light from each subject point in the scene comes in a straight line to the camera lens. The camera lens images this light on the film. The accompanying diagrams show how the location and size of each object in the scene are imaged, and how the geometric rules of similar triangles apply.

The mathematical formula that determines the size of objects in the image is:

$$\text{Image size} = \frac{\text{Subject size} \times \text{focal length}}{\text{Subject distance} - \text{focal length}}$$

where subject distance is measured from the lens. It can be seen from this that as subject size gets larger, image size gets larger. Also, when the focal length is greater, image size is greater. Conversely, when the subject distance is greater, or when the focal length is shorter, the image size is smaller.

Rectilinear Perspective. The perspective achieved in this manner is called rectilinear perspective because lines that are straight in the subject are imaged as straight lines. Nearly all pictures are made with cameras and lenses that produce this type of perspective.

There are two other types of perspective that are false perspectives (not typical of that provided by vision), but are sometimes seen. Panoramic cameras, in order to cover relatively wide angles (up to 360 degrees in one direction), essentially image on film that is positioned as the walls of a cylinder. Straight horizontal lines that fall on the lens axis level are imaged as straight lines, but all

other horizontal lines that are above or below that level are imaged as curved lines. This type of perspective is called cylindrical or panoramic perspective.

The other type of false perspective is created by lenses that have intentionally been made with severe barrel distortion in order to cover wide angles (up to 180 degrees), on a flat film surface. These are commonly called fisheye lenses. All straight lines in the subject are imaged as curved lines, with the concave sides of the curves toward the center of the field.

The principles of perspective (depth clues) that apply to rectilinear perspective apply, in large degree, to the other two types of perspective—with the exceptions noted.

The subjects in pictures are composed of shapes, lines, planes, and solids. The principles of geometric perspective show how subjects are placed on the film by the lens and, hence, how they are seen in the picture, or, as the artist might say, how they are drawn by the camera lens.

The series of diagrams show how the geometry of similar triangles explains the reproduction of the size and positions of objects on the film. These straightforward principles result in a number of depth clues that clarify how depth is seen in photographs.

True Perspective. With a given focal-length lens on a given format camera, a certain perspective of objects is obtained in a photograph. The photograph will give the sensation of the identical

Geometric Perspective

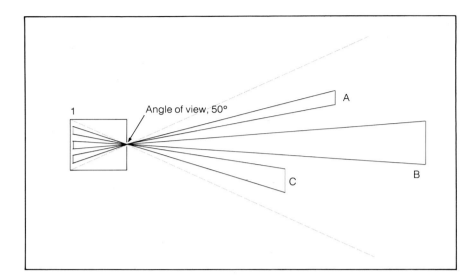

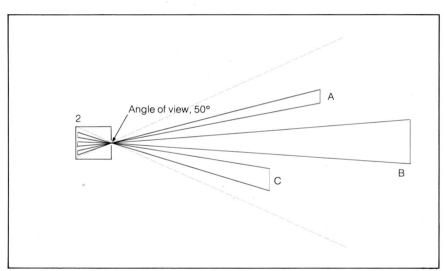

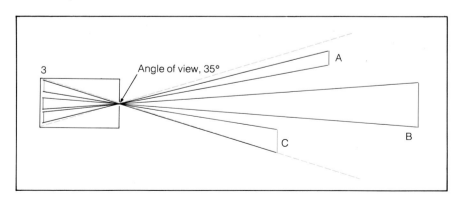

Diagram 1: Large-format normal lens. The location and size of objects imaged on the film by a pinhole illustrate the similar-triangle nature of image formation. The larger object (B) is further from the camera than object C, but appears to be the same size. The image is upside down on the film, and each point in the scene appears in a different location on the film. When a lens is used instead of a pinhole, the same result is obtained, but the geometry is slightly more complicated. The normal horizontal angle of view is about 50 degrees.

Diagram 2: Small-format normal lens. When a smaller format camera with a normal angle of view is used, the image of each object is smaller. However, all the image sizes are in the same proportion to each other and have the same relational positions on the film. If this smaller film were enlarged to make the same size print as the larger format camera makes, the perspective of the two photographs would be identical.

Diagram 3: Large-format telephoto lens. When a longer-focal-length telephoto lens is used on the same format as in Diagram 1, the images of the objects are larger. A smaller angle of view—about 35 degrees in this case—is covered. The images of the objects have the same proportional size to each other, and the same relative positions on the film. However, because they are larger in proportion to the format, they appear relatively larger in the print.

Geometric Perspective (continued)

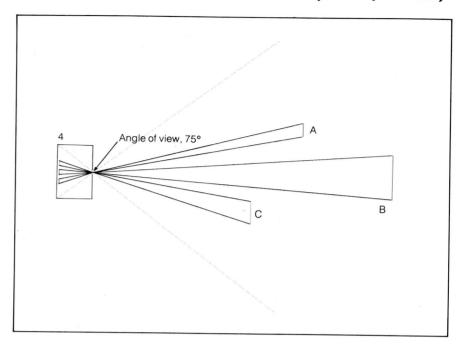

Diagram 4: Large-format wide-angle lens. When a shorter focal length, wide-angle lens is used on a larger format, the image size is smaller. If the focal length of the lens were the same as that shown in Diagram 2, the image size of each object would be the same as described. However, since the format is larger, a wide-angle view is covered—in this example, 75 degrees. Because of this wider angle of view, all the objects appear smaller in relationship to the entire picture area.

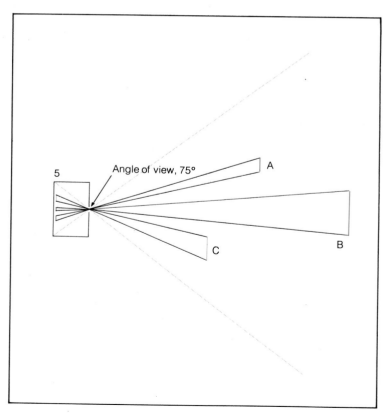

Diagram 5: Large-format, wide-angle lens; reduced camera distance. If the camera with the wide-angle lens is moved closer to the scene, so that the nearest object (C) is now as large as it is in the normal-lens picture, the relative sizes of the objects at different distances will change and the angular differences between them increase. The far objects (B) do not increase in size as much as the near objects do; so that the size differential increases. In perspective, this makes the distance of the objects that are far from the camera seem greater than in the normal-lens photograph, thus expanding the apparent picture depth.

Fish-eye lenses produce images in which most straight lines appear curved. This type of perspective is spherical, or barrel, perspective.

perspective only if the photograph is viewed in a certain, specified manner. When it it viewed in this manner, the viewing is said to be in *true perspective*. True perspective also relates to the magnification of the print.

The first rule of viewing is that the print be viewed square on; that is, that it be perpendicular to the line of sight. Also, the viewing eye must be aligned with the center of the print.

The second rule is that the distance between the eye and the print must be correct, so that the eye is in the same relative position that the camera lens was in relation to the film when the picture was taken. That distance can be found by the following formula:

True perspective viewing distance =
Camera lens focal length ×
Enlargement magnification

Perspective

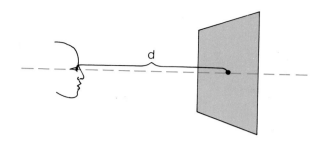

What this formula says is that if a print is a contact-print, the eye should be at a distance equal to the lens focal length. If an entire 4″ × 5″ negative taken with a normal 6-inch lens is enlarged 2× to an 8″ × 10″ print, the print should be viewed at 2″ × 6″, or 12 inches. If the same scene is taken on 35 mm film with a 2-inch lens, and the negative is enlarged 6×, then that print should also be viewed at a distance of 12 inches in order to achieve true perspective.

On the other hand, if a 4″ × 5″ negative is taken with a 20-inch telephoto lens and enlarged 2×, it should be viewed at 40 inches for true perspective.

When most photographs are viewed, the viewer is unaware of which focal-length lens was used. Most people do view 8″ × 10″ prints at about 15 inches, which is close, but not quite true perspective. They also view 3″ × 3½″ prints, 4″ × 5″ prints, and contact sheets of 1″ × 1½″ prints at the same 15-inch distance because it is difficult to view them much closer.

People tend to view larger prints from farther back. As a rule of thumb, it is comfortable to view a print from a distance that is twice the average of the length and width of the print. In a 16″ × 20″ print, the average length and width is 18 inches, and a comfortable viewing distance is 36 inches.

A 16″ × 20″ print is a 4× magnification of a 4″ × 5″ negative.

$$4″ × 6″ \text{ (normal lens)} = 24″,$$

which is the true perspective distance. When the print is viewed from a distance greater than the true perspective distance, the space in the picture appears to be expanded. To give true perspective to the 16″ × 20″ print viewed at 36 inches, a 9-inch lens should be used on the 4″ × 5″ camera.

If the original negative is taken with a 14-inch telephoto lens, then viewing the print from 36 inches will tend to compress the space between the objects. The true perspective distance would be:

$$4″ × 14″ = 64″.$$

Normally speaking, the knowledgeable photographer will try to give the viewer a perspective close to that of true perspective in most situations. However, he or she will know how to use longer- or shorter-focal-length lenses to compress or expand the space for expressive purposes.

For example, a small room photographed with a lens shorter than that required for true perspective will expand the space and make the room look larger.

On the other hand, a picture taken of a crowd of people with a lens longer than the true perspective focal length will compress the space between the people and make it look much more crowded than it really is.

True perspective is important in pictures taken for evidence. By using the true-perspective principle, the pictures of a crime or accident scene can present an honest view of the scene to the members of the jury.

Vanishing Point Perspective. Most camera lenses are made to image in a rectilinear perspective. That is, lines that are straight in the subject are straight in the pictures made of that subject. (The exceptions are the curvilinear or spherical perspective of fisheye lenses and the cylindrical perspective of some panoramic-type cameras.) In perception, lines parallel to each other meet at vanishing points. If the lines are perpendicular to the lens axis, the vanishing points are located at infinity—all other lines at all other angles meet at finite vanishing points.

We are used to seeing vertical lines as vertical, parallel to each other. In most pictures, the vanishing points of vertical lines are at infinity.

Distances in this interior picture, photographed with a wide-angle lens, look greater than they actually are. This is known as space expansion.

With a telephoto lens, planes appear squeezed together. This is known as space compression. Photo by Andreas Feininger; © 1949, Time Inc.

Perspective

We are accustomed to seeing vertical subject lines as vertical. This is accomplished by having the film vertical. Usually, for architectural photographs, a view camera is used, with the lens raised to encompass tall buildings. In two-point perspective, illustrated here, lines parallel to the ground meet at vanishing points (A in the diagram) on the horizon line (B on the diagram). The skyline (C) is often higher than the horizon line.

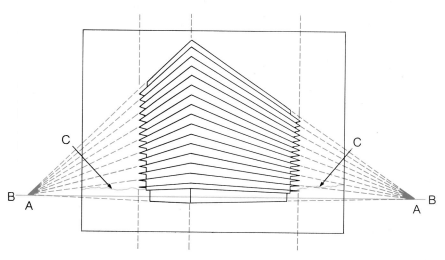

Converging or diverging verticals result when the camera is aimed upward or downward so that the film plane is not vertical. In most pictures, this gives the effect of surfaces that lean forward or tilt backward, so the visual sense of perspective is usually violated.

Lines parallel to the lens axis, or nearly so, start in at the edges of the picture and usually meet at vanishing points within the picture area. The foreground of most landscape pictures is composed of the ground plane. Perspective lines on the ground plane parallel to the lens axis move upward through the foreground and come together at vanishing points on the horizon. The horizon is the intersection of the ground plane and the sky plane.

(Left) When a camera is aimed upward, so that the film plane is tilted rather than vertical, vertical subject lines converge in the image. This makes the building appear to tilt backwards. (Right) In compositional use, converging lines are not always wrong. The photographer can use converging verticals as a creative treatment.

In most landscape pictures, the sky area appears to be a plane at a great distance, although in some pictures in which a large proportion of picture area is devoted to the sky, the upper part of the sky appears to come forward, like the inside of an inverted cylinder or bowl. In rectilinear perspective, the horizon is a straight, horizontal line, but in many landscape pictures, the actual horizon is completely or partially hidden by certain objects in the picture, such as hills, trees, or buildings. The usually irregular-shaped line that separates the sky from these terrestrial objects is called the sky line.

Height Perspective. In many landscape scenes, there are objects on the ground plane—rocks, trees, perhaps buildings, animals, or whatever. The place where an object rests on the ground plane is a clue to its distance from the point of view. Since the ground plane rises toward the horizon in the distance, the higher in the picture area (up to the horizon) that the object base appears on the ground plane, the farther away it seems.

Object-Overlap Perspective. The last two clues related to geometric perspective might be called the object-overlap clue and the diminishing object-size clue.

Most objects in pictures are opaque. When one object is closer to the point of view than another, and in about the same line of sight, part of the closer object overlaps and partially hides the farther object. It is obvious, visually, that the partially hidden object is behind the unobstructed

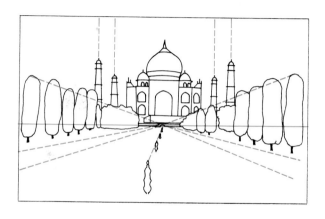

The ground plane rises from the bottom of the picture up to the horizon. If the camera is aimed downward, the horizon line rises in the picture. Lines on the ground plane, parallel to the camera axis, rise to a vanishing point on the horizon. This illustration also demonstrates these other depth clues: height perspective, object overlap, diminishing size, light and shade, cast shadow, and aerial perspective.

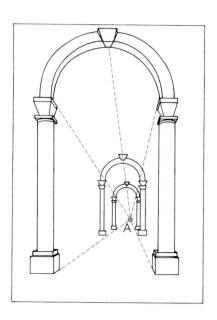

Interior linear perspective follows much the same principles as those of exterior perspective. The floor is the ground. When the ceilings are included, they act as upside-down ground. When the camera is aimed squarely at a wall, the vanishing point (A in the diagram) is behind that wall. Vertical lines, which are parallel, meet at infinite vanishing points.

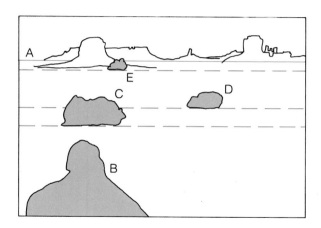

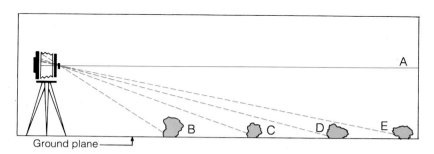

Ground plane

The intersection of the ground and the bottom edge of the frame is closest to the camera. The horizon (A in the diagrams) is the farthest distance, as well as the upper edge of the ground plane. Therefore, the higher on the ground plane an object is located, the farther from the camera it is. The diagram at left shows a ground-plane view of the positions of objects B, C, D, E relative to the camera.

object, so that the unobstructed object is closer. In many scenes, this overlapping is repeated many times, giving many visual clues as to the relative distances of the objects, and giving a perception of depth.

Diminishing Size Perspective. Human vision has an attribute called "size constancy." From experience, we are familiar with the size of common objects such as people. We know, for example, that most adult people are from about 5 to 6 feet tall. If in a picture there are two people, and one is twice as large as the other, we do not assume that in reality one person is larger. We assume that the larger person is closer and that the smaller person is farther away, and that in the original scene both people were about the same size. In the same way, we have a size-constancy evaluation of all familiar objects: trees, bushes, rocks, fences, buildings, animals, and so on. The distance clue that results from the size-constancy factor is often called the "diminishing object-size" clue, because the farther away an object is from the point of view, the smaller it appears.

In pictures, inclusion of objects that are familiar enough that viewers have developed a size constancy for them helps establish the *scale* of the picture. Scale helps the viewer interpret the actual size of the objects in the picture, especially if a near true perspective is also achieved.

Light and Cast-Shadow Perspective

The three-dimensional form of any object is more difficult to perceive if it is lighted very diffusely than if it is illuminated with direct sunlight from angles that cause part of the object to be fully lighted and other parts to be shaded. The shape of the lighted and shaded portions gives us visual clues on the "volume" or form of the object. When a number of such objects are included in a picture, the total impression of volume and depth are increased.

When the lighting is from grazing angles, the volume of the tiny surface details of objects become more apparent, which is the reason this type of lighting is called texture lighting. In addition, with sidelight one edge of all objects is

(Above) A strongly lighted subject, especially with back or side lighting, shows its form clearly. Note how clearly the cubic structure of the buildings can be seen. The tree-trunk form is strongly suggested by texture, light, and shade. Visual distance is achieved by the linear and light-shade elements. (Right) A diffusely lighted subject, like this barn, shows little form. In this type of photograph, visual distance is usually achieved by aerial perspective.

brightly lit, while the other side is shaded. This leads to better outlining of the objects against their background, increasing the sense of depth due to enhanced object-overlap perspective.

With backlighting, when the entire shape of each object is outlined with light while the front of each object is shaded, the sense of volume of each subject is decreased. But, the sense of distance between objects is increased, giving an overall increase in depth sensation.

With 45-degree frontlighting to sidelighting, shadows of objects are cast upon the ground. The length, depth, and shape of the shadows give visual clues to each object's volume. This enhances the clues to volume provided by the light and shade effect on the object itself.

The distance between the shadows cast on the rising ground plane gives clues to the overall depth of the scene.

Aerial Perspective

The photographer normally treats air as a perfectly transparent medium through which light travels and through which he or she takes pictures

Aerial perspective is the most effective way to show the relative distances of objects that are a long way off. This photograph demonstrates various aerial perspective effects: contrast, brightness, color saturation, hue shift, and sharpness.

Perspective

Aerial perspective is effective in black-and-white as well as color photography. Here, the frieze of silhouetted trees forms a close plane, beyond which the increasing brightness of midground and background reveals relative distances. The strong blacks that can occur in close objects account for much of the effectiveness of compositional framing.

with that light. For most photography at moderate distances, this is essentially true.

However, when photographs are taken of subjects at great distances, the air is less than perfectly transparent, and its presence shows in pictures in the way distant objects are imaged.

Air contains evaporated moisture, dust, smoke, and other extremely fine particles that tend to scatter light. The amount and mix of vapors and particles vary with conditions such as the relative humidity, temperature, winds that stir up dusts, sources of smoke, and so forth, so that the degree of scattering varies. The effect of scattering also changes with the direction of the light. In general, however, the effect of this light scattering on the appearance of objects is proportional to the distance, so that visually, and in pictures, these appearances are distance clues, and the overall effect is called *aerial perspective.* While the effects are additive, they vary with conditions, and they are discussed individually.

Loss of Contrast. At close distances, the luminance of each area in a scene is the direct result of the reflectance of the surface and the amount of light falling on it. White objects in the sun have the highest luminance; dark objects in the shade have the lowest. The typical scene is full-scale; that is, it has a relatively long luminance range.

When the same objects are at a great distance, the light from the higher luminance objects is scattered slightly by the air (and its contents) so that, viewed from a distance, the darker portions do not look as dark. The contrast has been reduced. The first aerial-perspective effect is loss in contrast.

When there are objects both near the camera and at a distance, the difference in contrast provides a strong distance clue.

Increase in Brightness. In addition to scattering the light, the particles in the air are illuminated by the sun so that there is an added level of overall brightness (luminance) to the objects seen through the air. So, in addition to the loss in contrast, the objects seen and photographed at a distance have an overall increased luminance, and are seen and photographed as lighter than they would be at close distances.

Loss in Color Saturation. The preceding two effects not only change the contrast and brightness of tones, they affect the saturation of the colors of

objects seen at a distance, both because the colored light is scattered and because the somewhat desaturated blue color of the aerial haze is added over the original color of the object. The original colors appear less saturated when seen and photographed at a distance than they do when seen close up. This effect is only perceived in color photographs, not in black-and-white.

Shift in Color Hue. The moisture and particles in the air scatter light of short wavelengths to a greater degree than they scatter long wavelengths. This means that the ultraviolet and blue light wavelengths are scattered most. It also means that the color of the haze through which we see and photograph objects at great distances is bluish in color, and hence, adds a veil of blue over the original colors of the objects. If the color film has a relatively high ultraviolet sensitivity, and no ultraviolet absorbing filter is used, the color shifts even more toward blue.

Many color films have ultraviolet absorbing filters coated on their surfaces to reduce the amount of blue in distant objects. The reason for this is that the eyes do not see the ultraviolet, and when it is photographed, it appears blue, and somewhat false. The use of an ultraviolet absorbing filter such as a 2B filter or skylight filter makes certain that the ultraviolet radiation will not be photographed, and that the distant objects will have only the blue cast as the eyes see it.

Loss in Sharpness. Because of the atmosphere and its contents, there is some loss in definition in distant objects, both as seen and as photographed. This is due to the lowering of the contrast and the scattering of the image light. This effect can be heightened by setting the far limit of the depth of field just short of infinity when taking the picture, throwing the extreme distance slightly out of focus. When the slight loss in definition is added to the other effects of aerial perspective, sense of distance is heightened.

(Above left) Contrasty colors in the foreground are saturated with good dark tones. Because of aerial perspective, the contrast in the distance is lowered (no blacks), the tones are lighter in brightness, there is little color saturation, and the hues shift toward the blue direction. (Left) While the normal hue shift in distant objects is toward the blue, low-angle sunlight can change the hue to warm oranges.

Perspective

Degrees of Atmospheric Effects. The degree to which the atmosphere introduces its effects depends largely on:

1. The distance.
2. The amount of haze and dust.
3. The direction of the light.

It is the distance that makes the atmospheric effects work as aerial perspective; the farther away the object is, the more the effects show.

The ultimate extremes in moisture content in the air are fog or, if you are in the mountains, low clouds that act as fog. In fog, objects can be completely obscured by the atmosphere in just a few feet; thus, the feeling of distance between objects at various close distances can be exaggerated. At the other extreme, in the mountains when the air is very clear, there can be almost no atmospheric effect, and distant objects can appear as clear and contrasty as closer objects.

Fortunately, the degree of effect can be seen by the eye and on the ground glass, so that the photographer can judge the aerial perspective before taking the picture.

Maximizing and Minimizing Aerial Perspective. Sometimes the photographer wishes to increase or decrease the atmospheric effects. In color, the best that can be done is to use the ultraviolet absorbing filter, which helps to a small degree to decrease the effect.

In black-and-white photography, a considerable amount of control over aerial perspective can be obtained by the use of filters (with panchromatic films). The relative amounts of increase and decrease given by various filters are shown in the accompanying table.

Use of a deep red filter or an infrared filter, such as the No. 87 filter, with infrared film gives the greatest possible decrease in the effects of aerial haze when the haze is composed of moisture. None of the filters have much effect when the haze is dust or smoke.

Use of a deep red filter with infrared film reduces aerial perspective to a minimum.

FILTERS TO CONTROL AERIAL PERSPECTIVE		
Filter Color	**Filter Numbers**	**Effect on Aerial Perspective**
Deep Blue	47, 47B	Increases by a maximum amount
Light Blue	80C, 80B, 80A	Increases by a moderate amount
Clear	2B, 1A (Skylight)	Decreases slightly
Yellow	8, 15	Decreases somewhat
Orange	21	Decreases moderately
Light Red	23A	Decreases considerably
Deep Red	25, 29	Decreases most

Perspective Distortions

One apparent distortion of perspective has been discussed earlier—the effect on space and the thickness of objects that is evident when serious deviation from true perspective occurs.

Edge Distortion. Another apparent distortion occurs when spherical objects (people's heads, for example) are placed near the edge of the format in wide-angle pictures.

The accompanying illustration shows how a series of flat circles are imaged across a wide field so that they look natural. It also shows how the width of spheres placed in the same positions as the circles are not imaged as equal widths, but the imaged width is increased near the edge of the format by the geometry of rectilinear imaging. The same distortion occurs with cylinders.

This effect shows frequently in banquet and group pictures taken with extreme-wide-angle lenses. The heads of people near the edges and corners of the picture are badly distorted. This does not occur in pictures taken with panorama cameras (cylindrical perspective).

Tilt Perspective Distortion. One of the human vision constancies is that vertical lines are parallel. The only way to get vertical lines to image parallel in pictures is to have the film vertical. The tilt that occurs when the camera is aimed upward or downward was mentioned earlier in this article.

When the camera is aimed upward, parallel lines in the image converge toward the top. If a building is being photographed, the convergent perspective makes the building look as if it is tilting over backwards; hence the name tilt-perspective distortion.

If the camera is aimed downward, parallel lines in the image diverge toward the top, making a box, for example, look larger at the top than at the bottom.

Especially in professional architectural and advertising photography, it is important to image vertical lines vertically, even though the camera is aimed upward or downward. This is usually accomplished by using a view camera and maintaining a vertical back although the rest of the camera is aimed up or down. The accompanying diagrams show how this is done.

Correction of tilt perspective distortion can also be accomplished, within limits, on cameras that do not have swings and tilts. The use of extreme-wide-angle lenses, such as a 17 to 20 mm lens on a 35 mm camera, permits the camera back

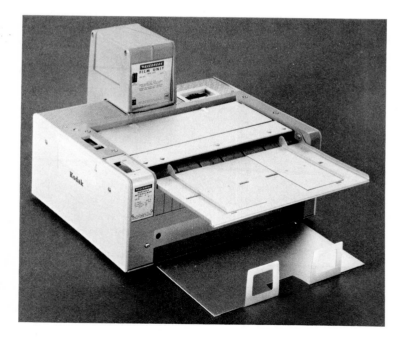

Typical isometric perspective is easily achieved with a view camera. If the camera is simply aimed downward, the verticals become divergent. But, by keeping the film plane vertical and by lowering the lens, perspective is achieved with parallel verticals.

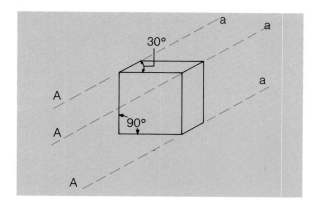
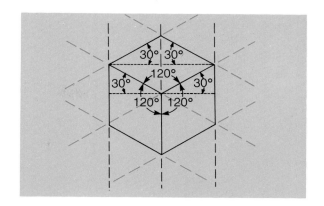

(Left) A form of oblique perspective is easily achieved with a view camera. A long-focal-length lens must be used to keep the diagonal edges nearly parallel (the vanishing point of the lines A–a would be at infinity). With a short-focal-length lens, lines A–a would meet at a vanishing point close behind the subject. (Right) Isometric perspective is difficult to achieve with a camera, and is rarely used in photography. A close approximate is achieved by placing the camera, with a long-focal-length lens, above the subject and in front of its front edge. The film plane is kept vertical while the lens is lowered to show the top of the subject. Diagonal and vertical vanishing points are at infinity.

to remain vertical and still cover considerable height in the picture. The unwanted extra subject matter always resulting from the use of this method can be cropped off when printing. If the lens does not quite image the top of the subject (a building, for instance), the camera can be aimed up slightly, resulting in only slight convergence of the vertical lines. These can then be made parallel again when enlargements are produced.

The use of the camera adjustments to "correct" perspective is discussed in detail in the article VIEW CAMERA.

Oblique and Isometric Perspective

Artists have used these two types of perspective for years, and photographs of block-type structures and appliances are usually made with one of these two types of perspective.

Oblique Perspective. Oblique perspective shows the front face of the block as a rectangle and usually shows two other faces as trapezoids. There is no way to obtain this perspective in photography without using the swings and tilts on a view camera.

To show the top of the block, the camera must be higher than the block. In order to show the side,

the camera must be to one side of the block; in order to have the front face of the block appear as a rectangle, the camera back must be vertical and parallel to the front face. The two accompanying diagrams show how this is accomplished by having the lens lower than the film center and shifted to one side. If these corrections are not used, the front face is imaged with no two sides parallel.

Isometric Perspective. Isometric perspective is so named because of the equal angles that result when this perspective is drawn. The viewpoint is diagonally 45 degrees from two sides of the block and is higher than the block so that the top shows. This is usually drawn so that the lines representing the three faces shown meet at 6 equal 60-degree angles.

The camera viewpoint is placed on a line that bisects the front two faces of the block, and is raised to a position higher than the block. It is not essential that it be raised high enough to make 60-degree angles. In order to keep the three vertical lines vertical in the image, the back is maintained in vertical position by using the drop front on the camera. To gain even more drop, the camera bed can be tilted downward, and the camera back and front swung to vertical positions.

Perspective

Panoramic Perspective

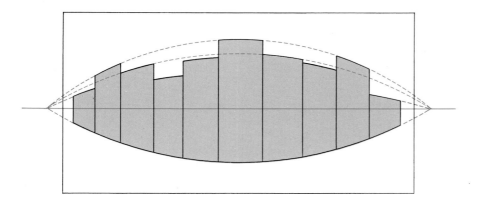

True panoramic perspective of a row of buildings. When a photograph is taken with a panoramic camera, perspective is changed gradually as the camera rotates. Horizontal lines curve to meet at a common vanishing point

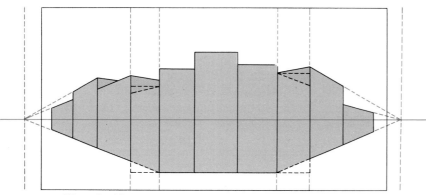

All vertical lines straight and parallel when film is vertical

Jointed sectional perspective. A sectional panorama, composed of several different pictures taken with a normal camera lens, will demonstrate changing magnifications and perspectives as the camera angle is shifted. When the sectional panorama is joined, the perspective of the horizontal lines changes at each point; each picture has its own vanishing points, and the combined result is odd. To avoid this, picture all objects at a distance, with a single horizon in the center and no other horizontal lines in evidence.

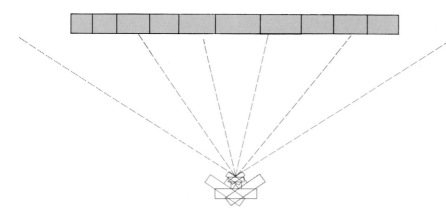

Jointed sectional perspective (top view). Colored lines indicate the views encompassed by shifting camera angles.

Without the use of the camera adjustments, all the parallelism between vertical lines is lost in the image, and divergent distortion results.

Perspective in Sectional Panorama Pictures

In the article PANORAMIC PHOTOGRAPHY, mention is made of taking a series of pictures of a long horizontal subject by rotating the camera about a vertical axis, and later joining the pictures together to form a panoramic view.

Because of the rectilinear perspective of the normal camera lens, this method only works well when there are no important horizontal lines, like in the tops of a number of buildings.

The magnification of objects at a given distance from the camera is constant across the field. This is what gives rectilinear perspective. However, when one picture of a subject is taken, and then another with the camera rotated about the vertical axis of the lens, the line of objects will have changing magnifications because they appear at different distances from the camera. Their images get smaller the more distant they are.

Further, if the first picture faces a row of buildings, the horizontal lines will be parallel. When the camera is rotated, the buildings will be photographed at an angle, and the horizontal lines will no longer be parallel. As a result, when the pictures are joined, the perspective of the horizontal lines will change at each joint, giving an odd, jointed perspective. If a wide-angle lens is being used so that the angular rotation of the camera is great, the change is very abrupt.

The panoramic camera changes the perspective gradually as it rotates, giving a continuously changing perspective, and the horizontal lines are curved instead of having a series of abrupt changes.

If the camera is horizontal, so that the horizon is in the center of the picture, if all objects are at a distance, and if there is just scenery with no horizontal lines other than the horizon, this type of perspective distortion does not show.

Perspective in Portraits

Many of the same geometric and light-and-shade perspective principles used in making landscape, architectural, and advertising pictures apply as well to making portraits.

To fill the frame with the head and shoulders of a subject with a normal camera lens, the camera must usually be about 3 feet from the subject. This results in apparent expansion of the head depth when the finished portrait is viewed from a normal distance. The head appears longer from front to back, and the nose appears oversized.

To get a reasonable-appearing head perspective, the camera distance should be about 6 feet for such subjects. To fill the frame with the head and shoulders requires a lens of about twice normal focal length. For three-quarter views, a lens about 1½ times the focal length, with the increased subject distance, renders an acceptable perspective. A normal lens creates an acceptable perspective of full-length figures and groups of figures because the camera must be farther away to take in the entire subject.

Because of the changes of appearance in the shape of a spherical object near the edge of a picture taken with a wide-angle lens, such lenses must be used with care in making pictures of people.

• *See also:* BARREL DISTORTION; ENLARGERS AND ENLARGING; FILTERS; LANDSCAPE PHOTOGRAPHY; LIGHTING; OPTICS; STEREO PHOTOGRAPHY; TELEPHOTOGRAPHY; VIEW CAMERA; WIDE-ANGLE PHOTOGRAPHY.

Petzval, Josef M.

(1807–1891)
Hungarian optician and mathematician

Petzval was the pioneer in the design of photographic lenses by mathematical methods. The famous Petzval portrait lens was the first such objective designed for photographic use. It combined very good achromatism with a large aperture, which was required to obtain short exposures with the very slow daguerreotype plates. It was manufactured by Voigtlander in Vienna. Until quite recently, this basic lens design was used for portrait lenses and for motion-picture projection lenses.

Petzval showed that the curvature of field of such a lens was inseparable from astigmatic correction, and that both astigmatism and field curvature could not be corrected simultaneously with the types of glass known at the time. His mathematical expression of this condition is known as the "Petzval sum" and depends only upon the powers of the lens elements and the constants of the glasses used. Thus, the sum can only be reduced to zero (indicating a flat field) by the choice of glasses, and so must be done at the very beginning of a lens design.

Petzval also designed the so-called "orthoscopic" (distortion-free) lens for landscape photography and reproduction work.

• *See also*: LENSES; OPTICS.

pH

A measure of the acidity or alkalinity of a solution, pH is expressed on a logarithmic scale from 0 to 14. Numbers from 0 to 7 are acid, those from 7 to 14 alkaline; a solution reading exactly 7 is neutral.

pH is measured in various ways. Where only an approximate reading is required, the measurement is made by adding one of a number of so-called indicator dyes to the solution. As an example, Bromcresol Purple is yellow when the pH of the solution is less than 5.2 (acid), and purple when the solution is at 6.8 or higher. Thus, it is often used in acid stop baths to indicate the point at which the bath is nearly neutral and hence exhausted: As long as the bath remains yellow, there is sufficient acid in it; when it turns purple, it is just about neutral. There are a great many indicator dyes, and by using them in combination, it is possible to pinpoint the pH of a given solution fairly closely.

Where more precise results are required, the procedure is to use an electronic pH meter, which employs a special electrode pair connected to a sensitive meter. Dipping the electrode into the solution produces a definite voltage that can be read by the meter. For convenience, the meter is usually calibrated directly in pH numbers rather than in voltage.

Phenol

Carbolic acid, hydroxybenzene

A preservative for gelatin solutions and other adhesives; rarely used in photography.
Formula: C_6H_5OH
Molecular Weight: 94.11

These colorless crystals, or white crystalline masses, have a strong and characteristic odor. They are soluble in water, benzene, alcohol, ether, and glycerin.

CAUTION: Phenol is poisonous and caustic.

Photoelasticity

Photoelasticity is the photographic technique of determining the distribution of stress in bodies under complex loading situations. In scientific and industrial applications, the technique provides an excellent visualization for stress analysis. To begin the process, a transparent model of the actual object is made and subjected to stresses proportional to the stresses that will be applied to the actual object. The model is then photographed using the methods outlined in this article.

pH OF COMMON PROCESSING SOLUTIONS		
	pH	Processing Solutions
Alkalinity	14	
	13	
	12	Developers with sodium hydroxide (12.0)
	11	
	10	Developers with sodium carbonate (10.2)
	9	Developers with *Kodalk*-Balanced Alkali (9.8–10)
	8	Developers with borax (8.5–9.0)
Neutral	7	
Acidity	6	Exhausted stop bath (5.5)
	5	Plain hypo fixers (5.2)
	4	Acid-hardening fixers (4.1)
	3	Fresh stop bath (3.5)
	2	
	1	

Polarized Light

Unpolarized light consists of light waves vibrating in all directions. A polarizer passes predominantly the light vibrating in the plane parallel to the polarizer axis (called the plane of polarization). If a second polarizer (usually called the *analyzer*) is added so that the plane of polarization is perpendicular to the first, no light will pass. (See the accompanying diagram.)

Double Refraction or Birefringence

Many transparent materials such as calcite and mica produce double refraction; that is, they divide light into two components, or beams. The beams travel at different speeds and are polarized at right angles to each other. In photoelastic stress

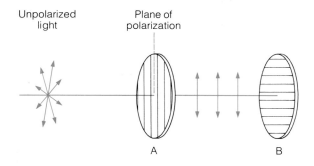

If a second polarizer is added so that the plane of polarization is at right angles to the first, no light will pass.

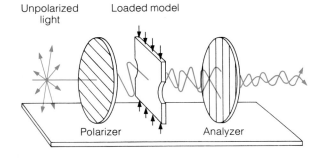

Incident plane-polarized light is divided into two components polarized at right angles by a model under stress.

analysis, incident plane-polarized light is used to reveal the presence of strains in many transparent materials such as glass, gelatin, celluloid, Bakelite, Catalin, Marbelete, Fosterite, Plexiglas, cellulose triacetate, and some epoxy resins. These transparent materials are not normally double refracting, but become so when strained.

Polarized light passing through such a material under stress is divided into two components, each vibrating in the direction of the principal stresses and each traveling at a different speed (see illustration). When the two beams reach the analyzer, the vibrations in the same plane as the plane of the analyzer are transmitted, and the others are blocked. This produces a pattern of bright and dark lines that indicate the variations of stress in the material. When illuminated by a white light source, these stress patterns appear as colored lines. With a monochromatic (narrow-band color) light source, the lines are black.

Lines Produced

Two types of lines, *isochromatic* and *isoclinic*, are produced. A typical pattern with isochromatic and isoclinic lines is shown in the accompanying illustration.

Isochromatic Lines. When the two polarized rays transmitted from the model are out of phase, the lines are known as *isochromatic* lines. When white light is used, the isochromatic lines are colored. One frequency is canceled by interference at each point of double refraction (coinciding with maximum stresses), leaving a colored line that is white light minus one frequency. The analysis of the various colors and patches will indicate the magnitude of difference between the principal stresses. In other words, the magnitude of the principal stresses controls the degree of birefringence and, therefore, the extent to which the polarized rays are out of phase.

When monochromatic light is used, the isochromatic lines are black. With monochromatic light, it is possible to identify 12 to 15 series, or orders, of stress lines. On the other hand, with white light, the colored lines become indistinct beyond the fifth or sixth order. White light is probably the more useful, particularly for work with small stresses, because it tends to yield less confusing patterns.

Isoclinic Lines. When the plane of the incident polarized light coincides with the direction of one of the principal stresses, the light passes straight through the transparent model. If the analyzer is at right angles to the polarizer, no light is visible, and the black lines observed are known as *isoclinics*. The isoclinic lines are always black and are superimposed on the isochromatic lines.

The isoclinic line corresponding to any stress inclination can be determined by rotating both the polarizer and analyzer, but always keeping their planes of polarization at right angles. The two illustrations of the stress pattern of a compressed ring show isoclinics with the polarizer and analyzer rotated 45 degrees.

Circular Polarization. In some investigations, the isochromatic lines can be examined more easily when the black isoclinic lines are removed. This can be done by placing quarter-wave (Q) retardation plates on each side of the model *between* the polarizer and analyzer. The retardation plate resolves an incident plane-polarized beam into two components, one of which travels through the Q plate more slowly (one quarter-wave out of phase) than the other. The combination of a polarizer and quarter-wave plate yields light that is nondirectional in nature; this is called *circularly polarized light*. Photograph C shows the isochromatic stress pattern obtained using the same model shown in photographs A and B, but with circularly polarized light. Light-field or dark-field backgrounds can be obtained by rotating one of the quarter-wave plates 90 degrees.

Photographing Stress Patterns

The best results for photographing isoclinics are obtained with a dark-field arrangement, since black isoclinics are produced. The light-field arrangement is favored for photographing isochromatic lines, because the edge of the model is more apparent.

Equipment

Light Source. Theoretically, the ideal light is a high-intensity point source, used with condensers. Small quartz-halogen lamps make fairly good point-light sources. However, excellent results have been obtained with an opal diffuser and an electronic flash, without using a point source and condensers. If you have the necessary equipment, try both lighting systems. The condenser system may be preferred if quantitative measurements are to be made from the photographs. The diffuse system, however, is simpler and almost as good.

Filters. The following filters can be used for photographing stress patterns.

Light Balancing. Balance a point-light source by using the appropriate conversion filter for the color temperature of the lamp and the type of color film used. Place the filter on the camera lens, not between the polarizer and analyzer. A light-balancing filter should not be necessary when electronic flash is used with daylight-type color film.

Monochromatic. Use a filter such as Kodak Wratten gelatin filter No. 25 for monochromatic techniques. The filter can be placed over the light source or after the first condenser, but not between the polarizer and analyzer.

Polarizers, Analyzers, and Quarter-Wave Plates. (See the following diagram.) The polarizing screen, P (polarizer) must be large enough to intercept the entire light beam. Polarizing sheet material is supplied by Polacoat Incorporated, 9750 Conklin Road, Blue Ash, Ohio 45242, and Polaroid Corporation, 549 Technology Square, Cambridge, Massachusetts 02139. The other polarizer, A (analyzer), should be of high optical quality for use over a camera lens.

The quarter-wave plates, Q_1 and Q_2, are usually made of sheet mica selected for freedom from flaws. Synthetic plates made by Bausch & Lomb, Incorporated, Rochester, New York 14605, are satisfactory. Other Q plates have been made by using suitably stressed glass or two sheets of cellophane crossed at the appropriate angle.

Condensers and Diffuser. (See the accompanying diagram.) The condenser, C_1, should be larger than the area of the model to be photographed. The focal length is not critical, but C_1 must be mounted to produce a parallel beam of light through the model, M, to C_2, the second condenser. C_2 converges the light so that it can pass into the camera lens. As mentioned previously, a diffuser, such as opal glass, can be used between the model and the light source in lieu of condensers C_1 and C_2.

Camera and Film. Use any through-the-lens viewing camera, such as a single-lens reflex camera or view camera, and select a moderately high-

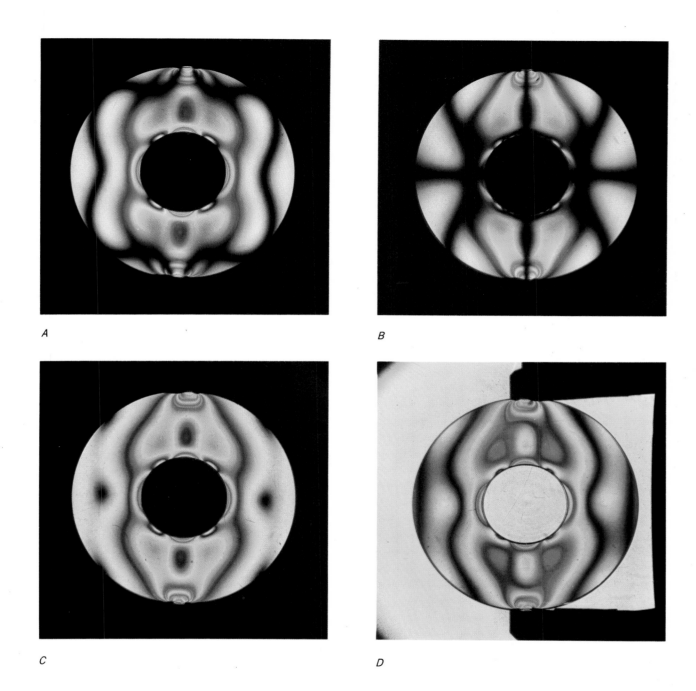

These photographs show stress patterns of a ring compressed diametrically from top and bottom. The black lines are isoclinic and the colored lines are isochromatic. Photo A was made with the polarizer axes parallel and at a 90-degree angle to the principal stress. Photo B shows the isoclinics with the polarizer axes at a 45-degree angle to the principal stress. In photo C, isoclinic lines have been practically eliminated by using quarter-wave plates to obtain circularly polarized light. Photo D is the same as photo C, except that one of the quarter-wave plates was rotated to obtain a light-field background.

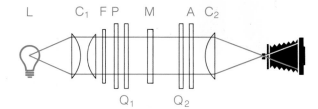

contrast film for black-and-white photographs. Most color films are suitable for use. Often the results of color photography can be beautiful as well as informative.

Model

You may need to photograph stresses appearing in manufactured material, such as epoxy derivatives, to determine what stresses are occurring in the manufacturing process. Or, a scale model can be made of an object in which the amount and areas of stress are to be studied. The model should be made of a suitable transparent material (such as one of those mentioned earlier in this article) that is birefringent when stressed. The model should be a thin section, ¼ inch, or less, in thickness. The model should be cut or sliced very carefully so that stresses are not introduced while cutting. Use extremely sharp machining equipment, and finish the cutting with light cuts. You can scribe fine lines on the model to use as reference marks in the photographs.

Loading the Model. Apply stresses to the model, similar to those that the real object will encounter, and photograph it at various levels or conditions of load. When movement is present, use electronic flash as the light source.

Model for Three-Dimensional Stress Analysis. With some materials, such as Fosterite, it is possible to have three-dimensional models fabricated that can have stresses "frozen" into them by heating the model to about 121 C (250 F), then loading it and cooling it slowly to room temperature. The model can be sliced into sections for analysis of the stresses frozen into it.

Taking the Picture

Proper exposure settings will vary greatly, depending upon your particular setup—light source, filtration, model, film used, and so forth.

You will need to experiment and bracket your exposures.

Isoclinic lines can be difficult to photograph because isochromatic lines are always present. They show up best with a point-light source and a good condenser system. Use white light with high-contrast film. The isochromatic lines are of various colors, but the isochromatic colors will be less distinguishable than the black isoclinics, and the isochromatics will tend to blend to about the same density. You can reduce the isochromatic lines even more by treating the negative in Kodak farmer's reducer.

If the model contains scratches or fingerprints, you can often improve the sharpness and general appearance of the stress patterns by coating the surface of the model with a light, clear oil, such as Nujol or Halowax, and then wiping it clean.

• *See also:* POLARIZED-LIGHT PHOTOGRAPHY.

Photofabrication

Photofabrication is a technique of working metals and nonmetals with the aid of photography and chemicals. At the heart of the method are the photosensitive resists—solutions of resins in organic solvents that become light-sensitive when applied in a coating to the chosen material and dried. After exposure, the unwanted areas of the resist coating are removed by the developer, leaving a resist pattern that possesses extremely high chemical resistance.

How Photosensitive Resists Work

When exposed to ultraviolet radiation through a photographic transparency, a negative-working resist "cross-links" or polymerizes in the areas that are struck by the ultraviolet radiation. The image formed by the ultraviolet radiation and defined by the clear areas of the transparency is insoluble in the developing bath. The opaque areas of the transparency act as a mask and allow those portions that have received no exposure to be dissolved in the developer. The soluble portions wash away and leave a tough, chemically resistant image in minute relief on the surface. This image acts as a clearly defined mask for etching, plating, or some other type of surface alteration.

Ultraviolet radiation striking the surface of a positive-working resist layer will render that layer *soluble*. The unexposed resist areas are *insoluble* in the resist developer. Positive resists will require a transparency with image values the reverse of those used for exposure of negative resists to produce similar results in the final surface treatment.

Chemical Milling

Chemical milling is a method of, first, selectively masking portions of a metal surface, and then using an etchant to remove exposed portions of the metal *chemically*. Photosensitive resists form a barrier to the penetration of etchant when they are suitably exposed and processed. Photographic techniques allow production of precise parts and provide methods for making each part the same as the last. Chemical milling is especially useful for working metals and foils where physical action might distort, set up strain in, or otherwise change the character of, the metal. With this process, thin or brittle metals can be worked and the process yield will remain high.

Plating and Electroforming

In both plating and electroforming, a photosensitive resist is used to form a stencil through which metals can be deposited on a surface. The radiation-hardened and developed photoresist image forms a nonconducting pattern for the plating process. Plating may be used as a method for adding a design to a surface, as a preliminary step before etching, or to add metals with distinctive properties that are dissimilar to those of the base metal.

Electroforming is normally used to produce such highly detailed articles as fine-mesh screens and evaporation masks. In electroforming, the resist defines a pattern on a metallic mandrel, which serves as the electrical conductor for electroplating. After an article is electroformed on the mandrel, it can be stripped away and the original image is available for reuse. Because of the support given by the mandrel, very fine parts can be made with little damage.

The Photofabrication Process

All photofabrication processes have in common the use of a line transparency and a photoresist-coated surface. The photographic transparency defines the area of exposure on the photo-resist coating. The resist, when exposed and developed, forms a stencil that confines further chemical operations to the unprotected portions of the surface.

These sequences show the effects of exposure and subsequent development on negative-working and positive-working resist coatings. (The cross-hatched areas show hardened resist.)

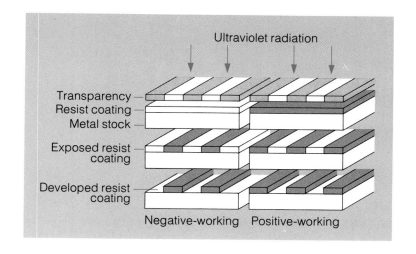

The typical photofabrication process proceeds with these steps:

1. Prepare the master drawing or artwork.
2. Produce, from the artwork, a film transparency for photoresist exposure control.
3. Prepare and coat a surface with photoresist.
4. Expose the photoresist surface, controlling the area of exposure with the transparency.
5. Process the resist to form a stencil.
6. Proceed with etching, plating, or electroforming.

Artwork

Whether the end product is to be a printed circuit, a chemically milled part, an integrated circuit, or a nameplate, the result will be only as good as the initial planning and execution of the original artwork. To produce a part by the photofabrication process, one needs a master or working transparency of the desired pattern. This is obtained by first making a master pattern and then photographically reducing this master artwork to the required size.

For most purposes, a piece of artwork is prepared at two to several hundred times the actual size of the finished part. This is done to make sure of dimensional accuracy on the photographic transparency, since any inaccuracy in the preparation technique is reflected in the accuracy of the finished part.

NOTE: The word "transparency" is used to denote either a negative or positive photographic image on film or glass plates. This term is chosen to avoid the necessity of distinguishing image values each time.

Since one of the basic processes for photofabrication—etching—is subtractive (material is removed), it may be necessary to make the artwork elements slightly oversized or undersized to compensate. When etching to give lettering designs in relief, the elements become smaller due to

sidewise etch. For the reverse case—etching the lettering into the surface—the design grows larger with metal removal.

Removing the Resist

Removal of the resist image after etching or plating depends on many factors. These include the thickness of the coating, whether or not the resist has been postbaked, and compatibility of the metal surface with the particular stripping solution. Consequently, any commercial stripper formulation should be evaluated both on its performance under a given set of conditions and on its compatibility with a particular surface. There is no "universal" resist stripper.

• *See also:* NAMEPLATES, PHOTOGRAPHIC; PHOTORESIST; PRINTED CIRCUITS.

Photo-Finish Photography

Photo-finish photography uses special cameras, film, and processing to quickly produce a sharp, accurate photograph of the contestants in a race as they cross the finish line. Photo-finish pictures are most widely used to determine the winner and the subsequent order of finish in horse racing, but they are also used for greyhound racing and for important athletic events such as the Olympic Games. These photographs provide racing judges with precise, impartial evidence for determining official results, which in many cases would be difficult or impossible to do with the unaided eye. In addition, they provide a permanent record of the results.

Conditions for Making the Photographs

Because photo-finish photographs are used to decide the winner and become official documents, they must be very accurately made. There are four conditions that must be met:

Correct Perspective. The camera must be exactly aligned with the finish line, which is usually at a right angle across the width of the track. A high camera position is an advantage in obtaining visual separation in the photograph; most photo-finish cameras are located on the roof of the judging stand.

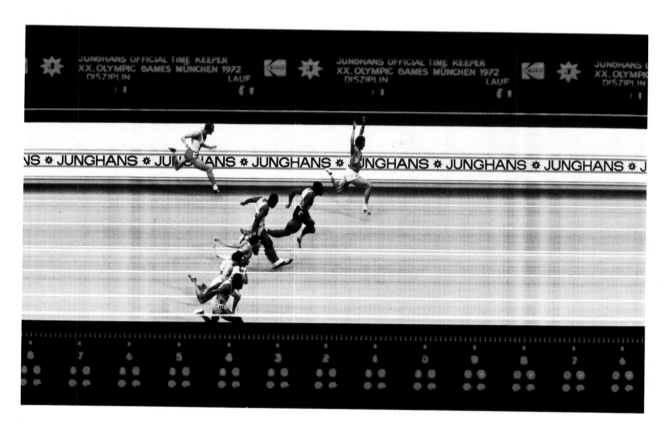

The cameras used for track events like the Olympic Games operate in the same way as those used for horse racing. Although, black-and-white film and rapid processing are normally used, this photo from the 1972 Munich Olympic Games was made on Kodak color film. Photo courtesy of Junghans GmbH.

Excellent Sharpness. The photograph must be sharp enough to make accurate judging possible. Sharpness includes correct focus, adequate depth of field, and sufficient "stopping" of motion.

Correct Timing. Photographs ideally should be made just as the horse's nose or the runner's chest reaches the finish line. Photos made a moment earlier or later might show contestants in an incorrect order of finish. Because of its special design, the slit camera—used almost universally for photo-finish work today—makes correct timing automatic.

Rapid Access. Since spectators and contestants are anxious to know the results, only a few minutes can elapse between the finish of a race and the availability of the processed photograph. By using specially-designed film, highly active processing chemicals, and high temperatures, photo-finish negatives are ready for use less than half a minute after the race.

Evolution of Photo-Finish Photography

In the early years of photography, slow lenses and emulsions demanded long exposures. As a result the images of even slow-moving objects were blurred, and photographing anything as fast as a running horse was out of the question. From 1840 to the 1870's various improvements reduced exposure times from minutes to seconds, and finally to fractions of a second.

By 1878, photography of motion had progressed to Eadweard Muybridge's silhouette

Photo-Finish Photography

photos of a trotting horse. These proved that at certain moments all four hooves are off the ground at once, and revealed that the way painters had portrayed running horses for centuries was wrong. These pictures were also good enough to suggest that photography would be a valuable aid in judging race finishes. However, tripping the camera by hand was not accurate enough, and stringing a trip-wire to the shutter after the horses had passed in the first part of a race was not practical.

It was not until the 1930's, when photoelectric cells became available, that it was possible to trip the camera accurately and automatically when the winning horse crossed the finish line. But these photographs revealed another problem: The second and third place horses might or might not be in the picture, and their positions might change before they actually crossed the finish line. Photocell triggering of a still camera did not offer any reliable way to trip the camera exactly when the "place" (second) and "show" (third) horses reached the finish line.

One solution to this problem was to use a motion-picture camera. To minimize the distance that the horses moved between frames, high-speed cameras that made as many as 250 frames per second were used. These were quite successful but made hundreds of photographs of the end of each race, leaving the photographer to find the two or three that were of interest. That was a time-consuming task and, if the race was very close, made it difficult to obtain immediate results.

Clearly, neither the conventional still camera nor the high-speed movie camera was ideally suited to photo-finish work. What was really needed was a camera that would make a continuous picture of everything that crossed the finish line over a selected period of time. The problem was solved by a Hollywood motion-picture engineer named Lorenzo del Riccio.

Del Riccio realized that if the image of moving subjects is seen through a narrow vertical slit and is recorded on a film that moves past the slit at the same speed as the subjects, the result will be a continuous photograph of the subjects in exact order, no matter what time or distance intervals are between them. Del Riccio's principle is used in nearly all photo-finish cameras today.

The Photo-Finish Camera

There are several names for the photo-finish camera: It is called a *slit camera* because it photographs through a slit; a *streak camera* because objects standing still become streaked images on the film (although moving objects are recorded sharply); and a *strip camera* because it produces an image on a long strip of film. Probably "slit camera" is the most descriptive phrase.

The slit camera is neither a still nor a movie camera, but it shares some of the features of both. It provides a sharp, still image of moving subjects, and it uses moving film. However, the still picture records an unbroken succession of moments rather than a single, "frozen" instant, and it provides a single, continuous image rather than a series of separate frames.

The slit camera does not have a shutter; instead, a plate with a slit only about 0.25 mm ($^1/_{100}$ inch) wide is located between the lens and the film. Although the lens field may be wide enough

A modern slit photo-finish camera is a precise optical-electronic instrument. The highly accurate quartz timing unit on the bottom prints elapsed times along the edge of the film, which permits reading each contestant's time directly on the photo-finish picture. Photo courtesy Photochart, Inc.

to include an entire horse, the slit permits only a fraction of that image to reach the film at any one time. The slit is exactly aligned with the finish line, so that as a horse crosses the line, the tip of its nose is imaged through the slit first, then the rest of its nose and head, the neck, the shoulders, body, tail, and, in turn, the following horses.

If the film remained stationary, all these image bits would pile up on one another in the same narrow strip of film. But a precision electric drive in the camera moves the film past the slit at the same speed as the image of the horses, typically 1 or 2 inches per second. In this way, each new part of the image passing through the slit falls on a different portion of the film. In effect, the combination of moving film and fixed slit "wipes" a continuous image onto the film.

A photo-finish camera usually has a built-in exposure meter that relates lens apertures to various rates of film travel. An optical system in the camera exposes the track name, the date, and other information onto the edge of the film; this makes the identification data a permanent part of each image.

The camera may also include a sophisticated electronic timer that will expose elapsed times onto the film as the horses finish. A lightproof take-up compartment for exposed film and a built-in film cutter make it possible to remove the exposed portion for processing immediately after each finish.

Film and Processing

The film used in photo-finish cameras is usually 35 mm in width, but it is unperforated and comes wound on reels in 100-foot lengths. The amount used for one photo finish varies, depending on how far apart the horses are at the finish and what focal-length lens is used on the camera. Frequently a photo-finish negative will be a strip of film about 2 feet long. If the horses are spaced far apart at the finish, the camera must run longer and the negative strip will be correspondingly longer.

The films used for general-purpose photo-finish work are panchromatic and similar to Kodak Plus-X pan film in characteristics; however, they have hardened emulsions to allow rapid processing at high temperatures. Typical processing uses concentrated, active chemicals at 37.8 C (100 F); development time ranges from 5 to 15 seconds, and

fixing takes another 5 seconds. Immediately after fixing, the film is rinsed in water and placed in a glass carrier while wet. It is ready for projection to the judges, using a modified filmstrip projector, or for making prints in a standard enlarger.

Instant-print film is used in some photo-finish cameras where the entire back of the camera is moved past the slit during exposure. The length of the film limits the number of contestants that can be photographed with this method, but the fact that no darkroom is required is convenient.

Photo-Finish Setup

Photo-finish cameras are operated from a permanent darkroom so the results can be processed immediately. There are generally two cameras, one mounted above the other, with their lenses aimed through lighttight portholes in the darkroom wall. Both cameras are precisely aligned with the finish line, and they are securely mounted on sturdy platforms. While both are aimed directly at the finish line, one has a long-focal-length lens that covers only the area at the inside of the track where the winning horses nearly always are when they cross the finish line; the other has a shorter-focal-length lens that covers the entire track width in case a horse happens to be running "wide." At most tracks, a mirror complex is installed on the far side of the track, directly opposite the camera lenses so that two views are recorded on each film simultaneously, one from each side of the track. This is helpful in distinguishing which horse is first across the line in very close races.

Processing trays, projector, enlarger, and stabilization print processor are at hand in the darkroom. Everything is organized for routine procedures both for speed, and to make certain that a usable record is made of every single race. This is not an insignificant achievement, because a track may have as many as 1000 races in a season.

To record the end of a race, the photographer observes the action through a lighttight port and starts the camera motors when the horses approach the finish line. As the horses go by they "streak" their images onto the film. After the last horse has passed, the photographer stops the motor, cuts off the exposed film strip, and processes it. As previously described, the results are ready for viewing within 30 seconds. If a print is required, another 30 to 60 seconds may be required.

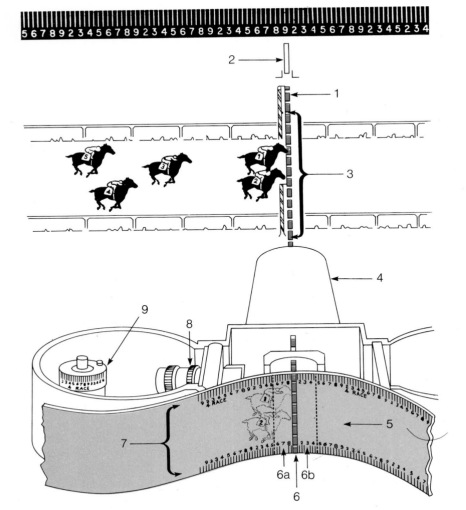

Photo-finish camera and setup (for clarity, the image on the film has been reversed): (1) racetrack finish line; (2) mirror complex; (3) field of vision; (4) camera lens; (5) film; (6) vertical aperture; (6a) stationary edge; (6b) adjustable edge; (7) guide registrations; (8) lens recording registrations; (9) data-bearing cylinder.

Slit-Camera Pictures

Considering how unusual the camera is, the most surprising characteristic of photo-finish pictures is that they look so much like conventional photographs. However, there are several important differences:

Perspective. There is no perspective from left to right; everything in the photograph is seen directly perpendicular to the lens axis. That is because each part of each horse is photographed only at the finish-line position. In a normal photograph only the part of a horse directly at the finish line would be seen along the lens axis; the rest would be seen at an angle either to the left or to the right.

Background. The background is a series of parallel streaks running from side to side. These are hoofprints, shadows, posts and railings, and all other stationary details on the racetrack. Because it is standing still, each light or dark subject area is stretched out into a streak by the film moving past the slit.

Distortion. The horses or athletes may have distorted legs (or arms); in some cases the entire body may be distorted. The distortions occur because the body moves forward at a fairly constant speed—matched by the film—but the legs and arms move back and forth. While they are moving backward, relative to the body and film movement, they will be distorted into a streak by

This photo-finish picture shows the narrow victory of Affirmed over Alydar in the 1978 Belmont Stakes. The slit photo-finish camera automatically photographs each horse (or athlete) exactly at the finish line, and permits determining winners by fractions of an inch. The top portion of the picture is a mirror image, formed by a narrow trackside mirror. Since the film moves horizontally, the mirror image extends the entire length of the photograph. The white "finish line" in the photo is actually superimposed when the enlargement is made. It can be placed anywhere in the picture, as long as it is accurately vertical—confirmed by the edge numbers. Photo courtesy of Jones Precision Photo Finish, Inc. and Jerome P. O'Neill, Jr.

the camera. Legs looking like this are called "rubber legs." If a contestant is moving much slower than usual, it will take a longer time to pass across the area covered by the slit, hence the image will be stretched out or lengthened. An especially fast contestant will show just the opposite effect—being unusually squeezed or compressed.

Finish Line. Since the finish line is stationary, it does not appear in the finished photograph. *All* parts of the picture are taken at the finish, so this doesn't matter. Every contestant in the photo is crossing the finish line, which means that every one of them has run the full distance. (In a conventional instantaneous photo, some would not yet have finished while others would already have passed the line.) When two contestants finish close together, a white vertical line may be added to the print during enlarging, in order to separate them. The line will be placed on the horse's or greyhound's nose, or on the athlete's chest. As long as it is accurately vertical, this line can be placed at the required position on the print because each point is at the finish line.

• *See also:* ACTION PHOTOGRAPHY; HIGH-SPEED PHOTOGRAPHY; MAREY, ETIENNE JULES; MOTION STUDY; MUYBRIDGE, EADWEARD JAMES; RAPID PROCESSING; SPORTS PHOTOGRAPHY.

Photoflood Lamps

"Photoflood lamps" was formerly a trademark of General Electric Company for incandescent lamps operated at higher than normal voltage. Known in England as "overrun" lamps, photoflood lamps (photolamps) have very high efficiency; a 250-watt lamp is said to produce as much light as a normal lamp consuming 750 watts. Because of the high burning temperature, the life of these lamps is very short. The original No. 1 (250-watt) photoflood lamp had a life of only two hours, which was later extended to four hours by improvements in manufacture. The No. 2 photoflood lamp, burning 500 watts, has a six-hour life.

The photoflood lamp is made in a variety of sizes and shapes, including several in reflector-type envelopes, eliminating the need for any special lamp fixture. Some photolamps are made of blue glass, which raises the color temperature from 3400 K (white bulbs) up to about 4900 K. This is close enough to daylight color film balance to use without filtration for many requirements. An 82A filter can be used to achieve a closer color balance.

• *See also:* INCANDESCENT LAMPS.

Photogrammetry

Photogrammetry is defined as the science of making measurements from photographs. Originally, it was essentially a technique of aerial photography and stereoplotting used in aerial surveying. After World War I, many private firms and government agencies went into aerial photography; World War II then accelerated the growth of this technology. Since then, new materials, equipment, and methods have evolved to make photogrammetry so advantageous that it is now standard for virtually all topographic mapping. While its original use was in aerial surveying (and it is still used for this purpose), a variety of techniques for other purposes has been developed.

In practice, all this is by no means simple. An aerial photograph is *not* a map. Uncorrected photographs, although usable for interpretation, must be corrected before accurate measurements can be made. Quality photographs are fundamental to the success of an aerial photogrammetric project.

Scale

The basic principle of photogrammetry is simple enough. Here we will first define scale. Suppose aerial photographs are to be taken from an airplane flying at an altitude of 10,000 feet with an aerial-type camera having a 12-inch focal length lens. The exposures are about 9 inches square on long rolls of aerial film. Since the focal length is exactly 1 foot and the lens will be focused at infinity, the scale of reduction is equal to the altitude of the plane—that is 1:10,000. If the altitude were 20,000 feet with the same 12-inch focal length lens, the scale would be 1:20,000, and so on. It is now more common to use aerial cameras with a 6-inch, or a half-foot, focal-length lens. Then if the plane were flying at 10,000 feet, the scale would be 1:20,000. A simple formula is

$$S = \frac{1}{H \div F}$$

where: S is the scale, H is the height above the ground in feet, and F is the focal length of the lens in feet. Scale is always referred to as that on the original aerial-camera film.

From this, the making of measurements and drawing of maps from such photographs would seem to be a very simple task.

Altitude. In practice it is by no means simple. For one thing, there is no height information in any one photograph, but this poses no great problem as will be explained later. Also, it is assumed that the altitude from which the aerial exposures were

Flight pattern for obtaining overlapping vertical photographs. The aircraft moves in parallel and overlapping paths; pictures are taken so that they overlap both along the line of flight and between the flight paths. Photo courtesy Wild Heerbrugg Instruments, Inc.

made is accurately known, which is almost never the case. The ordinary airplane altimeter is not very accurate at best; in addition it is a barometric device and indicates elevation above sea level. To know the actual height of the aircraft above the terrain, the elevation of the ground at any point must also be known. Some so-called "absolute altimeters" have been built; they usually work on a radar principle, but it is necessary in this case to have some means of knowing the altitude from which each frame of film is taken and having the figure recorded on the film itself.

Even then, the problem is not solved. Assume that the aircraft is flying at an average altitude of 10,000 feet and that the scale of the photograph is 1:10,000. But in the middle of one given photograph is a broad hill or land rise 200 feet high. Then all details on this hilltop are 200 feet closer to the aerial camera than the remainder of the scene, and therefore the scale is proportionately larger; that is, details on top of this hill are recorded at a scale of 1:9800 rather than 1:10,000.

There are further difficulties. For precise mapping, the aircraft should be flying perfectly level; if, for instance, it is tilted several degrees to the left or right, then the distance to the ground will be greater on one side of the photo than on the other, and the photos will have different scales on the two edges.

In short, the use of photographic mapping is limited by lack of reliable information as to the true scale of the photographs. In practice, it is usually necessary to send out a surveying party to locate certain major objects in the photographs and to measure the distance from one to the next, thus establishing an exact scale for the final map.

Once this has been done, the use of photographic methods does, indeed, facilitate the making of a map. When using old methods, it is necessary for the ground party to identify and locate every object in the map area and to measure its location, altitude, and other major parameters. With photographs, it is possible to have the ground party locate only major landmarks and establish

Comparison of a black-and-white panchromatic photo (left) and a black-and-white infrared photo (below left) of a forested area shows the ability of infrared film to reveal differences in vegetation, in a way which the panchromatic film cannot. Photo courtesy Carl Zeiss, Inc. and Keuffel and Esser Co.

their coordinates; then the draftsmen, using the photographs, can adjust the scale of each small section and fill in the details from the pictures.

Mosaics

Paper prints of aerial photos can be assembled as pasted-up composites or mosaics. Uncorrected prints can be used for making mosaics of small areas, provided that the errors in the photos are not excessive.

A rectifying enlarger provides a way of making corrected prints from aerial negatives for controlled mosaics. At the present time, controlled mosaics are seldom used for precise measurements of terrain features because of the limits of the accuracy as previously discussed under the explanation of scale. They can, however, be used for photointerpretation. Contour lines and other features can be added to controlled mosaics.

Making Corrections

A variety of errors must be corrected in the overlapping aerial photographs, so that accurate, measurable maps can be made.

Stereoplotting. One method for making these corrections is stereoplotting. The first step is to make either full- or reduced-size prints on film or glass plates (for maximum dimensional stability) of each of the aerial negatives. These prints are called "diapositives."

An overlapping pair of diapositives is positioned in the stereoplotter and the images are viewed directly by the operator or the images are projected on the plotting table and examined in this manner. In the viewing method, the height measurements are made by observing a floating dot in the stereoplotter. This involves two reticles, one for each eye, having a dot at the center of each, and supported at a fixed height above the photographs being viewed. At the start, the reticles are adjusted so that the dots are directly over a given point on top of the highest elevation. With the stereoplotter correctly adjusted, the dots will fuse and appear as a single dot, resting directly upon the chosen point. If the reticles are moved—without changing their spacing—to a point over a lower elevation, the dot will still appear single, floating in space above the ground. By changing the separation of the reticles, the dot can be caused

to rise or fall, in this case being lowered until it rests upon the ground at the lower elevation. It is then necessary only to measure the amount the reticles were moved to determine the difference in elevation, with due regard to the scale of the aerial photographs.

Projection. The projection method accomplishes the height measurements by utilizing two projected images, again from diapositives from a stereo pair and the dots previously mentioned. A small white screen is supported upon a vertical track, and the entire unit can be moved to different parts of the image area. At each selected point, the screen is raised or lowered until a chosen detail fuses into a single image, and the elevation can be read off a vernier on the height adjustment of the screen unit to the proper scale.

There are many other devices used in the making of maps from aerial photographs; all work on principles similar to those mentioned above, varying in speed, convenience, and precision.

The Map

This translation or plotting can be done in several ways, depending largely on the equipment being used. Some equipment is essentially manual. The plotted map made from the corrected stereo image can take several forms: pencil or ink on paper or film, or lines scribed on film base coated with a layer that can be cut and removed.

Provided the angle of view is known, it is not absolutely essential that the photograph be made vertically; if the camera has a known tilt, the photographs made can later be corrected photographically (for small angles of tilt) or geometrically (for large angles).

Tilt correction for small angles is done by making corrected prints in an enlarger utilizing the Scheimpflug principle. Adjustment of scale to facilitate drafting can be done at the same time.

More sophisticated plotting equipment has the ability to automatically record and reproduce information in a variety of forms. Plotting can be done so as to yield a hard-copy plot, magnetic tape, punch cards, or a combination. The magnetic tape or punch cards can be used to provide paper printouts of data, to automatically plot in pencil or ink on scribing material, or to provide prints on photographic film.

New Methods of Recording Ground Data

While the science of photogrammetry is essentially one of aerial photography and of stereoplotting, some new methods of recording ground data from aircraft are now being used to supplement the traditional photogrammetric methods. One of these methods involves the use of side-looking airborne radar (SLAR) to penetrate some types of earth cover in order to reveal features that cannot be seen by a camera. Another method uses heat-sensitive devices to detect points of heat concentration or temperature variation. Both procedures are proving to be of great value in the analyses and control of problems affecting the environment.

Underwater Photogrammetry

Photogrammetric methods were originally developed for photographic recordings made from the air, but their utilization in water is likely to be of greater significance. Much has been done to develop means by which the physical nature of an object existing in water can be recognized. Of course, the physical properties of water, including density, refractive index, light transmission, pressure, and others, pose problems of many kinds.

Uniform illumination is of paramount importance. Light characteristics in various waters will not be the same, and there will be transmission losses due to scattering and absorption. These create problems for underwater photogrammetric photography that are quite different from those for normal underwater photography. Nevertheless, photogrammetry can provide underwater maps with precision not achievable by other means.

Precise maps are important, not only to engineers who must place valuable equipment on the sea floor, but also to the marine geologists and biologists, chemical and physical oceanographers, and acousticians.

Microphotogrammetry

On a miniature scale, photogrammetric methods can be used to prepare three-dimensional models of microscopic objects. This is done by making two photographs of the object through a microscope, shifting it a definite amount between exposures. A stereo pair is produced, and when enlargements are made, the vertical dimensions of the object can be measured using a stereoscope and the floating-dot reticles, exactly as is done with aerial photographs.

• *See also:* AERIAL PHOTOGRAPHY; SCHEIMPFLUG PRINCIPLE; THERMAL PHOTOGRAPHY; UNDERWATER PHOTOGRAPHY.

Further Reading: Baker, Wilfred H. *Elements of Photogrammetry.* New York, NY: Ronald Press Co., 1960; Higgs, Gary K. *Photogrammetry and Aerial Photographic Interpretation.* Ann Arbor, MI: A.W.M. Company, 1975; Moffitt, Francis H. *Photogrammetry,* 2nd ed. Scranton, PA: Thomas Y. Crowell Co., 1967; Spurr, Stephen H. *Photogrammetry—Photointerpretation with a Section on Application to Forestry,* 2nd ed. New York, NY: Ronald Press Co., 1960; Wolf, Paul R. *Elements of Photogrammetry.* New York, NY: McGraw-Hill Book Co., 1974.

Photograms

Photograms are photographs made without a camera. A photogram is made in the darkroom by placing opaque, translucent, or transparent objects on a sheet of photographic paper, exposing the paper to light, and then processing it. The resulting print will have a dark background and silhouettes of the objects in white. By using black-and-white materials and adjusting the exposure, you can create a black background or any shade of gray. With color materials, the background can be any color desired. When translucent and transparent objects are used, there will be shades of gray or color as well as clear whites.

Photograms can also be made by placing a flat object in the negative carrier of the enlarger and projecting it onto the paper. A glass negative carrier is necessary to hold the subject in a flat plane. The best subjects for this type of photogram are flat nature objects, such as leaves, feathers, transparent insect wings, weeds, and grasses. Since a negative is not used, image degradation is held to a minimum, and enlargements produced by this method will have superb sharpness and faithfully reveal the most minute detail.

More sophisticated photograms can be made by arranging objects on a sheet of glass suspended above the paper to obtain a softened or blurred outline. By combining this technique with objects placed directly on the paper, you can simultaneously produce sharp and blurred images. You can also make multiple exposures and add or remove

The dried weeds used in this photogram were simply laid on the paper, unpressed, and the paper was then exposed. The butterfly is a costume jewelry pin. (For more information on photograms, see the article on Greeting Cards.) Photo by Penny Illingworth.

objects to obtain overlapping silhouettes in different shades of gray. With color materials the overlapping silhouettes can be various shades of the same tone or completely different colors.

Photograms can be printed with negatives, too. Simply place the objects on the paper, place the negative in the enlarger, and print them both at the same time.

Exposure times have to be found by trial and error. Making test strips without any objects will give the time of exposure for different tones.

• *See also:* SPECIAL EFFECTS.

 Photographic Organizations

A listing of some of the many organizations associated with photography is provided here. Letter abbreviations precede the full name. For membership details or more information, write to the particular organizations that interest you.

AASP—American Association of School Photographers, Inc., 3555 Cowan Pl., Jackson, MS 39216.

ARPA—American Racing Press Association, c/o Judy Stropus, 68 Weston Rd., Weston, CT 06880.

ASC—American Society of Cinematographers, Box 2230, 1782 N. Orange Dr., Hollywood, CA 90028.

ASMP—The American Society of Magazine Photographers, also known as The Society of Photographers in Communication, 205 Lexington Ave., New York, NY 10016.

ASP—American Society of Photogrammetry, 105 N. Virginia Ave., Falls Church, VA 22046.

ASP—American Society of Photographers, 65 Church St., Willimantic, CT 06226.

ASPP—American Society of Picture Professionals, Box 5283, Grand Central Station, New York, NY 10017.

APA—Architectural Photographers Association, 435 N. Michigan Ave., Suite 1717, Chicago, IL 60611.

API—Associated Photographers International, Box 206, Woodland Hills, CA 91365.

AFP—Association of Federal Photographers, 7210 Tuler Ave., Falls Church, VA 22042.

AGER—Association of Graphic Equipment Repairmen, Box 230, Lynn, MA 01902.

APPA—Atlanta Press Photographers Association, Box 562, Atlanta, GA 30301.

BPA—Biological Photographic Association, Box 1057, Rochester, MN 55901.

BPPA—Boston Press Photographers Association, Inc., Box 122, Boston, MA 02101.

CPPA—California Press Photographers Association, Inc., 2452 40 Ave., Sacramento, CA 95822.

CPPA—Chicago Press Photographers Association, 211 E. Chicago Ave., Chicago, IL 60611.

CPPA—Colorado Press Photographers Association, 1711 S. Newport Way, Denver, CO 80202.

CWPPA—Colorado-West Press Photographers Association, 614 Palmer, Delta, CO 81416.

CNPA—Connecticut News Photographers Association, 180 Goodwin St., Bristol, CT 06010.

CPPA—Copperstate Press Photographers Association, Box 465, Tempe, AZ 85281.

DPPA—Dakotas Press Photographers Association, 2929 8 St. N., Fargo, ND 58102.

DGP—Deutsche Gesellschaft für Photographie, Neumarkt 49, Cologne, West Germany.

EFLA—Educational Film Library Association, 43 W. 61 St., New York, NY 10023.

EPIC—Evidence Photographers International Council, 10322 Lake Shore Blvd., Cleveland, OH 44108.

GATF—Graphic Arts Technical Foundation, 4615 Forbes Ave., Pittsburgh, PA 15213.

GTA—Gravure Technical Association, 60 E. 42 St., Suite 858, New York, NY 10017.

HGCNPA—Houston-Gulf Coast News Photographers Association, 12411 Longbrook, Houston, TX 77072.

IPPA—Illinois Press Photographers Association, 3345 W. 91 St., Evergreen Park, IL 60642.

INPA—Indiana News Photographers Association, 3930 Ivory Way, Indianapolis, IN 46227.

IPANY—Industrial Photographers Association of New York, c/o Sanford Speiser, Columbia Records, 51 W. 52 St., New York, NY 10019.

IPNJ—Industrial Photographers of New Jersey, 232 Central Ave., Caldwell, NJ 07006.

IFPAI—Information Film Producers of America, Inc., Box 1470, Hollywood, CA 90028.

ICHSP—International Committee of High-Speed Photography, 10703 E. Nolcrest Dr., Silver Spring, MD 20903.

IFPA—International Fire Photographers Association, 588 W. De Koven St., Chicago, IL 60607.

IPA—International Photographers' Association, Inc., 2063 N. Leavitt, Chicago, IL 60647.

IPL—International Photographers Local 659, (IASTE & MPMO), 7715 Sunset Blvd., Hollywood, CA 90046.

IPMPI—International Photographers of The Motion Picture Industries, Local 644, 250 W. 57 St., New York, NY 10019.

IPOA—International Photo Optics Association, Inc., 1156 Ave. of the Americas, New York, NY 10036.

ISP—International Society for Photogrammetry, Prof. Dr. Ing. L. Soliani, Instituo di Geodesia del Politechnico, Piazza Leonardo da Vinci 32, 20133 Milan, Italy.

ISCC—Inter-Society Color Council, Dr. Fred W. Billmeyer, Jr., Secretary, Dept. of Chemistry, Rensselaer Polytechnic Institute, Troy, NY 12181.

KAMHFP—Kappa Alpha Mu Honorary Fraternity in Photojournalism, 135-F School of Journalism, Univ. of Missouri, Columbia, MO 65201.

MPPA—Michigan Press Photographers Association, Box 1731, Grand Rapids, MI 49501.

MPPA—Milwaukee Press Photographers Association, 355a E. Van Norman Ave., Cudahy, WI 53110.

NAPET—National Association of Photographic Equipment Technicians, 1240 Mt. Olive Rd., NE., Washington, DC 20002.

NAPM—National Association of Photographic Manufacturers, 600 Mamaroneck Ave., Harrison, NY 10528.

NDCC—National Directory of Camera Collectors, Box 4246, Santa Barbara, CA 93103.

NFLPA—National Free Lance Photographers Association, 4 E. State St., Doylestown, PA 18901.

NMA—National Microfilm Association, 8728 Colesville Rd., Silver Spring, MD 20910.

NPPA—National Press Photographers Association, Box 1146, Durham, NC 27702.

NPPA—Nebraska Press Photographers Association, 206 Avery Hall, University of Nebraska, Lincoln, NE 68508.

NJPPA—New Jersey Press Photographers Association, 91 Douglas St., Lambertville, NJ 08530.

NYPPA—New York Press Photographers Association, 225 E. 36 St., New York, NY 10016.

ONPA—Ohio News Photographers Association, 1446 Conneaut Ave., Bowling Green, OH 43402.

ONPA—Oklahoma News Photographers Association, 830 Crestview, Ada, OK 74820.

PPPA—Pennsylvania Press Photographers Association, 1919 S. Broad St., Lansdale, PA 19446.

PCMI—Photo Chemical Machinery Institute, 1717 Howard St., Evanston, IL 60201.

PMA—Photo Marketing Association, Inc., 603 Lansing Ave., Jackson, MI 49202.

PA—Photographic Administrators, Inc., c/o Leonard Silverman, 3 Province Lane, Glen Head, NY 11545.

PASF—Photographic Art & Science Foundation, Inc., c/o Frederick Quellmalz, 111 Stratford Rd., Des Plaines, IL 60016.

PCI—Photographic Credit Institute, 370 Lexington Ave., New York, NY 10017.

PHSA—The Photographic Historical Society of America, c/o Eaton S. Lothrop, Box 41, Simsbury, CT 06070.

PMDA—Photographic Manufacturers & Distributors Association, Inc., c/o Norman Lipton, 369 Lexington Ave., New York, NY 10017.

PSA—Photographic Society of America, Inc., 2005 Walnut St., Philadelphia, PA 19103.

PIA—Photography Instructors' Association, c/o John Silengo, Box 6491, Torrance, CA 90504.

PPALI—Press Photographers Association of Long Island, 5 Firelight Court, Dix Hills, NY 11746.

PPGF—The Professional Photographers Guild of Florida, Box 1307, Homestead, FL 33030.

PPA—Professional Photographers of America, Inc., 1090 Executive Way, Des Plaines, IL 60618.

PPSF—Professional Photographers of San Francisco, 44 Montgomery St., San Francisco, CA 94104.

PSPPA—Puget Sound Press Photographers Association, 16823 1 SE., Bothell, WA 98011.

RCPP—Rose City Press Photographers, 3796 Hulsey SE., Salem, OR 97302.

RPS—Royal Photographic Society, 145 Audley St., London, WIY5DP, England.

SFPC—Société Française de Photographie et de Cinématographie, 9 Rue Montalembert, Paris VII, France.

SPE—Society for Photographic Education, Box 1651, FDR Station, New York, NY 10022.

SMPTE—Society of Motion Picture & Television Engineers, 862 Scarsdale Ave., Scarsdale, NY 10583.

SNOPP—Society of Northern Ohio Professional Photographers, 23611 Chargin Blvd., Beachwood, OH 44122.

SPAR—Society of Photographers' & Artists' Representatives, Box 845, FDR Station, New York, NY 10022.

SPSE—Society of Photographic Scientists & Engineers, 1330 Massachusetts Ave. NW., Washington, DC 20005.

SPIE—Society of Photo-Optical Instrumentation Engineers, 338 Tejon Place, Palos Verdes Estates, CA 90274.

SPT—Society of Photo-Technologists, Box 19308, Denver, CO 80219.

SFNPA—South Florida News Photographers Association, Inc., Box 3107, Miami, FL 33101.

UPS—Underwater Photography Society, Box 15921, Los Angeles, CA 90015.

USSPPG—United States Senate Press Photography Gallery, U.S. Senate, Rm. S-317, Washington, DC 20510.

UPA—University Photographers' Association of America, c/o Photographic Services Dept., Austin Peay State Univ., Clarksville, TN 37040.

UIPPA—Utah-Idaho Press Photographers Association, 1948 S. 3 St., Salt Lake City, UT 84111.

WHNPA—White House News Photographers Association, c/o Norman J. Driscoll, 1515 L St. NW., Washington, DC 20005.

Photography

The first use of the word *photography* is generally attributed to Sir John Herschel with its appearance in a paper he presented in 1839. The word is derived from the Greek *photo* (phos), meaning light and *graphia,* meaning writing. It was offered as an improvement on the word heliography (sun-writing) and similar terms.

Photography is usually defined as the process (science and art) of recording permanent images on light-sensitive materials. The term is frequently extended to include the recording of images with other types of radiation such as x-rays, infrared, and ultraviolet. The photographic material undergoes a photochemical change upon exposure to radiation; this change may be visibly apparent, but it usually is not. Subsequent physical or chemical treatment is usually used to greatly amplify the effects of exposure (development) or to render the image permanent (fixation).

A conventional and restricted concept of photography involves image formation with a lens, latent-image recording on a light-sensitive silver-halide emulsion, and a chemical process to develop and fix the image. The definition in the paragraph above encompasses a much broader usage. While the term *photograph* usually implies a paper print or reproduction, the end product of a photographic process does not necessarily have to be an image that is directly visible or immediately recognizable. Methods of optical reconstruction or playback are required to completely reproduce the information stored in the images of stereo pairs, motion pictures, or holograms. The image may not be intended for viewing at all; it may serve as a data recording or storage medium (as in spectrography) or as an intermediary (as in photolithography).

Authorities disagree on the inclusion of some image-recording techniques within the meaning of photography. However, those imaging systems that depend upon electronic recording, processing, and display, such as television, are usually excluded by the definition. (The case of magnetic recording of television images for subsequent playback *has* been included by some authorities.) Some systems that use electronic processing but whose final image is recorded on film or paper, such as satellite "photographs" and scanning electron microscope images, are ambiguous; their output is frequently described as a "photograph." Although *all* photographic methods and processes are not touched upon in this Encyclopedia, the diversity of topics that are included demonstrates the breadth of the term *photography*.

  ## Photointerpretation

When one looks at a photograph, various objects are seen. Some of these objects may be readily identifiable, while others may not. What is seen and identified sometimes depends upon the training and background of the individual. In any event, what is seen can be communicated to anyone who may ask about the objects in the picture. In other words, one is "interpreting" the photograph—or doing "photointerpretation."

In a similar way, the trained photointerpretation specialist is capable of communicating to others the kinds of information contained in aerial photographs. In effect, the photointerpreter decodes the information and acts as a communications expert for those who are unfamiliar with, or do not understand, the images they see.

The photointerpretation of aerial photographs can be useful in a great many fields. It is being done for agriculture, archeology, geology, geography, forestry, ecology, military intelligence, natural-resource examination and management, soil analysis, land planning, land usage and control,

and oceanography. Several examples of the effectiveness of these techniques are presented here.

Agriculture and Forest Management

With today's emphasis on conservation and natural resources, lumbermen are vitally concerned that no forest area be overcut or destroyed irreparably. They are also interested in the condition of their cutting stock. Is disease present? Are there enough mature coniferous trees in a certain stand to make a full-scale logging operation profitable? What is the condition of a certain stand of trees marked for cutting? These questions and others like them can be answered through the use of skillful photointerpretation.

In black-and-white photographs and in some color photographs, deciduous and evergreen trees appear about the same in color. However, if a photograph of these trees is made on an infrared-sensitive color film, an immediate differentiation can be made. This is because healthy deciduous trees have a much higher infrared reflectivity than do healthy evergreens; the differences are shown distinctly in color infrared photographs.

Further advantage can be taken of such infrared reflectance when deciduous trees are studied for possible disease problems. Although healthy foliage has a high infrared reflectance, unhealthy foliage has little. This loss of infrared reflectance is one of the first detectable changes that occur in many trees or plants when their foliage becomes diseased. In an infrared photo, this change can be easily detected before any visible change has occurred.

In agriculture, aerial photography and photointerpretation can be used to detect the early stages of certain plant diseases. Again, advantage can be taken of the presence or absence of infrared reflectance. Citrus growers, for example, can have color infrared photographs taken of their groves. From these it is possible to estimate the extent of certain types of diseases.

Planning

The complex problems faced by planners today can often be helped a great deal through the use of aerial photography. While the planner may not conduct the actual interpretation of a series of aerial photographs, the data they contain can be of immeasurable usefulness. Answers to such questions as where to locate a new highway and how to

Regular color film may not pick up subtle differences in forest areas. In the infrared photograph, the varying hues of red indicate the presence of a number of different tree species. In addition, the presence of diseased trees, ("A" in the upper left corner) is evidenced by a variation in color. The area of the infrared photograph marked "B" indicates the presence of a stream not readily apparent in the regular color photograph.

extend an existing one can be obtained—at least in part—by accurate photointerpretation. For instance, it may be advisable to locate a highway in a different area than the one originally intended because the topographical features of the terrain do not allow a highway to be built, except at great cost. The question of where to locate the highway so that a minimum reduction in tax revenues occurs can be answered by aerial photography.

New communities, as well as old ones, can realize benefits from photointerpretation. One of the most notable applications of this technique was in the planning of Brasilia, the capital city of Brazil. This tremendous job of photointerpretation required a survey of some 20,000 square miles, of which 80 square miles were selected as the building site. In contrast to the years required for a land survey, the entire area was photographed, maps were made, and the necessary topographical, geological, and other environmental factors were analyzed in a period of 10 months—and at a considerable reduction in cost.

Photointerpretation can provide information for community planning. The area marked "A" in this photograph indicates the presence of a trailer park. The definite pattern in which the trailers are laid out, and the presence of several detached sheds, indicate that the park has been established for some time, and that some of the residents have taken up a relatively permanent status.

Photointerpretation

Water Resources and Water Pollution

Considerable concern exists over the problems of water pollution and the availability of new water supplies. Several severe water problems that have occurred in recent years have made stringent control measures necessary. Vigorous measures to abate pollution have been taken. Also, steps are now being taken to conserve the supplies of fresh water available to communities.

Aerial photography and photointerpretation can offer a rapid means of studying these problems. For example, it is possible to determine the depth of snow from an aerial photograph if suitable ground-control devices are used. Snow is very conspicuous on an aerial photograph. Low-level aerial photography can be used to make close-ups of snow-depth markers; high-level aerial photography can be used to estimate the size of the snow field. From data gathered over a period of time, it is relatively easy to follow the growth and depletion of a snow pack. This in turn can be an aid to more effective management of that water-supply area.

Serious water-pollution problems can likewise be pinpointed by aerial photography. Some definite indications of pollution problems have been documented. In such cases, aerial photography, combined with accurate photointerpretation, can make the extent of the problem much easier to see than it would be from the ground.

In the study of water resources, photointerpretation can indicate a number of conditions. The aquamarine discoloration about the periphery of the lake, first noted in this photograph, was later found to be not algae, as was originally assumed, but a lightweight soil.

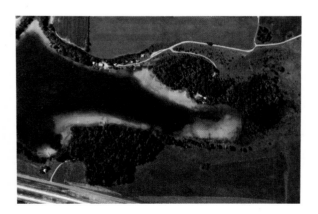

Geology

In the hands of a trained geologist who is also versed in photointerpretation, an aerial color photograph can become an outstanding source of information. It is not uncommon, therefore, to see aerial photography being used to determine the possible existence of mineral deposits, or to estimate the feasibility of drilling for oil.

The techniques of photointerpretation may also be used in geology to determine the likelihood of landslides occurring in populated areas. In certain areas, for example, landslides have occurred as the result of heavy, prolonged rain. Shale and shale-like soils have a tendency to retain moisture; they will eventually slump, causing a landslide. Conversely, sandy-type soils do not retain moisture readily, and thus provide a better home-building site. Such differences between soil types may be determined by the use of color aerial photography.

Range Management and Zoology

The importance of aerial photography and photointerpretation in range management and zoology is steadily increasing. From aerial photographs, different species of animals can be identified, and the condition of the rangeland can be determined. This capability has made aerial photography very helpful in the intelligent management of living resources.

Aerial photography can yield accurate inventories of animals and tell the wildlife manager the condition of their feeding grounds. In addition, the wildlife manager can use aerial photography as a law-enforcement tool to prove illegal hunting or fishing in areas that would be difficult to reach by land or water. Often, such activities are documented so successfully that they make conviction a certainty.

Obtaining the Aerial Photographs

In cases where existing aerial photographs do not satisfy the requirements of the user, new photographs can be obtained by contracting with one of the many aerial photographic firms. In other instances, the user may prefer to do the aerial photography. In either case, it is best to understand fully what is needed before the photographic mission is flown.

This stereo pair of photographs is interesting since it demonstrates the ability to predict the kind of crop yield expected from a particular field. Stereoscopic comparison of the two fields marked "A" and "B" indicated that the yield of field "B" will be much lower than that of field "A". Mottled coloration of field "B" indicates that ground is visible under the crop cover.

Do-it-yourself aerial photography is becoming increasingly attractive, especially for a small job (consisting of only a few photographs, which are not to be used for making maps). Such photography can be done with a 4″ × 5″ press camera or an aerial-photography camera. The latter is preferred because it is much more rigid in construction. The press camera has an easily collapsed bellows and can be damaged if struck by the air blast from the slipstream of the aircraft. High-wing monoplanes, which provide an unobstructed view of the ground, should be used. Helicopters are also very useful in this work, particularly because they can provide the photographer with a relatively stationary platform.

Stereograms

One specific aspect of photointerpretation that has not been mentioned is the use of stereograms (stereoscopic photos). When stereoscopic photographs are viewed correctly, they impart a much higher degree of realism to the scene under study. Buildings assume height, valleys assume depth, and small but significant items in the photograph are not overlooked. Whenever possible, a photointerpretation mission should be flown with the idea that stereoscopic photographs are to be produced. From an interpretation viewpoint, the increased accuracy will more than offset the slight additional cost.

Stereograms are best examined with a stereoscopic viewer or stereoscope. This is a device that magnifies the stereogram slightly, and at the same time reconstitutes it into a single, three-dimensional picture. Sources for stereoscopes can be found in publications such as *The Optical Industry & Systems Directory*, and *Photogrammetric Engineering and Remote Sensing*.

• *See also:* AERIAL PHOTOGRAPHY; PHOTOGRAMMETRY; STEREO PHOTOGRAPHY.

Further Reading: American Society of Photogrammetry. *Manual of Photographic Interpretation.* Menasha, WI: George Banta Company, 1960. Avery, T. Eugene, *Interpretation of Aerial Photographs,* 2nd ed. Minneapolis, MN: Burgess Publishing Company, 1968. St. Joseph, J. K. S., *The Uses of Air Photography.* New York, NY: John Day, 1966. Strandberg, C. H., *Aerial Discovery Manual.* New York, NY: John Wiley & Sons, 1967.

Photointerpretation

 **Photojournalism**

Every news photographer is an eye-witness reporter. The picture and caption combine in a unique and most effective way to reproduce the actuality of an event. Photographic coverage of the news has become the most realistic and informative aspect of journalism with the greatest reader interest. The fusion of the visual and verbal methods of communication has created a medium with its own characteristics—photojournalism.

Although the reporting of events with words has existed for centuries, the process of reproduction and mass distribution of photographs is less than a hundred years old. Two critical developments contributed to the modern practices of photojournalism.

History

William Henry Fox Talbot invented a practical, workable method that produced a negative in the camera, from which positive prints could be made. He first reported it to the Royal Society in London in January, 1839.

The introduction of the halftone process, which made possible the quick and inexpensive reproduction of a photograph in conjunction with words set in type, occurred with this photograph of Shanty-town, a squatter's camp in New York, made by Henry J. Newton. It appeared in the *New York Daily Graphic* on March 4, 1880, as a result of Stephen Henry Horgan's experiments.

These two technical advances are the foundation of modern visual communication. But their concept of telling the news pictorially goes back to the primitive cave paintings of prehistoric times. Words are composed from alphabets that were originally pictures, and the Chinese alphabet today is a collection of picture ideas that are combined to form mental images.

A Tradition. The great artists, Hogarth, Goya, and Daumier were also journalists. The words "Yo lo vi" ("This I saw") are scribbled under one of Goya's gruesome war scenes of the battle between Spanish partisans and Napoleon's troops in 1810. Certainly, the concept of picture reporting is as old as man's drive to tell a story through drawing

pictures. The use of the camera merely makes the pictorial presentation of the information more efficient, faster, and available to more people.

The photographic process has certain inherent characteristics that the photojournalist recognizes and emphasizes. They are:

1. The production of fine detail and texture.
2. The accurate rendition or willful distortion of perspective through proper choice of lens and viewpoint.
3. The infinite range of tonal values from light to dark that may be combined or extended at will.
4. The ability to stop motion—to capture the decisive instant or the exact moment.

The photojournalist knows that the lens has a different standard of values than the eye. The camera discovers significance in things that seem unimportant. It also may be deficient in those areas where the eye is attracted psychologically. It teaches a new way of observing the commonplace and enriches the visible world of infinite detail. It opens up new vistas and bares the aspects of people and their environments with unequaled precision.

The men and women in this specialized field must be technically competent. They find it necessary to use many devices: cameras, lenses, and lights. But their techniques are used only to obtain more freedom, to make the mechanics of taking the picture so simple that they can concentrate on the subject, the idea, and the event. They realize that a picture is a reflection of what they see and understand, and their job is to mirror the world.

Evolution. Today's photojournalist is a product of evolution in photography, a process that started in 1839 when Daguerre made public the details of his method.

The Daguerreotype. The use of the daguerreotype for portraiture established the medium as a superb means of creating a likeness. The portrait painter was virtually put out of business by the photographer. An outstanding example of the early effectiveness of the photograph as an accurate record was Mathew B. Brady's portrait of Abraham Lincoln. When widely reproduced and circu-

Lincoln attributed his first election as President to this portrait by Mathew Brady. Many woodcuts and lithographs of this picture were circulated, and helped to dispel the notion that Lincoln was a rough and uncouth backwoodsman. Photo courtesy Arthur Rothstein from his book Photojournalism.

lated prior to the presidential election of 1860, Brady's photograph helped dispel the notion that Lincoln was a rough and uncouth backwoods character. The serious, thoughtful, and dignified appearance of Lincoln in the portrait, plus the extensive distribution of the picture, caused Lincoln to give Brady credit for helping him become president.

Early Coverage of Historical Events. The camera as an accurate recording instrument and the existence of the concept in the minds of the public have been fundamental factors in the development of the photojournalist. Coupled with this is the idea of the camera and its trained observer functioning as a witness to events.

When Roger Fenton photographed the Crimean War in 1855, the long tradition of the photojournalist covering history-making events began. Fenton's pictures could not be published, although wood engravings of some of the scenes were made and printed in the *Illustrated London News*. It was impossible to show the action of war

Joe Rosenthal's 1945 Pulitzer-prize winning photograph, "Marines Plant Old Glory on Mount Suribachi," (commonly referred to as "the flag raising on Iwo Jima") was the inspiration for numerous reproductions in various media. As Rosenthal made the laborious climb up the steep mountain, sidestepping Japanese mines, he wondered whether a picture at the summit would be worth the effort. Photo © Wide World Photos, Inc.

with the slow, wet collodion process used. But even in the dull landscapes of the battlefields, there was a sense of reality that had never existed before.

Considering the primitive methods used, the work of Mathew B. Brady in documenting the Civil War was remarkable. He and his staff produced 7000 wet-plate negatives, that, according to his catalogue, were taken on the spot during the progress of hostilities, and represent grim-visaged war exactly as it appeared. These photographs, now in the Library of Congress, have influenced war photographers ever since. Here, for the first time, the special quality of photography, which is so important to the photojournalist, became evident: the strong sense of realism and truth; the participation with the photographer present at the scene and as a witness to the event.

Modern-Day War Coverage. Since the days of Brady, improved photographic techniques and faster methods of transmission have made war photography more significant and the photographer a more vulnerable witness. In order to obtain pictures with dramatic emphasis, the photographer has had to be exposed to danger as great as, if not greater than, the combatant. In modern times, an outstanding photojournalist who carried on in the tradition of Brady, was Robert Capa. Starting with the Spanish Civil War in 1935, Capa photographed the battle fields of his times for 20 years. His tragic death came when he stepped on a land mine while covering the war in Indo-China.

Documentary Photography. The documentary photographer made a substantial contribution to photojournalism. While all unretouched photographs are documents in the sense that they can be accepted as evidence or proof, the term documentary has been applied more specifically to photographs that not only present facts, but comment on them. The most effective documentary photographs are those that convince their observers with such compelling, persuading truth that they are moved to action. An early example was the work of William H. Jackson, who photographed the natural wonders of the West in 1870. Jackson's photographs of the Yellowstone area convinced Congress of the importance of preserving the region for the public, and the first National Park was created.

In 1890, Jacob Riis, one of the first to use flashlight powder, photographed the sordid slums of New York and used these pictures to help his crusade for housing reforms. In the early 1900's another effective commentator with the camera, Lewis W. Hine, was the first to employ the photostory as a journalistic device. His coordinated pictures and captions on child labor, immigrants, and coal miners, had a strong influence on the passage of legislation designed to correct these social injustices.

Under the stimulation and encouragement of Roy E. Stryker, the Farm Security Administration photographic project used the camera most extensively to interpret and comment. From 1935 to 1942, photographs of agricultural conditions, widely reproduced in newspapers and magazines, made the public aware of the need for rural rehabilitation and thereby affected farm legislation. In addition, the thousands of photographs, now in the Library of Congress, synthesized the best trends in modern photography and influenced the attitudes of many of today's photojournalists. The idea content of these photographs, combined with fine technique and artistic perception, resulted in pictures that had a profound effect on the observer.

Photojournalism Today

A writer uses words, phrases, sentences, paragraphs, and stories to present observations. In the same way, the photojournalist has a visual language composed of news pictures, feature photographs, sequences, photo essays and picture stories.

The goal of a news photographer is the publication of a single picture or sequence that is direct, straightforward, factual, and realistic. It may record an incident of interest to the community, present a well-known personality, or isolate a significant action. It may show conflict, tragedy, or emotion. Working under the pressure of events, the photographer who covers the news fights against time. He or she seeks the essence of the story, shoots it, and rushes the exposed film back for quick processing.

Improvement in the technique of news coverage means that a photographer must do more than be physically present at a scene. The photojournalist must be an artist, a skilled craftsman, and a reporter. Today's photographer of news events has risen above the mere button-pusher. Such a photographer has developed an instinctive insight and sensitivity to news events, so that the pictures translate the news into human terms and emotional values that the reader can appreciate.

The news photographer is most successful when three basic factors are operating:

1. Presence—getting to the spot where the action is taking place.
2. Instinct—knowing when to take the picture.
3. Anticipation—being prepared for coverage of the event with the proper mental attitude and physical equipment.

The Decisive Instant

The appreciation of the exact moment, the decisive instant, to take the picture is an instinctive action on the part of the news photographer that is somewhat comparable to the absolute pitch of the musician. Virtually anyone can be taught the mechanics of operating a camera. News sense can be sharpened by experience. But every great news photographer has a unique attribute that cannot be

The appreciation of the precise moment when a photograph should be made is instinctive. Henri Cartier-Bresson's "Banks of the Marne" (1935) captures, in a single picture, the full essence of a French working-class family's summer picnic. Photo © Magnum.

cultivated. It is an unconscious awareness of the unusual and unexpected, an attraction to and perception of the momentous event, an instinctive reaction that causes the photographer to make the picture at the height of the unfolding drama.

The coverage of a rapidly moving story requires foresight and preparation. Mechanically, the news photographer must have equipment in readiness and good repair. The photographer should be able to choose the right camera and lens for the job; a telephoto lens may be needed or perhaps an unobtrusive 35 mm camera. Mentally, the photographer should be alert, familiar with the background of the story, know the names of the principals, foresee the direction of the action, and anticipate the sudden or extraordinary act that makes a more revealing photograph.

The Feature Photograph

A feature photograph is a single picture of an event that is of continuing interest, creating a mood, presenting information, recording a timely subject, as opposed to recording spot news. It often embodies elaborate technical effects and unusual compositions, but it may also be extremely simple. The photojournalist who produces feature pictures

Margaret Bourke-White's image of a black chain-gang laborer is part of a much larger photo-documentary about social injustice in the rural south of the 1930's, which she did with Erskine Caldwell. Photo © 1938, Time Inc.

works carefully and has time to evaluate and to consider the approach.

Although major publications consider features a specialty, some photographers alternate between covering spot news for the daily paper and shooting features for the Sunday supplement. It becomes necessary for them to adjust to a change in pace. Instead of compressing the story into a few pictures, as with spot news, in producing feature photographs the event can be covered comprehensively and more of the atmosphere can be interpreted. The photojournalist working on a feature assignment does not have the drama, excitement, and pressure of spot news work. On the other hand, he or she can exercise more control. The subject, lighting, and composition can emphasize the specific details that the photographer wants to show.

In analyzing the subject, the feature photographer must be able to select the significant. The selection of what to photograph is just as important as the technique used for making the picture. The process of selectivity starts with a thorough knowledge of the subject. In this way, the photographer can analyze the important elements. Composition is then utilized to make the resulting selection interesting and effective.

Arthur Fellig, known professionally as "Weegee," entitled this fortuitous picture of two bejeweled dowagers and a shopping-bag lady "The Critic." Photo reproduced courtesy of Aperture, Inc.

Certain photo stories may be composed entirely of pictures with short captions. This grimly dramatic series illustrates the death of a suspected Viet Cong officer on a Saigon street in February, 1968. (A) Disarmed and bound, the prisoner is escorted by Vietnamese Marines. (B) He is brought before National Police chief General Nguyen Ngoc Loan. (C) Loan orders the Marines to move away, levels his pistol, and shoots the prisoner in the head. This photo won the 1969 Pulitzer Prize. (D) Loan reholsters his weapon and walks away saying, "They killed many Americans and many of my men." As Loan walks off, a soldier watches the prisoner die.

A

B

C

D

E

F

G

The Sequence

A photo sequence or picture series consists of more than one photograph dealing with the same subject. It may tell a story, describe a scene, record an event, or reveal a person. The sequence or series is most effective when it creates several visual images all containing highlights of revealing action.

A photo sequence is thus an amplification of a single picture. It is justified when it reveals more. It may require the use of special sequence cameras. In producing a sequence, many exposures are edited down to those that are most effective. Finally, it requires continuity that may be created by the action of the subject, the event, or through the consistency of the photographic technique.

The Picture Story

The picture story is a planned, organized combination of news and feature photographs that presents a complete, detailed account of an interesting and significant event, personality, or aspect of contemporary life in narrative form. Sometimes called a photo essay, it represents the most complicated type of work done by the photojournalist. It requires the knowledge and the use of the greatest variety of techniques; the ability to direct people and their actions; the application of diplomacy, tact, and persuasion; as well as a considerable amount of physical energy.

Photographic narration is a relatively new means of communication, resulting from the blending of words and pictures to tell a story.

(Below and facing page) This picture story, published in Look *in 1954, illustrates the use of pictures within a text story. The text, subordinated to the photographs, is written so that both information and mood enhance the visual effect. The picture layout was made before the words were written. Photos by James Hanson; courtesy of Arthur Rothstein from* Photojournalism.

Homecoming brings gladness, reflection and a solemn visit to the churchyard

At a family reunion, Nick shows off by squeezing into his old regional costume and demonstrating folk-dance steps. As a surprise, he had brought costume from U.S.

Outfitted for Norwegian winter, Nick shaves his face over a washbasin in the same bedroom he used as a boy. Modern touch in the house is a radio.

Karolina, Johannes's wife, and Nick enjoy leafing through family album. Other items of family lore include 100-year-old Bible, Nick's schoolbooks.

In the Lygra cemetery, Nick takes flowers to his mother's grave. The Lutheran church, where Nick and other children were confirmed, is attended by Lygra people and also from nearby islands. Since the congregation is too small to support a full-time pastor, Sunday services are held only once a month.

Nick may never see Norway again, but he has satisfied an American's curiosity about the quiet life he left

The old schoolroom has its orderliness disturbed by a former pupil's return, following the award to a bank, where Nick collected school-day savings of $30.

Leaving his old home at the end of his visit, Nick waves good-by to three generations of the family. To catch the ferry to Bergen, Johannes's son Trygve rows Nick out to the stream, where he will be picked up. To a former son, Lygra will remain a compact, quiet island society he will always remember and love.

The modern newspaper and magazine use this picture language in three ways. Probably the most commonly used approach is the combination of pictures and words in such a way that the story is told by related pictures arranged in continuity. The words occupy less space than the photographs, and although they are very important, the words are subordinate to the pictures, and are presented in the form of short, related captions.

Another type of picture story is the kind that requires no captions at all. A brief headline, a word with each photograph, or perhaps a general text block is all that is necessary.

The third form of photographic narration is the use of the picture story continuity within a text story to increase readership by making the story visually appetizing. Reader tests show that the connected picture story used as illustration often gets twice the readership given to the text it accompanies. The text also benefits from the picture story, often getting twice the attention it would receive if it were presented alone.

The ability to capture a particular moment in an ongoing event is part of the skill of the good photojournalist. (Above) Photographer Sal Veder waited at the airport with the family of a returning POW from Vietnam; then, as they ran toward him, he took this 1974 Pulitzer Prize-winning photograph. (Left) One of many grim moments in the Vietnam war was the public suicide of a Buddhist monk to protest the ruling regime. This remarkable example of spot news photography by reporter Malcolm Browne has a visual impact equal to the millions of words written about that crisis. Photos © Wide World Photos.

(Right) The dramatic resuscitation of an electrocuted lineman was phototgraphed by Rocco Morabito, a local newspaper photographer on his way to another assignment. This photo was the 1968 winner of the Pulitzer Prize. (Below) The sinking of the Italian liner Andrea Doria was one of history's great maritime tragedies. Struck by another ship on a foggy night off the Nantucket coast, she finally sank almost twelve hours later. From a plane overhead, photographer Harry Trask recorded her last moments, and won the 1957 Pulitzer Prize with this photograph. Photos © Wide World Photos.

Ideas

Every picture story starts with an idea, and these ideas come from a variety of sources. They may originate from an editor or a photographer on the staff of a publication. They may come from the inventive brain of a press agent, a free-lance writer or photographer, a faithful reader, or an interested citizen.

The photojournalist creating picture stories gets ideas in various ways. The photographer seeks stimulating experiences, talks to people, travels, and reads newspapers, books, and magazines. Ideas result from the stimulation of an old experience to a new expression. The successful photographer tries photographic techniques. Picture ideas are often achieved by knowing how to convert ideas from words into visual terms. In producing a picture story, the photojournalist must also be aware of the slant of the publication that will use the material. Different publications will require different approaches to a picture story.

In shooting a picture story, the photographer has to keep several points in mind. A lead picture can combine many elements of the basic idea in one dramatic, story-telling, well-composed photograph. A beginning and an end to the picture story allow the photographs to start at a given point and flow smoothly from one statement to another with a logical conclusion.

The photojournalist creating the picture story tries to achieve as complete coverage as possible. This means shooting many more pictures than are required for the final layout. In some cases, the photographer may compose a shot in both horizontal and vertical arrangements, as well as for possible use on a left or right page. On an average picture assignment, a photographer will often make as many as 36 exposures for every one that is published.

The picture story or photographic essay, when it becomes more than a mere number of sequence pictures, offers the photographer the most elbow room as a communicator. It can give some of the greatest creative satisfactions. If photographs speak more powerfully than words, they reach their apex of meaning and influence in the picture story. It is a medium that lends itself to penetrating the economic, social, and psychological problems of people's lives.

Equipment

Except for special purposes, the news and magazine photographer has adopted the 35 mm camera. With improved films, lenses, and cameras, it is virtually impossible to distinguish quality differences in the printed reproductions of photographs made with small- and large-format cameras. The photojournalist may now carry several cameras, lenses, and related equipment. Motor-driven film advance allows fast working and provides striking sequences.

Lighting

With respect to lighting, the photojournalist is concerned with realism. Supplementary light is necessary only to raise the level of illumination so that an adequate exposure is possible. Such lighting should be natural, unobtrusive, and in keeping with the subject. To achieve a natural effect, photographers often use only the light that is available. Many assignments can be covered with fast films and fast lenses.

Where additional light is required, a popular device is the portable electronic flash. This type of unit operates on replaceable or rechargeable batteries and permits hundreds of flashes to be made without interruption. Frequently, light is directed or bounced against a wall or ceiling to create a more realistic and natural effect. When several lights are used, photo cells can provide synchronization.

Sometimes, several electronic-flash units will be set up in a given area for zone lighting. This permits the photographer to move freely within the zone and obtain adequate exposures. As emulsions have become faster, lighting equipment for use by the photojournalist has become smaller and less powerful.

Legal Considerations

Every photojournalist must be aware of the basic legal aspects of his or her rights to take photographs as well as the risks involved in their use. It is important for the photographer to know where he or she can operate.

In general the press photographer may legally photograph any person, scene, or occurrence in a public place; or any person, scene, or occurrence that may be observed from a public place.

Any public building may be photographed, but a private building such as a famous hotel or sporting arena may create difficulties. In a case involving Madison Square Garden and Universal Pictures, the motion-picture company made a film about hockey and used Madison Square Garden as the locale for the film without the consent of the Garden. The court decided that damages would have to be paid to the Garden for the publication of pictures of its building and the use of its name and publicity.

The government prohibits photographing of money and securities, but this does not mean that photographers must avoid all such subjects, since the law is designed to prevent the photographer from passing off the securities as real money or securities. Thus, it is legal to photograph money, stamps, or securities, being passed from hand to hand or on a table.

As far as personalities are concerned, the problem is more complicated. In 1926, a federal court held that a public man or woman cannot claim a general right of privacy. This means that a person who is a candidate for public office or who holds a public office, or one who is a statesman, artist, or author, has limited claim to the right of privacy. A politician, an entertainer, a sports figure, or someone involved in a crime or accident may be in a position of great public interest; for that reason, no complaint can be brought with respect to the taking or using of that person's picture.

Picture Ownership. Every photojournalist is faced with the question of who owns the picture. The person who possesses the negatives and prints may not necessarily be the legal owner of the photograph. Whoever pays for the shooting of the picture owns it. A staff photographer for a newspaper or magazine, therefore, has no rights to the photographs he or she makes for that publication. If a free-lance photogrpher has been hired by a publication to perform an assignment for it, the publication then owns the rights to the photographs that are made. It is possible for a photojournalist to license some rights and not to sell all the rights. The photographer can license the publication to use the picture for a special purpose or for one-time publication, or for a limited time.

Copyright. Every photographer who makes a photograph for his or her own purposes is protected by the Copyright Statute. The law recognizes that the real value in a photograph is not just the paper, chemicals, and materials involved, but the skill, intellectual labor, and mental effort that make the photograph possible. The photojournalist should be aware that the law reserves copyright for the photograph from the moment the picture is taken, even before publication. Under the new Copyright Act of 1976 which became effective January 1, 1978, both unpublished and published photographs can be registered with the Copyright Office in Washington. When a copyrighted photograph is to be published, the copyright symbol should be affixed to it, along with the name of the owner and the new date of publication. Forms for copyrighting photographs can be obtained free of charge from the Registrar of Copyrights, Library of Congress, Washington, D.C. A statutory copyright in the United States now lasts for the life of the originator plus 50 years. The originator may be the photographer, but could be the commissioner of the photograph in a work-for-hire situation. Any commissioning contract should address this point. (*See:* COPYRIGHT.)

Selling Photos

Whether or not he or she has copyrighted the photographs, the photojournalist, especially the free-lancer, must be extremely careful in selling them to a publication. Most magazines and newspapers like to obtain complete ownership and rights to a picture, including the right to sell it later and to syndicate it to other publications. The photojournalist should read the fine print of any letter of contract so that his or her rights in the photograph are not abrogated. The best procedure in selling a photograph is to license its use for a specific purpose or for a limited period of time.

Although for the most part, professional photojournalists are affiliated either as staff employees or by contract with a given newspaper or magazine, a large number of published photographs come from freelance or amateur photographers.

The amateur gets involved in photojournalism usually because he or she is the only one present at an important news event with a camera. The amateur who succeeds under these conditions is usually a very capable photographer who appreciates the visual significance of news. He or she also understands the need for speed in getting the photographs to a publication. An outstanding example of this is the series of photographs made in Atlanta, Georgia, of the Hotel Winecoff fire by Arnold Hardy, who sold his pictures to the Associated Press and later won a Pulitzer Prize.

Submitting Story Ideas. On the other hand, the professional freelance photographer rarely works on speculation, but will contract for a specific job with newspapers and magazines either personally or through an agent. Occasionally, the photographer submits story ideas, and asks if the publication is interested in their execution. The free-lance photojournalist is usually very versatile, technically proficient, and ready to go anywhere, anytime.

One effective way to obtain assignments is to channel a flow of ideas, tailored to the specific publication, into the editor's office. These ideas should be written out in the form of a brief paragraph stressing the visual aspects of the subject. Even if the percentage of those accepted is low, the editor will become conscious of the free-lancer's news sense and imagination.

Photo Agent. Another method of keeping in touch with the picture market is to employ an agent. The greatest market for photographs at present is in New York City, and for those who live in other places, representation there is important. Picture agents are always eager to see the work of photographers and will offer their opinions in person or by mail. If a photographer's work indicates a potential salability, the picture agency can contribute many valuable hints and suggestions. Some agencies employ full-time editors to advise photographers, to contact editors, and to help create assignments. The agent's commission will vary, depending upon the services offered. Some agencies have film processed, purchase supplies, and provide office space. Others limit themselves to contract assignment and picture sales.

Although New York City may be a primary picture market, many news agencies and national magazines have bureaus all over the world. If a photograph or story having national significance has been produced, the local newspaper will be made aware of its value and arrange for its distribution.

When a free-lance photographer does not use an agent, dealings with a publication should be governed by a thorough understanding of its rates and working conditions.

Television and Electronic Communication

For many photojournalists, an area of concern is the possibility that television may replace the printed page as the prime medium of visual communication. It is certainly the best source for bulletins and live, on-the-spot coverage of important news. But it is a medium with no permanence. The picture on the printed page, on the contrary, is archival, convenient, and infinitely retrievable. It may be examined as long and as often as desired. With a blend of meaningful words and skillful layout, it becomes more than a witness to an event. It can provide information, interpretation, and insight that transcends the transitory, electronic image of television.

However, the technical devices associated with electronic communication have created a change in the method of distributing photographs. One of the great assets of the still photograph is its rapidity of transmission. At present, a cooperative network of agencies and syndicates can transmit a picture to any part of the world within an hour via cable, radio, and satellite.

Now, with an ingenious combination of laser light and a dry-process photographic paper, the Associated Press moves its pictures world-wide with greatly improved sharpness and clarity. The use of digital transmission minimizes interference and, in addition, makes computer storage of images practical.

As a result of exposure to all forms of photography, the present generation has developed an increased sophistication and awareness of the pictorial image. This audience demands pictures that convey information quickly and concisely. In order to communicate effectively, the photojournalist must get to the point immediately. Neither the reader's time nor the resources of paper, printing, or film can be wasted. Every picture must have value and importance. This requires the cooperation of the creators of the images and those who use them.

• *See also:* COPYRIGHT; DOCUMENTARY PHOTOGRAPHY; HISTORY OF PHOTOGRAPHY; LEGAL ASPECTS OF PHOTOGRAPHY; NEWS PHOTOGRAPHY; PICTORIAL PHOTOGRAPHY.

Further Reading: Edom, Clifton C. *Photojournalism: Principles and Practices.* Dubuque, IA: William C. Brown Co., Pubs., 1976; Feinberg, Milton. *Techniques of Photojournalism.* New York, NY: John Wiley & Sons, Inc., 1970; Logan, Richard H. *Elements of Photo Reporting.* New York, NY: Hastings House Publishers, Inc., 1971; Life Library of Photography. *Photojournalism.* Hastings on Hudson, NY: Time-Life Books, 1971; National Press Photographers and Edwin Bayrd. *The Best of Photojournalism.* New York, NY: Newsweek, 1977; Rothstein, Arthur. *Photojournalism,* 3rd ed. Garden City, NY: Amphoto, 1973.

Photomacrography

Photomacrography is the technique of making photographs of subjects having details too small to be seen with the naked eye. The term should not be interchanged with *macrophotography*—the making of large photographs, such as photomurals. Another laboratory technique is *photomicrography,* which is photography through a microscope; this term should not be confused with *microphotography*—the making of small photographs, such as microfilms. The important distinction to observe here is the difference between photomacrography and photomicrography, since they both furnish magnified images of differing characteristics.

The practical magnification range in photomacrography is 2× to 50×. Since photomicrographs can also be made over most of this range, it is obviously not possible to define either one on the basis of magnification alone.

The techniques employed in each field, however, do offer definite distinctions. Photomicrography is done with a compound microscope—one with both objective and eyepiece lenses. Photomacrography is done with a simple microscope setup—one with an objective lens only.

There are other points of difference. Photomicrography involves the use of very particular optical imaging components. Photomacrography, on the other hand, can be done with camera lenses and with cine lenses, as well as with macro lenses specifically designed for the technique. Another

practical factor is the difference in the lighting procedures used. Photomicrographs are made with focused microscope lamps and condensers. Photomacrographic subjects are lighted by the methods of close-up photography.

Resolution of Detail

Depth of field is based on geometric optics. The data it yields are satisfactory in close-up photographic techniques. However, in photomacrography, physical optics and diffraction have to be considered. This leads to the concept of "depth of detail." Depth of detail indicates a depth range over which detail of a given fineness or separation is delineated satisfactorily. The criterion is 6 elements per millimetre in the magnified image on a print to be viewed at 12 inches.

Pointlights have a counterpart in close-up photography, called catchlights. These are the tiny, specular reflections that arise in small, shiny structures of the subject. In close-up subjects, the catchlight is just a highlighted part of each of these structures. In photomacrographic subjects, the pointlight usually covers the entire fine-detail element, and thus its size and separation usually constitute the resolution in the print. Lighting has a bearing on the size of the pointlights and also upon the delineation of fine structures.

No optical system images a theoretical true point as a point, but rather as a small blur. Diffraction, aberration, magnification, and focus result in imaging a tiny pointlight as a larger blur circle. The size of this blur circle governs the resolution of the photograph because the edges and tone details of non-pointlighted structures are rendered to the same degree of sharpness as the pointlights.

Subject Shape

It is well known that photomacrographic subjects present difficult depth problems. The more rounded or three-dimensional a specimen is, the greater the depth requirement. A whole orange presents more depth in its shape than does a thin slice of the orange. The shape factor is defined as the depth (or thickness visible from the camera viewpoint) over the longest dimension. Thus, the orange has a larger shape factor than the pebbled surface of the slice.

As objects having the same shape factor become smaller in their long dimension, they also become more difficult to photograph from the depth standpoint. The situation becomes critical in photomacrography—an insect's egg that is 1 mm in diameter can never be photographed to the same size as a 1:1 record of an orange, with sharpness equal to that in the orange photograph.

Since blur circles increase in size because of diffraction as the lens is stopped down, an unlimited reduction in the size of the lens aperture does not solve the depth problem.

Two-Dimensional Subjects. Such subjects require careful attention to good resolution and, since little depth is involved, this is readily obtained. In lighting relatively flat but rough-surfaced specimens like a butterfly wing, a texture, or glancing, illumination is needed. Many botanical cross sections have to be transilluminated with carefully focused light. The practical magnification limit for two-dimensional subjects is $m=50$, because of the apertures available with lenses for photomacrography.

Three-Dimensional Subjects. Subjects in this category present the additional requirement of recording depth and shape. Carefully arranged lighting for the purpose of showing both shape and texture are needed for tiny specimens. The size of a specimen also calls for particular attention to the size of the light source. For example, a bare, clear glass bulb with a filament coil 1 mm in diameter permits the recording of fine detail. The practical limit for three-dimensional subjects is a magnification of $40\times$ ($m=40$), because of depth problems.

Living specimens offer the greatest challenge in photomacrography. Essentially, the technique involves flash illumination that is bright enough for exposure, yet cool enough to preclude harming the specimens. Action fields, in which rapidly moving photomacrographic specimens locate themselves, both in focus and within the field of view of the camera, are used.

A study of the illustrations in this article will reveal that many photomacrographic subjects cannot be rendered with the same degree of subjective sharpness that exists in a needle-sharp photo-

Many small subjects cannot be rendered as sharply as larger subjects, and different criteria are necessary for judging their quality. (Left) A magnification of a piece of coral, photographed at f/22, yields just enough detail for a satisfactory record of the entire specimen. (Right) An overenlargement of a spicule of the same coral actually shows finer enlarged detail, even though it appears less sharp, than photo at left.

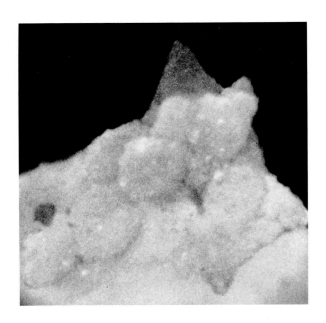

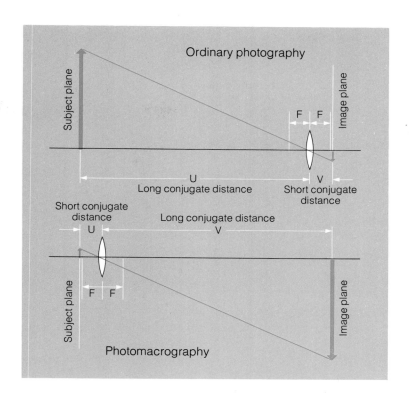

These diagrams compare the conjugate relationships existing in ordinary photography and photomacrography.

graph of a larger subject. The photographer should appreciate this limitation in the quality obtainable in a photomacrograph. Then he or she will be able to appraise the results and judge whether or not they could be improved. Time and effort should not be wasted in trying to achieve the unattainable. The photographer will have confidence in his or her work and will be able to counter with conviction any impossible demands of clients.

Equipment

The simple microscope for photomacrography can be obtained in many ways. Basically, a supported camera with a long bellows and a lens of short focal length constitutes the setup. Special lighting equipment has to be provided, and some form of focusing stage is needed.

Camera Setups. The accompanying diagrams demonstrate the difference between the subject-lens-film relationship in ordinary photography and the simple microscope relationship in photomacrography. It can be seen that the basic difference lies in the fact that the subject is at the long conjugate distance in ordinary photography, and at the short conjugate distance in photomacrography.

The following formulas define *m* and show how it is related to the other quantities.

F = focal length
m = magnification
u = subject distance
v = image distance
O = length of subject
I = length of image
f_r = relative *f*-number
f_e = effective *f*-number

Simple lens formula: $\frac{1}{F} = \frac{1}{v} + \frac{1}{u}$

Magnification: $m = \frac{I}{O} = \frac{v}{u} = \frac{v-F}{F} = \frac{F}{u-F}$

Lens to image:
$$v = \frac{Fu}{u-F} = mu = (m+1)F$$

Lens to subject: $u = \frac{Fv}{v-F} = \frac{v}{m} = (\frac{1}{m}+1)F$

Effective *f*-number: $f_e = f_r(m+1)$

The most often used factor in photomacrography is $(m + 1)$. It relates the bellows extension, v, to the magnification obtained with a lens of a given focal length, F.

$$v = (m + 1)F$$

With this simple formula, the photographer can determine the various dimensions for the setup. For example, if a 120 mm lens is used, and the extension is 420 mm, putting these figures into the above equation indicates that $m = 2.5$.

The other use for the factor is to calculate exposures when values have been found on the basis of the relative f-number, f_r—for example, figures obtained from exposure tables. Such values have to be multiplied by $(m + 1)^2$. When an exposure meter is used, the aperture dial should be set at the effective f=number, f_e.

Following is a list of equipment, and its essential features, especially manufactured for photomacrography.

1. A camera rack that permits a wide range of bellows extension.

2. An elevation rack that permits moving the entire camera to various heights for rough focusing.
3. A fine-focus rack for the lens front (optional when a focusing stage is available).
4. Facilities for interchanging lenses of focal lengths ranging from 120 to 16 millimetres.
5. A ground-glass focusing back with diagonal crosslines and a semi-clear circular area in the center.

Many 35 mm cameras are adaptable to making magnified images. Lenses with extended focusing threads provide 1:1 photography. Other cameras can be fitted with macro lenses and extension bellows, with a means for attaching a lens backwards. Tele-extenders are provided for some cameras to double or triple the image size. For outdoor or other hand-held use, the equipment should incorporate a coupling for maintaining an automatic diaphragm feature. Photographic dealers have data on the scope of the varied setups. The

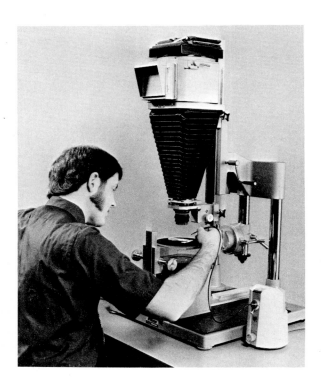

(Left) A 120 mm macro lens is used with a long bellows draw to project a 2.5 × image of the subject on the film. A ⅛-inch bundle of fiber optics provides a small-sized source. (Below) The texture within this fossil was rendered by using the fiber-optics bundle shown in photo at left. Specimen courtesy of William W. Pinch.

upper magnification limit they allow is usually about 6X.

Antivibration mountings are required in certain vicinities for the camera stand or for the optical bench. The use of electronic-flash illumination with inanimate subjects can alleviate the effect of vibration at low magnifications and low residual frequencies. Nevertheless, at high magnifications and vibration frequencies, the flashes are not of short enough duration to preclude blurring. For this reason, every effort should be made to install efficient mountings when vibration is a problem. The rubber-in-shear type is quite effective. It can be obtained from scientific-equipment suppliers.

Lenses. While the lens used for photomacrography should be of the highest quality, it does not have to be of very wide maximum aperture. Shutters are seldom needed in reflection photomacrography. An $f/4.5$ lens serves for final magnifications up to about 35X. Cine lenses from 16 mm cameras can be utilized at the upper limits of magnification.

Most good cine lenses have certain advantages over other lenses for photomacrography. For one thing, the back elements of the lenses usually have to be fixed very close to the rear of the barrel in order to clear the cine-camera mechanism. When cine lenses are mounted backwards on the photomacrographic camera, they provide the photographer with the maximum working space. A high lighting angle can then be adopted for three-dimensional specimens if needed. When a low angle is required, it is simple to shade the lens with a baffle to prevent flare.

Cine lenses generally have a negligible change in focal plane as the aperture is stopped down. This should be checked when other lenses are used. Also, since cine lenses are designed for use over wide focusing ranges, a lens of high quality maintains its corrections at various photomacrographic magnifications.

When pressing a cine lens into service, one with an aperture of about $f/2$ or $f/3.5$ should be selected. A lens with a wider maximum aperture is more likely to have more glass-air surfaces than one of simpler design. Interreflections from the surfaces reduce image contrast.

Regular camera lenses of complex design will most likely have to be placed backwards on the camera. The reason for this is that such lenses are designed to provide good definition in ordinary photography, where the front of the lens faces the longer distance. The front must also do this when the lens is used for photomacrography. Thus, the front of the lens should be directed toward the film when the image is larger than the object because the distance to the film is greatest. The photographer can make tests with the lens mounted each way, employing a subject that exhibits fine detail, in order to find out whether or not the lens ought to be reversed.

Enlarging lenses and those designed for microphotography usually do not need to be reversed because they are designed for working with nearly equal conjugate distances. Cine lenses always have to be mounted backwards; this is partly due to the barrel design.

Pupillary Magnification. The optical formulas for close-ups and photomacrography have been given for reasonably symmetrical lenses. However, asymmetrical lenses, such as retrofocus, wide-angle, and telephoto lenses, are widely used, especially with 35 mm single-lens reflex cameras. With these, the midpoint of the lens barrel can no longer be considered the plane of the diaphragm. Photographic tests will have to be made for determining the amount of magnification obtainable at a particular lens extension. A graduated scale can be used as a test object. The size of the image in a reflex viewfinder will indicate the amount of magnification being obtained (taking into account the difference between the viewfinder and the actual image at the film plane).

Another vital aspect to be considered is the effective aperture, which enters into exposure calculations if the camera does not read the *image* brightness directly. Depth-of-field figures are also affected by this asymmetry. These considerations are only needed for camera images at about 1:5 scale or larger in the close-up range. For photomacrographic magnifications greater than 6X, symmetrical lenses are needed.

The problem arises because the diameter of the beam of rays entering the front of the lens (through the "entrance pupil") is not the same as that leaving the back of the lens (through the "exit pupil"). In retrofocus lenses, the exit pupil is larger than the entrance pupil; in telephoto lenses, the reverse is true.

To determine whether a lens is symmetrical or asymmetrical, view a bright light source, first through the front of the lens (for the entrance pupil) and then through the back (for the exit pupil). The diameter of these pupils can be measured with a scale. The lens should be stopped down far enough for the iris to clear the lens barrel.

The ratio of exit over entrance pupil is called pupillary magnification factor (P). An exact 1:1 ratio indicates that the lens is symmetrical. To arrive at the effects of this factor for asymmetrical lenses, P is substituted in the effective-aperture and exposure calculations, and also in the geometric depth-of-field formula.

This factor is reasonably useful for ultraclose-up photography and photomacrography at magnifications below about 6×. Wherever the magnification factor (m + 1) appears in equations, it should be changed to (m + P)/P. When the lens is reversed on the camera for any reason, P must be changed to 1/P.

Thus, the exposure factor for a symmetrical lens, $(m + 1)^2$, must be changed to $(m + P/P)^2$, or the equivalent $(m/P + 1)^2$, for an asymmetrical lens. When the asymmetrical lens is reversed and 1/P is substituted for P, this becomes $(mP + 1)^2$.

Macro Lenses. The manufacturers of photomacrographic equipment supply macro lenses, which are meticulously corrected to work at a given magnification. They may not provide as good an image if used for other magnifications. For example, a 25 mm cine lens gives excellent results at m = 45, but a high-grade 10× macro lens would not perform as well at that magnification as it would at m = 10. For most photomacrography, lenses of 25, 50, and 75 mm focal length will suffice. A 100 mm lens can be included if a good one is available. Also, 16 mm macro lenses are available.

Shutters. When a shutter is not used, time exposures can and should be made by turning the light on and off; this avoids jarring the setup. It is preferable not to use a shutter. Flash exposures can be given under low ambient light by means of the open-flash technique. With this technique several electronic flashes can be used for one exposure if the setup is not jarred by the blast of heat or the photographer.

In transillumination setups, a shutter is usually needed. A detached shutter in a lens holder on the optical bench, or elsewhere in the light beam, can be employed. A flexible cable release should also be used.

Since lights are placed quite close to the lens in photomacrography, it is important to be certain that they do not shine on the lens surface, because this may lead to ghost images or excessive stray light. Ordinary lens hoods may not give sufficient protection. Improvised protection is always needed with reversed lenses because the rear element is exposed.

Covering Power. The rule of thumb for covering power in ordinary photography is that the focal length of the lens should equal the diagonal of the negative. Since the conjugate relationships are reversed in photomacrography, it is the long dimension of the specimen, not of the film, that governs the selection of the focal length of the lens to be used. A practical rule is that the lens focal length should be at least 1½ times the length of the specimen for camera and macro lenses. It should be 2¼ times for cine and microphotography lenses, since they have narrower angles of view than the other lenses.

Poor covering power shows up in the usual way. In a negative, the corners are lighter, thinner, and less sharp than the center. The reverse, with respect to density, is true in a transparency.

Focusing. Before the camera is focused, the bellows extension should be set and locked for the magnification desired. Rough focusing is done by moving the entire camera; fine focusing, by moving the specimen on a stage capable of smooth adjustment. In this way, the magnification is not changed, as would be the case if the lens were moved.

A slight modification of this procedure is permissible at magnifications of about 10× or over. Under these circumstances, the extension is relatively much longer than the distance through which the lens would have to be moved for making slight adjustments in focus. Then it is feasible to trim the focus with the lens adjustment provided on manufactured units.

Before the camera can be focused, the specimen must be within the field. Getting it there is quite difficult with the camera not yet focused, particularly at the higher magnifications—you cannot focus until the subject is centered in the ground glass, and it is impossible to center the subject unless it is approximately in focus.

The following procedure simplifies the problem immensely; the trick is to center the specimen in relation to the camera lens.

1. Make the distance from the specimen to the optical center of the camera lens a little more than the focal length of the lens. The lens should be wide open.
2. Visually locate the specimen as closely as possible on the subject-lens axis of the camera.
3. Look through the clear area in the ground glass, with the eye almost touching it, and use the camera lens as a magnifier for finding the specimen.
4. Move the specimen around until it is centered on the crosslines.
5. Bring the specimen a little closer to the lens. This will enlarge the image seen. Then the desired specific structure in the specimen can be centered on the crosslines.
6. Use an actual loupe, accurately focused on the crosslines, to focus the image in the plane of the ground glass at the clear spot.

An alternative centering method that can be adopted when it is convenient to illuminate the

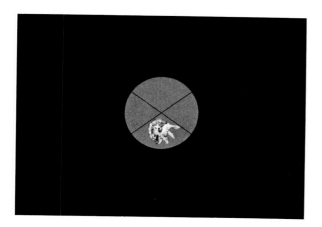

ground glass, is to shine a diffuse, axial beam of light onto the clear spot area. The specimen is then centered in the image of the clear spot formed by the camera lens. The specimen should be placed at such a distance from the front of the lens that the clear spot is roughly in focus on the surface to be photographed.

The loupe used to focus the image preferably should be of the Ramsden-eyepiece, or focusing-magnifier type, in which the focus is outside the front element to the extent of the usual thickness of the ground glass. With this type of magnifier, the aerial image can be focused through the clear spot. When the optical elements of a loupe and its focus are at some distance from the ground glass, the focus of the camera can be slightly inside or outside the ground glass and still appear visually sharp in the loupe. Therefore, parallax focusing must be done. When the eye is moved laterally across the loupe, there must be no apparent motion of a focused structure or pointlight with respect to the crossline. (*See:* VIEWING AND FOCUSING SYSTEMS.)

Focusing should be done with lens closed down to the desired aperture. Some lenses change their plane of sharpest focus when they are stopped down. At most photomacrographic magnifications, the plane of sharpest focus is almost halfway through the total depth limit. This is demonstrated by the curves in the accompanying diagram. However, these curves show that the near depth is always a trifle less than the far depth. Slightly out-of-focus detail, if it must be tolerated because of scanty depth, is less obtrusive when it appears at the back of the subject than at the front. These two facts indicate that detail near the camera should be favored slightly in focusing.

Checking Focus and Drift. Photomacrographic negatives may appear deceptively sharp because the wrong detail may be in focus. Therefore, before the setup is changed, they should be carefully examined with a magnifier to determine whether or not the focus is in the exact plane.

This illustration shows the appearance of the inside of the camera front as seen through the clear spot in the ground glass. The camera lens can serve as a loupe for locating the specimen prior to focusing.

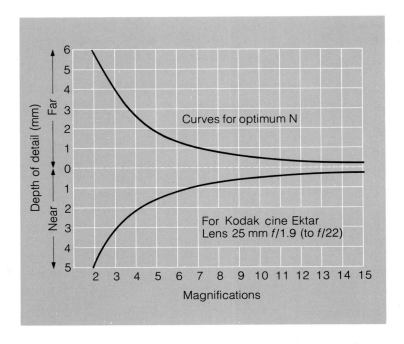

Depth of detail (mm)

Far — 6 5 4 3 2 1
Near — 0 1 2 3 4 5

Curves for optimum N

For Kodak cine Ektar
Lens 25 mm *f*/1.9 (to *f*/22)

Magnifications

2 3 4 5 6 7 8 9 10 11 12 13 14 15

These curves show the distribution of the depth with respect to the plane of sharpest focus. The magnifications plotted are those of the final photograph. These curves show that the near depth is always a bit less than the far depth. There is an optimum camera aperture for each magnification that provides the maximum practical depth.

An effect that may be confused with poor focus is the blurring caused by either camera vibration or subject drift during the exposure.

Exposure Meters. It is often practical to make direct exposure-meter readings at the location of the subject, but not to read the subject itself. The hand or the Kodak neutral test card (gray side) can be placed at the same distance and angle from the light source as the subject. The average hand reflects twice as much light (one stop more) than an 18 percent gray card. Meter readings should be made from a simulated camera-lens position. Incident-light meters can be placed in the subject position. The effective aperture, not the relative aperture, should be set on the dial, when either kind of exposure meter is used.

Only the main light should be turned on. Reflected accessory illumination will not appreciably affect the basic exposure time. Because of variations in equipment and working methods, it should be understood that any method of arriving at a trial exposure in photomacrography is approximate. Accuracy, to within plus or minus one stop of a usable negative, is reasonable to expect. Thus, the exposure arrived at by calculation serves as a practical starting point for tests.

Photoelectric Probes. It is more accurate to read the brightness of the image at the ground glass than it is to measure reflected or incident light, particularly when the short working distances of high magnifications are involved. It is not always possible to simulate subject lighting with the hand or a card. And, of course, transilluminated specimens cannot be read in this way.

Light meters especially intended for photomicrography are available and are capable of measuring extremely low brightness. They are suitable for use in photomacrography. They usually consist of a photoelectric probe, an electronic amplifier, and a galvanometer. An instrument of this type usually requires a source of electrical power, such as a regular power line or batteries. Very sensitive light meters of this type are available from several manufacturers of scientific equipment.

The image brightness of transilluminated specimens is usually very high. Therefore, any meter intended for reading the ground glass in a full program of photomacrography should have a long sensitivity range. It can then accommodate images from directly lighted and transilluminated specimens. A cadmium sulfide (CdS) cell—with sensi-

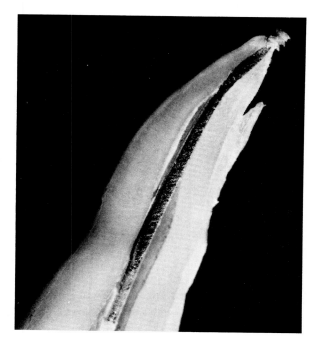

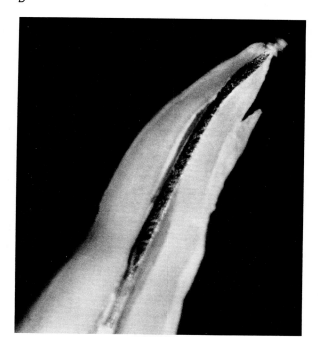

Both photos above show the apex of a human tooth containing a silver root-canal zone; the tooth has been sectioned to show details of the fit. In photo B, focus is too close to the near limit of depth of field. Photo C, showing the same tooth before sectioning, is greatly overenlarged for observation; the pointlights have been blurred by subject drift during a 4-minute exposure, not by an error in focusing. Specimens courtesy of Arthur C. McFeaters, D.D.S.

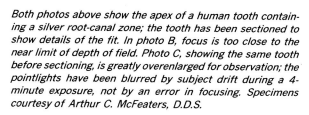

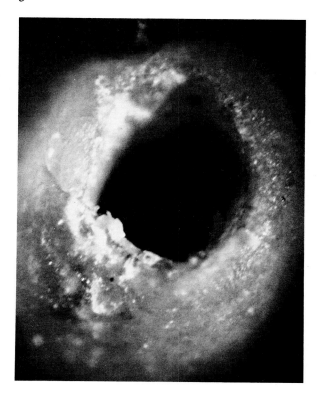

tivity at very low and very high levels—coupled to a microammeter, provides a simple, efficient, and quite inexpensive light meter. Some firms manufacture meters of this type specifically for photomicrography of all kinds, These are also applicable to photomacrography and are most practical if this work is done routinely.

Exposures. Many photomacrographic exposures have to be found by trial, especially flash exposures. Exposure times found for a certain magnification can be modified for another magnification by referring to the smooth curve in the accompanying diagram. For example, the exposure ratio for 5× and 20× is seen to be 9:110. Thus, if an exposure with a lamp at a certain distance is 2 seconds when $m = 5$, it will be 24 seconds when $m = 20$, provided the camera aperture is not changed.

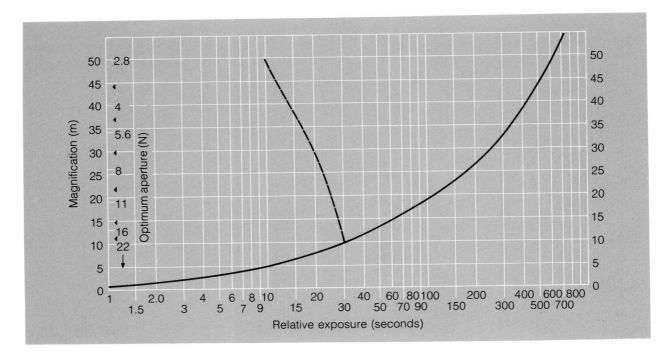

The solid curve indicates the relative increase in exposure time required at increasing magnifications. The curve is plotted for f/22 and based on a 1-second exposure at 1:1 (m = 1). It does not include compensation for reciprocity effects. Given along the magnification scale (m) are the optimum apertures (N) corresponding to the magnification ranges indicated. The dashed curve shows how the exposure times decrease for magnifications greater than 10 when the lens is opened to the optimum aperture. As an example, if an exposure time at m = 5 was found for a given lighting condition to be 9 seconds, the exposure time at m = 10 would be 30 seconds. The values are relative, so that 3 seconds at m = 5 would correspond to 10 seconds at m = 10. For long exposure times, adjustments in the values found must be made for reciprocity effects. Beyond m = 10, use of the optimum aperture allows shorter exposure times. Thus, at m = 10, N = 22; the relative value is 30. But at m = 40, the value is 14.

There is an optimum aperture for each magnification, so that the lens would be opened up at 20× to halfway between $f/8$ and $f/11$, whereas it could be set at $f/32$ for 5×. However, $f/22$ is the practical limit for most photomacrographic lenses. The change from $f/22$ to $f/8$–11 would reduce 24 seconds to about 5 seconds. Allowances would have to be made for departure from reciprocity law.

Lighting

Establishing suitable lighting for revealing the form and texture of specimens is the most important phase in technique for close-up photography and photomacrography. This holds true in any kind of photography since the basic principles are the same. The chief difference lies in the fact that the lamps have to be smaller for close-up work.

There are three elements in good lighting:
1. The main light, which models the shape of the specimen or reveals its texture.
2. The fill-in illumination, which throws light into the dense shadows so that the film can also record detail there.
3. The accent illumination, which serves either to separate the specimen from its surroundings or to lighten localized areas for introducing tone contrast.

Mirrors or matte reflectors are usually best for supplying fill and accent illumination. Using them eliminates the annoying multiple shadows that usually occur when more than one lamp is employed. However, two lamps can often produce good delineation of symmetrical subjects.

The formula for good lighting is a simple one: Start with the main light, and move it around until the key details are visible from the camera viewpoint; then add fill-in or accent illumination only when necessary.

Architectural lighting occurs naturally when the sun is 45 degrees above the horizon and at 45 degrees to the facade of a building. It is the most valuable single lighting effect for revealing structure and ornament. Such lighting can be produced by a single bare bulb. The modeling is enhanced when no lamp reflector is used, because the light beam is then smaller—the lighting is more "raw."

Since architectural lighting is quite directional, a fill-in reflector is valuable for photographing shiny specimens. This serves to soften the shadow areas. With living subjects, the reflector has to be moved in behind them slowly and carefully. A reflector placed behind the object serves to separate the specimen from the background.

When the subjects are photographed in natural surroundings, the photographer has to be on guard against colored reflections. A typical example might be the greenish cast over a pale grub photographed in the fold of a leaf. There is so much green light reflected from the foliage that it predominates over the direct light from the lamp. One way to circumvent this effect is to photograph the specimen on the edge of a stem or leaf. When the natural habitat of the specimen is the fold of a leaf, reflection can be minimized by cutting away all of the leaf except the part that is within the field of the camera. Sometimes, a pale magenta filter over the lens can be used to neutralize the green cast on the specimen, without unduly changing the color of the leaf.

Small Light Sources. Compactness is the key word in designating light sources for close-up photography. In photomacrographic lighting, use light sources of a size in keeping with the size of the subject.

Not only do small light sources furnish crisp modeling, they also make for smaller pointlights than those produced by larger sources. A catchlight (and also a pointlight) is the imperfect mirror image of the source. The larger the source, the larger the reflection.

The usual studio photographic lights produce beams that are too broad for close-up photography. They wash out fine detail and shape. Small sources provide much better modeling. Miniature desk lamps on flexible supports can serve to illuminate most close-up subjects. For ultra close-up photography, it is often better to use bare—without reflectors—clear glass bulbs. There are 500-watt projection lamps available with medium screw bases. For the smallest specimens, especially when they exhibit fine texture, 30-watt bulbs from microscope illuminators can be demounted and pressed into service. With such bare, unfrosted lamps, the filament represents a compact light source.

For photomacrography, the following light sources can be utilized (the color quality of the illumination is indicated in parentheses):

1. A miniature desk lamp, or inspection light, with a high- and low-voltage switch, and a flexible lamp support (approximately 3100 K).
2. A 30-watt microscope lamp with a tungsten bulb and a high-quality lamp condenser (3100 K).
3. A clear glass bulb removed from a lamp like the one described above. Any bulb to be used "bare" in such a way should have a single-coil filament about 1 mm in diameter. The end of the coil should be aimed at a slight angle toward the specimen to provide a very small source. The photographer should make sure that no shadow from the filament support is cast across the specimen (3100 K).
4. A 500-watt, 3200 K, projection lamp, such as DMS/115/120. It has a medium screw base, and is practical to burn at any angle for photography (3200 K).
5. A xenon arc. These are manufactured by microscope companies (Daylight).
6. A 100-watt zirconium arc (3200 K).
7. The flashtube from an electronic flash unit. The reflector should be removable from the light so that the tube can be used bare (Daylight).

The color temperature at which the lamps burn should be determined from the manufacturer's data. The customary light-balancing filters can be placed over the lens to provide the correct balance for color photography with various indoor color films.

Lighting Contrast. The ratio of the brightness from the main light (plus any spilled light) to that of the fill-in illumination is called the lighting contrast. The close-up photographer should learn to gauge this ratio visually, because it is difficult to calculate or measure reflected intensities from small subjects.

When two equivalent lamps are used at different distances, their intensities follow the inverse-square law—illumination varies inversely as the square of the distance—closely enough for practical purposes. Thus, a lamp at 16 inches would produce one quarter of the illumination of one at 8 inches. For practical purposes, spilled light can be neglected in establishing a lighting ratio by measuring lamp distances. The photographer can experiment with two lamps and learn the effects of various lighting contrasts.

As a general rule, a 3:1 ratio is suitable for black-and-white photography, and 2:1 for color photography. It is not feasible to establish or specify the contrast ratios in photomacrography. The photographer should study the appearance of the subject and the image, and learn to relate the effects he or she observes to similar effects in close-up photography. When mirrors are used, the inverse-square relationship can be applied approximately to the distance extending from the lamp to the mirror and back to the specimen.

Supplementary illumination changes the lighting contrast. Accessory lighting serves two purposes: (1) fill-in lighting that decreases the tone contrast of the image by brightening the shadows, and (2) accent lighting that increases the tone range by throwing extra light onto certain areas.

A backlight accents the edges of a specimen. It may not be possible to introduce backlighting in photomacrography. Yet, such accentuation should be kept in mind when good separation of the subject from its background is deemed advisable.

As a general rule, fill-in illumination should be provided with a shiny matte reflector, because the use of another light produces a double shadow that can falsify or reduce texture. A localized accent illumination can come from another lamp or from a mirror reflection of the main light.

Lighting Angles. The main illumination should yield a natural effect. Usually, the light should come from the camera side of the subject.

The angle between the main-light-to-subject axis and the front surface of the subject can vary from almost zero, just grazing the surface for texture lighting to 90 degrees in axial lighting. For good close-up or photomacrography lighting, establish the right lighting angle and direction visually by moving the main light around the subject until the pertinent shape and texture are clearly revealed.

Symmetrical Lighting. Symmetrical lighting is used for flat objects. The lighting is even on both sides, and the plane of the lamps cuts through the center of the central long axis of the subject. For small items, like postage stamps or similar subjects, two bare, clear lamps produce a fair rendition of the texture as well as an excellent portrayal of the design or inscription. The filaments are located at the 45-degree angles generally used for copying.

A slight modification in the copying setup can be effectively employed for photographing symmetrical specimens, such as mounted insects. This suggestion may seem to contradict the one-light principle. However, specimens with bilateral symmetry lend themselves to symmetrical lighting.

Axial Lighting. Axial lighting comes from very close to the subject-lens axis. Such illumination is yielded by a ring light; it is almost shadowless but does produce some modeling in surfaces closely parallel to the axis. Flat surfaces perpendicular to the axis are prone to reflect specularly into the lens. The ring light is useful for photographing details in depressions or crevices that are difficult to reach with other types of lamps.

Coins, cameos, and inscriptions can often be recorded by axial lighting. A clean, thin sheet of glass is placed in front of the camera between the subject and the lens, at a 45-degree angle to the subject-to-lens axis. Illumination is beamed toward the subject side of the glass at a 90-degree angle to this axis. The photographs are made through the glass. The light is partially reflected to the subject, perpendicularly to its surface, by the mirror action

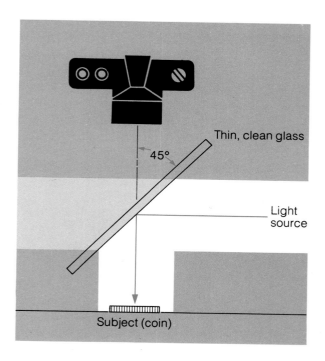

Axial lighting for small subjects is almost shadowless.

duce pointlights. Then enough axial illumination should be introduced to brighten the shiny parts without substantially lightening the rough, non-specular areas.

Transillumination. Transmission lighting or transillumination is produced by reflecting or focusing a beam of light through the back of a specimen. It is chiefly a photomacrographic technique but can be adopted for large specimens, such as thin mineral slices, large tissue sections, and skeletonized leaves. In close-up photography, the specimen is usually placed on a piece of transilluminated opal glass, or on clear glass through which a spotlight is focused. It is important to provide a black paper mask up to the edges of the camera field in order to preclude flare from stray light.

Transillumination photomacrography is adopted when thin or sectioned specimens are too large for photomicrography. The subjects are usually illuminated with a condenser system by suitably beamed transmitted light. In some

of the 45-degree glass. The rest is transmitted through the glass and is lost.

Light lost through the glass must not strike surroundings near the camera. Light from such surroundings can radiate back to the upper surface of the glass, where it can be reflected directly into the lens, causing flare. Even though there may be no reflecting walls opposite the lamp, light-colored objects, shiny objects, or the photographer's shirt, will be reflected into the camera if the objects are not removed or draped with a black focusing cloth. The shirt can be covered with a dark jacket or apron.

Axial lighting is required for the photography of smooth reflecting surfaces. Their surfaces reflect any other type of lighting away from the lens and thus would photograph dark.

Sometimes, a combination of oblique or cross-lighting and axial lighting delineates the desired detail. For example, a shiny metal surface with rough pits may record in an almost even tone under axial lighting alone. The oblique lighting should first be directed to model the roughness and intro-

This section of a millipede was photographed using transillumination: a beam of light carefully focused through the back of the specimen.

instances, when the specimens are quite large and do not exhibit critical detail, a simple angled mirror and diffusing-glass support can be used.

Matched camera lenses and specimen condenser lenses are available for equipment specifically manufactured for photomacrography, and should be used in accordance with the manufacturer's instructions.

When the amount of work does not warrant the purchase of such equipment or when the specimens are too large for it, setups have to be improvised. Some setups utilize highly corrected condenser systems from slide projectors. Such systems, if properly used, provide results of the best color and detail definition. A simpler and more practical system for those who have only single-condenser elements is also available, and is capable of producing excellent results.

Focused Illumination. A practical optical setup for transilluminating thin-mounted specimens is shown in the accompanying diagram. A clear bulb with a biplanar coil filament should be in the light source. To obtain results exhibiting good contrast and sharp detail, it is extremely important to select and adjust the optical components of the illuminating beam carefully. The specimen condenser should have a diameter 2 to 3 times that of the longest dimension of the specimen. Its focal length should be at least 1.5 times that of the camera lens used for making the photomacrograph, but preferably not greater than 2 times. The condenser should be clean and dust-free.

Dark-field Illumination. Some specimens in photomacrography may be transparent but practically colorless, having no natural color and being unstained. Standard transmitted lighting, therefore, will show little or no detail in the recorded image. Specimens of this type can often be photographed to advantage with oblique dark-field illumination. The accompanying diagram shows how light can be directed through a specimen at an angle of about 45 degrees from below. The direct light beam misses the camera lens, but light is diffused and scattered by the specimen. A clear beam, just large enough to cover the specimen, should be focused in the plane of the camera lens with the condenser lens. There should be no bright wall or object on the camera axis beyond the slide.

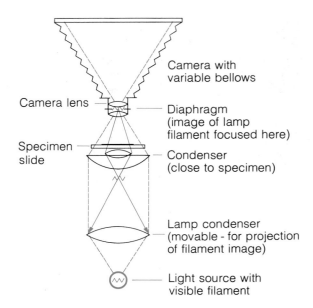

Camera with variable bellows

Camera lens

Diaphragm (image of lamp filament focused here)

Specimen slide

Condenser (close to specimen)

Lamp condenser (movable - for projection of filament image)

Light source with visible filament

(Above) In this setup for providing a focused light beam for transilluminating specimens, the dotted rays show the scheme most useful with large condensers. Alternatively, when only a specimen condenser of short focal length is available (the dotted lens), an aerial image of the filament can be projected and picked up by such a condenser (solid rays).

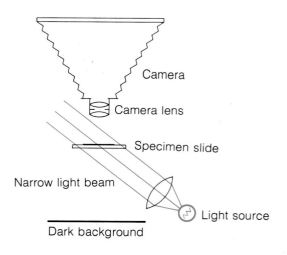

Camera

Camera lens

Specimen slide

Narrow light beam

Light source

Dark background

When arranging focused oblique dark-field illumination, the light is directed through a specimen at an angle of about 45 degrees from below.

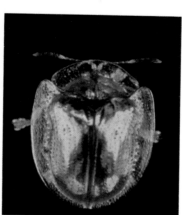

A gold bug undergoes remarkable color changes as it passes from an excited state to a relaxed one. A tent-lighting setup for diffused lighting was used to make this series. The specimen was placed on a piece of thin glass treated with an antireflection lens coating to avoid reflections. A mirror was inserted within the tent to give a degree of backlighting.

A brightly illuminated image against a dark background is produced by this technique. For added interest, a color filter can be placed in the illumination beam between the light source and the specimen to provide a colored image against a dark background.

Tent Lighting. The general purpose of tent lighting is to minimize specular reflections and to prevent dark areas from appearing in extremely shiny objects. Shiny metal surfaces pick up and reflect the relatively dark walls of the laboratory at other angles. The tent provides bright walls for the metal to reflect and reduces the brilliance of the specular reflections. A cylinder of translucent white paper often provides the most suitable tent. (*See:* TENT LIGHTING.)

There are other ways in which the cylinder setup can be used. For example, instead of a black-card background, a piece of opal glass can be used.

This can be transilluminated with light reflected off white paper. A small silvered mirror can be placed at 45 degrees under a clear glass specimen support, and transillumination can be effected with a spotlight. The silvered side of the mirror is turned upward, and the beam comes in at 90 degrees to the subject-lens axis. Such a setup can be used for photographing watermarks on subjects suitably treated to reveal them.

• *See also:* BRIGHT-FIELD ILLUMINATION; CLOSE-UP PHOTOGRAPHY; DARK-FIELD ILLUMINATION; ELECTRON MICROSCOPE; PHOTOMICROGRAPHY; SCIENTIFIC PHOTOGRAPHY; TENT LIGHTING.

Further Reading: Gibson, H. L. *Close-up Photography and Photomacrography,* publication No. N-16, 2nd ed. Rochester, NY: Eastman Kodak Co., 1975; Owens, William, ed. *Close-up Photography.* Los Angeles, CA: Petersen Publishing Co., 1975; Simmons, Robert. *Close-up Photography and Copying.* Garden City, NY: Amphoto, 1961.

Photomechanical Reproduction, Preparing Photographs for

When photographs are destined for printed reproduction, every effort should be made to be sure that the printer or platemaker receives the best print or transparency possible. Printers and platemakers have specific requirements that have to be met if a successful reproduction is to be attained. If followed, the guidelines in this article will not only help the printer to make the best possible reproduction, but they will also save time and money in plate-preparation costs.

Black-and-White Prints

A good black-and-white print made for halftone reproduction should have the following characteristics:

1. Detail in the shadows and modeling in the highlights.
2. The proper contrast—not too flat nor too harsh.
3. A glossy or smooth surface.
4. Generally, a size of from 1½ to 2 times larger than the size at which it will be reproduced.
5. *No* physical defects such as dust spots, cracks, scratches, or black spots.

Retouching. Some reproduction prints may need retouching. A skilled retoucher can help control distracting or unnecessary highlights, subdue overbright backgrounds, and enhance small details. However, it should be the photographer's goal to give the retoucher as little work to do as possible.

Layout. When more than one picture is to be used on a page, real economies can be effected by making all the prints to the same reproduction ratio and placing them into position on a layout. When it is not practical to paste them into a layout, savings in plate costs are still possible by making all individual prints to the same reproduction scale. These scaled prints should be made from the original negatives, not copies. Making scaled prints may increase the photographic costs, but it reduces the reproduction costs. Since the assembly of prints must be made eventually, it is less costly for the photographer to do this. And it is possible to compare the print quality at a point where reprints for tone or contrast are easily and inexpensively made.

Choosing a Paper. There are several criteria to consider when choosing a paper for prints to be reproduced in halftone. If a print is going to require extensive airbrush retouching, such as removing backgrounds or smoothing machine surfaces, then a smooth lustre surface is best. It accepts tempera-type retouching paints better than glossy-surface papers.

A disadvantage with lustre-surface paper is its relatively low density range. Because of the way the surface reflects light, the best blacks always reflect some light that dilutes their density. In order to make prints that have enough visual contrast and to get the blacks to look black, the tendency is to print with a slightly high contrast and to overcompress the black tones, losing shadow detail. This loses dark-tone separation, so that reproductions also lack shadow separation.

Conventional glossy papers can be left unferrotyped—giving a surface partway between that of a lustre and a ferrotyped glossy surface. Such a surface accepts most retouching and generally gives better tone reproduction than the lustre surface. The blacks of unferrotyped glossy paper are blacker than those on a lustre surface, so that better dark-tone separation is achieved.

With ferrotyped glossy surfaces, only a moderate amount of print retouching can be done, such as spotting. A moderate amount of transparent black-dye color can be added with the airbrush. Tempera-type retouching colors do not adhere well.

However, many photographs do not require extensive airbrushing. For such pictures, the highest print density range of the high-gloss surface provides the best tone reproduction in the original print, and in later halftone reproductions. The best blacks can be achieved with good dark-tone separation and good overall-tone separation. Such prints look good to clients and have the potential of making the best halftone reproductions.

Color Transparencies

All of the precautions that pertain to black-and-white prints apply to color transparencies with triple emphasis. They should be sharp where sharpness is needed. Highlights should have modeling. Shadows should not be lacking in detail. Contrast should be normal and density proper. The extra ingredient most important here is that the color balance be absolutely correct, with neutral highlights and shadows.

When transparencies are made in a studio, lighting and exposure can easily be controlled to fit the contrast characteristics of the film so that these characteristics can be achieved. However, the subject luminance range outdoors is often so great that either the highlight or shadow detail will be lost. Where possible, fill flash or the use of reflectors will bring the luminance range down to where the film can record both regions. In larger subjects, however, this is usually not possible. In these cases, it is best to expose for the highlights so that there will be good highlight detail in the transparency, and let the darkest shadows go black. This is the best compromise possible because the important detail will then be in the highlight region.

Viewing Standards. All of those concerned should place a great deal of importance on the color quality of the method of viewing transparencies for reproduction, and everyone should use the same type of viewer. The American National Standards Institute (ANSI) has defined a standard light source and viewing conditions.

The recommended standards for viewing conditions for *color quality appraisal* refer to three controlled conditions:

1. Original artwork and proofs are viewed under lighting of the same color temperature and color-rendering quality.
2. The viewing conditions provide that original artwork and proofs are viewed under conditions that reduce differences in appearance between the two when they are viewed together for comparison.
3. The areas surrounding the viewing areas have been designed so as to be similar in different locations and to minimize visual differences in their interpretation.

The conditions of most general interest for the viewing equipment are:

1. The color temperature of both the transparency illuminator and reflected copy/printed sheet is 5000 K.
2. The various wavelengths of light are in correct proportions to produce the 5000 K.
3. The transparency should have an illuminated border that is at least 2 inches wide on at least three sides of the transparency.
4. The position of the reflected copy or reproduction and the light source must minimize specular reflection.
5. The physical surface of the viewing booth and the surrounding viewing room must be neutral in color and make no color contribution to the viewing condition.

Further specific information on standards for viewing transparencies can be obtained from the American National Standards Institute, 1430 Broadway, New York, N.Y. 10018.

Retouching. As with black-and-white photographs for reproduction, some retouching is usually necessary on color transparencies. If a retoucher works on a transparency with dyes, he or she must be certain that the dyes used have the same photographic separation characteristics as the dyes contained in the transparency itself. *This is very important.* More correction fees are created by bad color retouching than anything else.

When more than the usual amount of retouching must be done, or when the contrast range of the transparency is greater than it is possible to reproduce photomechanically, dye-transfer prints can be made. The retouching is then done with the exact same dyes used to make the print. Density and contrast corrections are easily introduced during the making of the print. Although dye-transfer prints are relatively expensive compared to other color-print methods, the superior results and the ease and reproduction fidelity of retouching makes them worthwhile.

When a number of color photographs are to appear in a single spread, much money can be saved by doing all the original photography to the same scale, so that the transparencies can be ganged and separated or scanned together.

Duplicate Transparencies

When shooting all transparencies to the same scale is impractical, or when the original photography is done with a 35 mm camera, excellent presentation transparencies and reproduction copy can be obtained by duplication. An experienced technician can produce properly scaled, cropped, and color-corrected duplicate transparencies of a quality so high that they are difficult to distinguish from the originals. Therefore, the client receives from the photographer a complete package ready for the printer with no concerns for further preparation for reproduction.

• *See also:* COLOR SEPARATION PHOTOGRAPHY; COLOR TEMPERATURE; DUPLICATE SLIDES AND TRANSPARENCIES; GRAPHIC ARTS PHOTOGRAPHY; LIGHT BOXES.

Further Reading: Dentsman, Harold and M. J. Schultz. *Photographic Reproduction: Methods, Techniques, and Applications for Engineering and the Graphic Arts.* New York, NY: McGraw-Hill Book Co., 1963; Eastman Kodak Co. *More Special Effects for Reproduction.* Rochester, NY: Eastman Kodak Co., 1977; Yule, John A. *Principles of Color Reproduction.* New York, NY: John Wiley & Sons, Inc., 1967.

Photometer

A photometer is a meter that measures light intensity or flux. Early photometers, of the Bunsen type, were comparators; they were designed to produce a balance between the illumination to be measured and some standard light source such as a candle. Improved versions of these photometers utilized standardized incandescent electric lamps, and the sophisticated Lummer-Brodhun head took the place of the Bunsen "grease-spot" comparator.

Modern photometers are usually photoelectric instruments containing a light-sensitive cell, with or without amplification, and a meter to indicate the cell's response. Such a meter, if intended to measure the intensity of a source, is calibrated in footcandles, metrecandles, or lumens. To measure the brightness of an extended source or of a reflecting surface, the meter-cell is arranged to have a pickup limited to a fairly narrow angle; the meter is then nearly independent of distance from the source, and can be calibrated in candles per square foot, candles per square centimetre, lamberts, or footlamberts.

Exposure Meter

An exposure meter is simply a photometer, to which has been added a device by which shutter speed and *f*-stop combinations can be calculated, based on the meter reading and the sensitivity (speed) of the film. An intensity meter is used for incident-light readings, a brightness meter for reflected-light readings.

Densitometer

A densitometer is also a photometer, differing only in that it compares light from the standard against light from the same source after it has passed through the specimen (transmission densitometer) or reflected off the specimen (reflection densitometer) to be measured. The original transmission densitometer of Hurter and Driffield consisted of two lamphouses, each containing a standard candle, with apertures in one side; one had a holder for the specimen over the aperture. The Bunsen photometer head slid along a rail between the two lamphouses, and the transmission of the sample—hence its opacity and density— could be calculated by the inverse-square law. More modern comparator-type densitometers include the Martens densitometer, which uses a rotating polarizer and a beam splitter with a single light source, and the Kodak densitometer, which is similar but has a standard density wedge instead of the polarizing device.

Currently, many transmission densitometers are photoelectric; they measure the light transmitted through the specimen, and the meter scale reads directly in density. Such devices are precise and very easy to use, but are necessarily expensive if they are to have sufficient sensitivity to read densities upwards of 3.0.

Reflection densitometers are made similarly, but the light source is designed to illuminate the surface being measured at 45 degrees while the measurement is made at 90 degrees to the surface. Many densitometers are constructed for a dual function; they can measure either transmission or reflection densities with a minor set-up change.

• *See also:* DENSITOMETRY; EXPOSURE METERS AND CALCULATORS; LIGHT: UNITS OF MEASUREMENT.

Photomicrography

The technique of making photographs by means of a compound microscope is called *photomicrography*. It involves the coupling of a camera to a microscope and the efficient use of illumination. The quality of a photomicrograph depends almost entirely on the quality of the image produced in the microscope. A complete understanding of the principles and operation of the microscope is therefore a prerequisite to producing good photomicrographs.

Although any type of microscope can be used to make photomicrographs, the most common is the bright-field illuminated microscope. The specimen, or subject, may be dark, colored, or nearly transparent and appears against a bright, almost white background. Hence the term bright-field. This microscope is found in biological laboratories and in schools where biology is taught.

The Compound Microscope

A simple magnifying system uses a single lens unit to form an enlarged image of an object. An example is slide projection where a transilluminated transparency is enlarged to form a real image on the screen. If the screen were removed and a suitable lens located behind it and focused in the plane of the screen, the lens would form another image of the slide. This is the basic principle of "compound" magnifying found in a compound microscope. From the first, or primary, image a lens produces an enlarged secondary image, called a virtual image. That is the image the eye perceives. (See the following diagram.)

Microscope lenses are of relatively short focal lengths. The shorter the focal length, the greater the magnification at a given image distance. In a microscope, a high, two-stage enlargement is attained over a relatively short optical path with such short focus lenses.

The first lens in a microscope is the *objective,* since it is near the object. This lens projects a magnified image to a fixed position. The amount of magnification that the objective produces at this fixed distance is its magnifying power. The magnifying power of an objective may be 1×, 5×, 10×, 20×—up to 170×. The projection of the primary image takes place within the body tube of the microscope.

The second lens is placed in the body tube above the primary image. This lens is called the

Photomicrograph of black stem rust affecting a kernel of wheat.

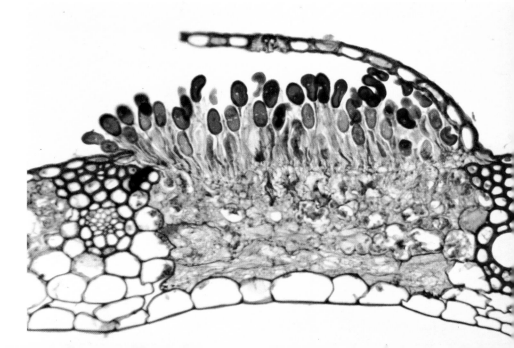

Photomicrography

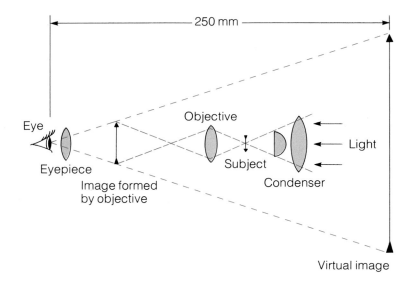

(Left) In this simplified diagram of the compound microscope, the intermediate image formed by the objective is enlarged by the eyepiece. The virtual image is seen by the eye. Alternatively, the eyepiece can project a real image into a camera. (Below) A professional photomicrography setup. Light source, optical system, and camera are in the same vertical plane and mounted on a rigid stand.

eyepiece, and forms a secondary, further enlarged image. The eyepiece, like the objective, is also classified in terms of magnifying power, and could be 5×, 10×, or higher—up to 25×.

The total amount of image enlargement, or magnification, produced within the microscope is found by multiplying the magnifying power of the objective by that of the eyepiece. A 10× objective and a 10× eyepiece then produce a visual magnification of 100×.

As light rays emerge from the eyepiece, they converge to a point called the eyepoint. This is the position that the eye normally seeks when you look into a microscope to see the whole image field. The distance from the eyepoint to the virtual image, or final image, within the microscope system is 254 mm (10 inches).

Instead of looking into the microscope, you can allow the image to be projected from the eyepiece to the film plane. If the film plane, or camera, is 254 mm from the eyepoint, the magnification at the film plane will be the product of the eyepiece and objective magnifications.

Objectives. Microscope objectives are usually classified in terms of magnifying power, mechanical tube length, numerical aperture, and their degree of optical correction; that is, whether they are achromats, apochromats, or fluorites. Some of this information and the focal length are usually imprinted on the objective mount.

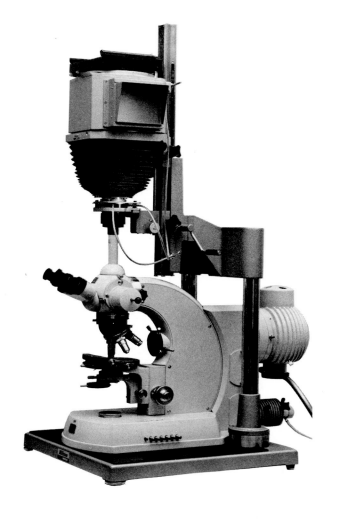

Photomicrography

The *achromat* is the most common type of objective used on any microscope. It is also the least expensive. An achromat is corrected for spherical aberration for one color only, usually yellow-green. It is corrected for chromatic aberration for two colors. If an achromat is used with white light, color fringes may appear in the outer margins of the image. When black-and-white film is used, these fringes may contribute toward a fuzzy image.

An *apochromat* represents the finest microscope objective available. It is corrected for spherical aberration for two colors (blue and green) and for chromatic aberration for the primary spectral colors of red, green, and blue. Because of this high degree of correction for aberrations, the apochromat is particularly suitable for color photomicrography and for the best resolution of fine details and the finest image quality. Apochromats, however, achieve their finest correction only when used with matched compensating eyepieces.

The third type of objective is known as a *fluorite,* or semiapochromat. Objectives of this type are better than achromats, but not quite as good as apochromats. They represent a compromise, both in quality and in cost. Like the apochromats, they should be used with compensating eyepieces for best performance.

For photomicrography, flat-field objectives used with compensating eyepieces are best to reduce curvature of field.

Numerical Aperture. In conventional photography, photographic lenses are always classified in terms of *f*-value, which is an indication of light-gathering power.

Microscope objectives, however, are not classified in terms of *f*-value. In microscopy, the concern is primarily with the ability of the lens to distinguish fine structural details in a specimen. The reason for obtaining a magnified image is to see the details within the specimen. This ability is expressed in terms of *numerical aperture,* or "N.A.," as it is usually called.

Mathematically, numerical aperture is expressed as the product of the refractive index (n) for the medium in which the lens operates and the sine of one-half the angular aperture of the lens (u). The formula then reads: N.A. $= n$ sine u. The sine relationship is a simple means for expressing the size of an angle as a number, the ratio of two sides of a right triangle. For lenses in air, the N.A. and *f*-value are related in this way:

$$f\text{-value} = \frac{1}{2 \text{ N.A.}}$$

Resolving Power. The ability of the optical system in a compound microscope to distinguish and separate fine structural details in a specimen is known as resolving power.* It is limited by the N.A. of the objective, but it also depends upon the working N.A. of the substage condenser. The higher the N.A. of the system, the greater the resolving power will be. Resolving power is also dependent on the wavelength of light. The shorter the wavelength, the better the resolving power.

Eyepieces. The purpose of the eyepiece in a compound microscope is to enlarge the primary image formed by the objective, and either to render it visible as a "virtual" image in the microscope or to project it as a "real" image that can be recorded in a camera.

For visual examination of the image in the microscope, any familiar eyepiece can be used satisfactorily. The most common eyepieces are called Huygenian and wide field. Although Huygenian eyepieces can be used with low- and medium-power achromatic objectives in photomicrography, color fringing and poor image quality may result if they are employed to make high-power photomicrographs. The principal advantage of wide field is in visual work, to scan a slide in order to find a suitable field for photography.

Some eyepieces are intended specifically for photomicrography; they are appropriately called photo eyepieces. Besides producing fair flat-field results, they are also color-corrected and, therefore, are advantageous in color photomicrography.

Eyepieces generally are produced with different magnifying powers, ranging from about 4× to 25×. The most common are those with a magnifying power of 10× or 15×.

Condensers. The third optical component of a compound microscope is called the substage condenser. The specimen slide is placed on a plat-

---

*However, this value is subjective. An image may be unsharp but may still be considered resolved.

form beneath the objective. This platform is called the stage; the substage area is beneath the stage. In some microscopes, light is reflected from a mirror and through the substage condenser to illuminate the specimen. Many microscopes today have built-in substage illumination, so a separate mirror is not used. In either case, however, the light is directed through the substage condenser and converges to a very small area at the position of the specimen. The light rays diverge as they pass through the specimen and form an inverted cone, whose base is just large enough to fill the aperture of the objective. The size of the light beam entering the condenser is controlled by the opening of a variable diaphragm beneath the condenser. This is called the "aperture diaphragm."

Any substage condenser should have centering screws so that it can be correctly aligned with respect to the objective. This is an important feature in photomicrography.

An achromatic condenser is highly recommended for all bright-field photomicrography, but particularly for use with color films. It is essential, however, that the condenser, whatever the type, be accurately centered with respect to the objective for good photomicrography. Loss of light and uneven illumination can result when the condenser is out of alignment.

Cameras for Photomicrography

An efficient microscope, used to best advantage with properly controlled illumination, is the image-forming part of a photomicrographic system. The camera is the means for recording the image formed by the microscope. If the quality of the image is the highest attainable, an excellent photomicrograph can be made. If it is not, then no film, camera, or camera refinement can improve the image quality in the photomicrograph. It is important, however, that the image should not be degraded in the camera or by any photographic technique.

Cameras with Integral Lenses. The simplest way to make a photomicrograph is to use a conventional, existing camera over the microscope. A fixed-focus camera is the simplest. A more elaborate camera offers focusing, a range of shutter speeds, and a variety of aperture settings. This type, obviously, provides more versatility in exposure control.

When a microscope is focused visually with a normal, relaxed eye, the image is considered to be at infinity. Therefore, the distance setting on the camera should be set at infinity. If the camera is placed over the microscope in the correct position, the microscope image will be in focus on the film plane.

The lens-aperture settings (*f*-numbers) on the camera do not control exposure in this work as they do in regular photography. The largest aperture

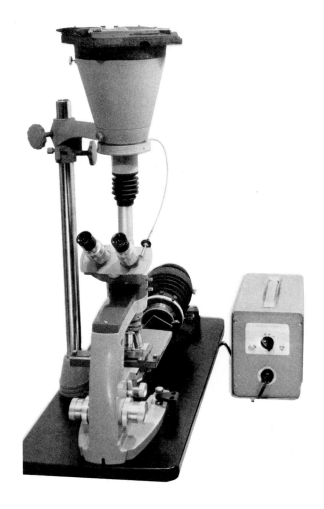

A typical photographic arrangement with "trinocular" microscope. This type of microscope provides binocular viewing for visual work and a third tube for photographing.

setting should be used—that is, the lens should be wide open. The effect of using smaller apertures will be to vignette the image; that is, to reduce the illumination at the edge of the field because of the restrictive action of the aperture.

The camera should be positioned over the microscope so that the eyepoint of the eyepiece is at, or very near, the front surface of the camera lens, as in the accompanying diagram. The eyepoint is the position *above* the eyepiece at which light rays are parallel after leaving the eyepiece. They then converge to form the photographed image. The position of the eyepoint can be determined by holding a piece of white paper right on top of the eyepiece, then slowly raising it. A bright circle will appear on the paper. This circle becomes smaller and then larger. The position at which the circle is the smallest is the eyepoint. The distance of the eyepoint above the eyepiece will vary with different eyepieces. If the eyepiece is changed, therefore, the eyepoint may appear in a different position. The distance may only be a few millimetres or it may be as much as 20 millimetres.

The camera can be held in place over the microscope by any available means. Attaching the

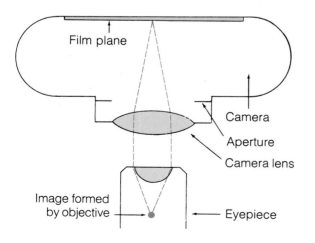

When a camera with an integral lens is properly positioned, the microscope eyepiece is focused so that parallel light reaches the camera lens.

camera directly to the microscope should be avoided. The camera should be held firmly in the correct position, but you should still be able to move the camera up out of the way or swing it to one side to look into the microscope and adjust image focus. The rule is: Focus the microscope and do not change the distance setting on the camera.

Exposure may be a problem with simple cameras having only one or two shutter speeds. With some cameras, setting the camera for "color" or "flash" selects the slower shutter speed or a larger aperture. This means that you must have a very bright image in the microscope and, of course, a very bright light source. The exposure time, or shutter speed, is usually very short and will be about 1/30 or 1/40 sec.

Normally, when an image is formed outside of the microscope, the magnification, as seen in the microscope (objective power multiplied by eyepiece power), is reproduced if the image is 254 mm (10 inches) from the eyepoint. An integral camera lens has a focal length shorter than 254 mm. Image (lens-to-film) distance becomes the determining factor for magnification of the photographed image. A camera with a 50 mm (2-inch) lens will record an image only about one-fifth the size of the image seen in the microscope. Magnification on film can be determined by the ratio between the camera-lens focal length and 254 mm, multiplied by the visual magnification of the microscope.

To determine the actual magnification recorded on film, you can place a micrometer slide under the microscope. The lines of the slide should be focused sharply and the image recorded. When the film is processed, you can measure the separation of the recorded lines and compare the measurement with the actual separation of the lines on the micrometer slide. For example, if two lines on the slide were 0.01 mm apart, and the same lines are recorded 0.5 mm apart, the recorded magnification is 50× (0.5 ÷ 0.01).

Cameras without Integral Lenses Many firms that manufacture 35 mm single-lens reflex cameras also offer microscope adapters. Normally, when a reflex camera is to be used over a microscope, the lens is removed from the camera and one or more extension tubes is placed on the camera in the lens position. A microscope adapter ring, containing the microscope eyepiece, is then fastened in the front extension tube. The whole assembly of camera, tubes, and adapter can then be placed on the microscope, fitting the microscope eyepiece and the adapter ring directly into the drawtube of the microscope. This assembly, in some designs, can be attached to a rigid stand that is supported independently of the microscope. This will prevent transfer of vibration from the camera to the microscope.

The micro-image is focused by adjusting the focus knob on the microscope while viewing the image in the camera's viewfinder. One disadvantage of this system is that the image is usually focused on a ground glass within the viewfinder. Critical focus of fine detail is difficult to achieve on a ground glass because of the coarseness of the ground surface. If a clear glass can be used in place of the ground glass, or if a clear area is present on the ground glass near the center, this disadvantage can be overcome.

Some firms that manufacture reflex cameras also offer an adjustable bellows, which is normally used in close-up photography. This bellows (with no lens attached) can be used on a reflex camera over a microscope and has the advantage of adjustability, so that magnification and the amount of recorded field can be varied for control of image composition. When the camera is used in this manner, it is advisable to attach the bottom plate on the bellows track to a rigid vertical stand.

With a reflex camera, magnification can be varied, a wide range of shutter speeds is available (usually 1 sec. to 1/1000 sec.) for exposure control, and the entire film frame in the camera can be filled. Also, many modern reflex cameras include a behind-the-lens metering system for monitoring the image brightness in exposure determination.

Photomicrographic Cameras. There are several commercially made cameras designed specifically for photomicrography. The most popular are those called *eyepiece cameras;* a feature generally common to cameras in this group is a beam-splitter eyepiece. The microscopic image can be viewed, focused, and composed by means of this auxiliary eyepiece. A rectangular area is often shown in the center of the field to indicate the portion of the field that will be recorded on film. (See the accompanying diagram.)

The film plane in a 35 mm eyepiece camera is in a fixed position, usually far enough from the microscope eyepiece so that only the central area of the field is recorded. This feature avoids the out-of-focus peripheral area caused by curvature of field, which is inherent in many microscope objectives and which would be recorded in a camera with integral lens. The distance from eyepoint to film may vary slightly for 35 mm eyepiece cameras of different manufacture, but is usually about 100 to 125 mm (4 or 5 inches). Since the distance is less than 254 mm (10 inches), however, a simple

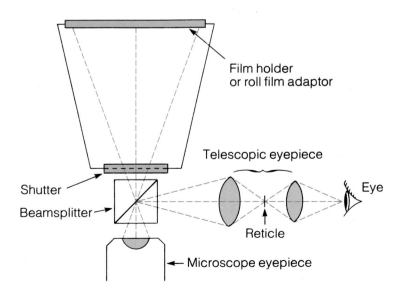

Eyepiece camera with fixed bellows. If bellows draw (the lens-to-film distance) is less than 254 mm (10 inches), a correction lens is often included to adjust the focus to the film plane.

correcting lens is incorporated so that the image seen sharply focused in the viewing eyepiece will also be in sharp focus in the film plane of the camera. The use of this correcting lens also provides that the microscope will be used at the correct optical-tube length.

Sheet-film cameras of the eyepiece type often reproduce visual microscope magnification, since the eyepiece-to-film distance can be fixed at 254 mm (10 inches). In addition to an observing eyepiece, these cameras often have a ground-glass back to facilitate both composing and focusing of the image to be recorded. Film size is usually 4″ × 5″. Because of this larger film size, greater magnifications can be recorded with these cameras than with roll-film cameras, especially 35 mm cameras.

Camera Vibration. Vibration in a camera setup can result from microscope manipulation, from drawing and replacing dark-slides in film and plateholders, from setting the mechanical shutter, and from vibration within the building. It is always good practice to wait a few seconds for vibration to cease before making the actual exposure. Even then, if the shutter is actuated manually, additional vibration can occur and may cause some unsharpness in the recorded image. For this reason, if the shutter is part of the camera, the use of a suitable cable release is strongly recommended. A self-timer can also be used to provide a means of automatic delay before the shutter is operated.

Microscope Illumination

Correct adjustment of the optical system of the microscope is, in fact, dependent upon an efficient system of illumination. An objective, for example, cannot be used effectively unless the substage condenser is properly adjusted and the substage diaphragm is set at the correct aperture. These adjustments are made by following the system known as Kohler illumination, which is described in a later section.

The light source itself should provide sufficient intensity to allow reasonably short exposure times. The lamp housing should be suitably designed to allow easy access to the light source and should contain those elements necessary for proper adjustment of the illumination furnished to the microscope.

When a color film is to be exposed, the light source should conform to, or allow suitable filtration to meet, the requirements of the film.

Light Sources. The most common light source in general brightfield photomicrography is the incandescent tungsten filament lamp, available in a wide selection of voltages and wattages. Most microscopes having built-in illumination utilize either a 6- or 12-volt coil filament lamp, which varies in color temperature from about 2700 K to 3200 K, depending on manufacture and electrical conditions at the time of usage. Operation of this low-voltage lamp is through a transformer that has several settings. The highest setting is usually suggested when color film is to be exposed, in order to provide the highest color temperature.

When a microscope does not have built-in illumination, an external illuminator must be used. Separate illuminators are available from microscope manufacturers or dealers.

The tungsten-halogen lamp is an excellent source for photomicrography. It emits high-intensity, efficient illumination because the coil filament is small and compact. Lamp life is about 50 hours, and it can be replaced easily and inexpensively.

Electronic flash lamps can also be used in photomicrography, specifically in photographing moving organisms. The illumination is of daylight quality and therefore is satisfactory for use with daylight-type color films. Since the flash is instantaneous, an auxiliary tungsten lamp of low brightness is usually necessary for purposes of alignment, for producing Kohler illumination, for focusing and composing the specimen image, or for general viewing of the specimen prior to photography. The flash should be synchronized with the operation of the camera shutter.

Because complete control of illumination is necessary, photomicrographic illuminators should contain both a lens to project an image of the lamp filament and a diaphragm to control the size of the illuminated field in the microscope. The lens is usually called a "field condenser"; the diaphragm, a "field diaphragm." Also, the terms "lamp condenser" and "lamp diaphragm" are used. (See the accompanying diagram.)

Methods of Illumination. There are two ways to illuminate specimens—by transillumination and by reflected light. The latter is used for photo-

(Below) The unpolished surface of an industrial diamond was photographed using surface light, rather than transmitted light. This technique is frequently used to photograph thick or opaque specimens. (Bottom) Printed micro-circuit photographed by reflected light. Magnification is 40×.

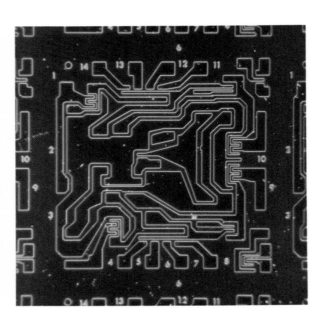

graphing the surfaces of thick or opaque subjects. It is accomplished with microscope lamps that project a small spot of light, or by special built-in ring or axial systems. Metallography utilizes the latter. The majority of subjects encountered in general photomicrographic work are examined and photographed by transmitted illumination.

The simplest setup involves the use of axial transmitted light. Rays of light are reflected from the plane surface of the substage mirror through the substage condenser, through the subject and the field around it, and into the microscope objective. (See the accompanying illustrations.)

A movable substage condenser permits accurate control and concentration of the light and the use of high-power objectives. The illumination should completely fill the diaphragm opening of the condenser with light of even intensity. The condenser must be properly adjusted to insure that the back lens of the objective is evenly filled with light. The plane, or flat, side of the substage mirror should always be used when a condenser is employed. The spherical mirror is used only in

Cone of light from the substage condenser with the apex in the specimen plane. The inverted cone fills the aperture of the objective. Critical focus of the condenser is necessary.

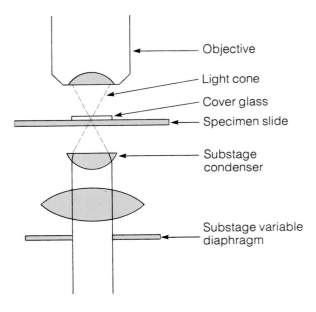

- Objective
- Light cone
- Cover glass
- Specimen slide
- Substage condenser
- Substage variable diaphragm

Photomicrography

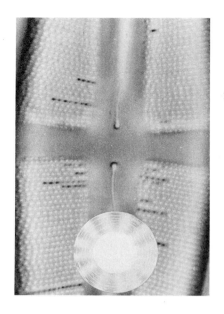 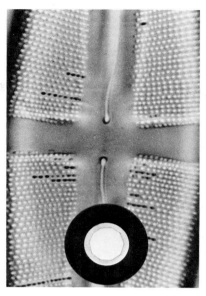 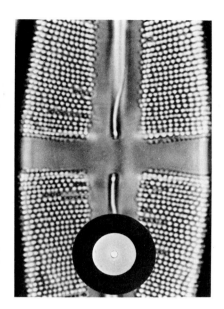

Adjusting the aperture diaphragm for optimum resolving power of the objective: (left) wide open; (center) correct aperture; (right) stopped down. The bright area should be four-fifths the diameter of the distant circle.

cases when a low-power objective is used without a condenser.

If the illumination system has not been properly adjusted, a photomicrograph may be disappointing—even if the highest quality optics have been used, the image has been focused critically, and the exposure of film has been correctly determined. The two basic requirements are that the whole illumination system be centered, and that the cone of light from the illumination system completely fills the aperture of the microscope objective, providing uniform illumination over the whole subject field.

Kohler Illumination

This is the most common system of illuminating a microscope specimen in photomicrography. It can be used in visual work, too, because it provides best image quality and highest resolution.

The chief practical advantage of this technique is that, when the elements are properly aligned, a uniformly illuminated field is provided, with practically no restriction as to the structure of the light source. Hence, it is possible to employ a nonuniform source (such as a coil-filament tungsten lamp) or a high-intensity source of small area (such as a zirconium arc or a xenon arc).

Essentially, the method of producing Kohler illumination in photomicrography consists of focusing an image of the lamp collector in the plane of the object and image of the lamp filament in the plane of the aperture diaphragm. In effect, the lamp collector becomes the source of illumination.

The steps in establishing Kohler illumination follow:

1. Focus on a thin, transparent specimen.
2. Stop down the field diaphragm to a small aperture. While looking into the microscope or at the ground glass of the camera, focus the condenser to obtain a sharp image of the field diaphragm in the specimen plane.
3. The image of the field diaphragm should be centered in the observed field. If it is not centered, alignment of the lamp to the mirror or

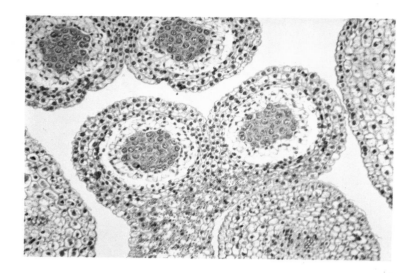

Cross section of a lily bud magnified 200×, photographed on Kodak Ektacolor professional film, type S.

lamphouse adjustments are not properly made and must be corrected.

4. While still observing the diaphragm image, open the field diaphragm until its diameter is equal to, or just slightly greater than, the entire microscope field as seen.

5. Check alignment of the lamp with respect to the lamp collector. A quick check of alignment can be made by placing a piece of thin white paper over the field diaphragm and focusing the lamp collector to produce an image of the lamp on the paper. The image of the lamp should be centered within the outline of the diaphragm.

6. Adjust the lamphouse so that the image of the lamp is centered on the mirror. Adjust the mirror so that the image reflected by it onto the aperture diaphragm is centered on the diaphragm. Focus the lamp collector to produce a sharp image of the lamp filament on the aperture diaphragm.

7. Adjust the field diaphragm until it falls just outside the field of view. The principal functions of the field diaphragm are control of image contrast by minimizing flare and control of the size of the illuminated field. This diaphragm has no effect on image brightness. If brightness is affected, the microscope is not adjusted for Kohler illumination.

8. Focus on the specimen and remove the eyepiece from the drawtube of the microscope.

9. Look down the tube. The back lens of the objective will be visible as a bright circle. (This step is aided by the use of a pinhole eyepiece.) The centered lamp-filament image (Step 3, preceding) will also be visible.

10. Reach below the condenser and adjust the opening of the aperture diaphragm until its edge is seen within the bright circle. The correct setting occurs when the diameter of the diaphragm image is about 0.8 that of the back lens image.

If the edge of the diaphragm image is not visible, the aperture diaphragm is open too far. If it is left this way, the effect will be a loss of contrast in the image of the specimen. Poor image quality will result.

If only a very small diaphragm image is visible, the diaphragm opening is reduced too far. The effective numerical apertures of the objective and condenser are thus reduced, and poor resolution results. Also, pronounced interference fringes appear in the specimen image. Such fringes produce low image quality.

Proper adjustment of the aperture diaphragm cannot be overemphasized if the best image quality is desired.

Built-In Illumination

The present tendency in modern microscopes is toward more convenient and compact illumination systems. Many microscopes include illuminators built into the base. The illumination provided to the specimen is usually a modified type of Kohler illumination. The lamp in its holder can be moved with respect to the nearest lens and can also be rotated in the lamp housing. This serves the same purpose as focusing the lamp condenser and setting alignment screws for on-axis adjustment.

Color Photomicrography

The film characteristics to consider in selecting a color film for photomicrography are size, speed, and the ability of the film to record specimen colors as accurately as possible. Other factors are contrast, granularity, illumination, and color balance.

In photomicrography, 35 mm reversal color films are most often used. Normally, if tungsten illumination is used with the microscope, a color film balanced for artificial light should also be used. Daylight-type films are suggested when the light source has daylight quality. Sources such as the xenon arc or electronic flash give this illumination.

Rendition of Color. The many biological stains used in specimen preparation, such as tissue sections and smears, represent all of the colors of the visible spectrum. Color films, however, show considerable differences in sensitivity and response to various colors. For this reason, the color of one stain may record better on one color film than on another. It depends on where *that* color appears in the spectrum and how sensitive the color film is to *that* region of the spectrum.

There is no one color film that will record all specimen colors accurately. If specimen colors must be reproduced with reasonable fidelity, it

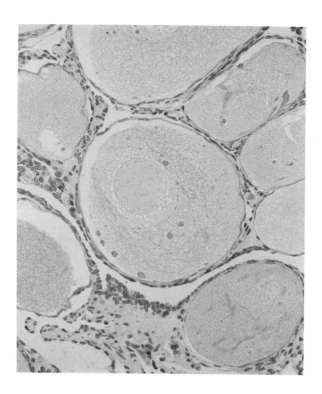

Ovary of amphiuma magnified 100×. Hematoxylin and eosin stains were used. A didymium filter enhanced the eosin stain color. The specimen was photographed on Kodak Ektachrome film, 6116, type B.

may be necessary to experiment with different films to find one that is most suitable.

Filters. The ultimate function of both the microscope and the illumination is to produce the best possible image of a specimen. A photomicrograph is a record of this image on a photographic, or light-sensitive, material. If the specimen is colored, as with biological stains, then the image will also be colored and will be recorded ideally on a color film. If a colored image is to be recorded on a black-and-white material, the colors must be reproduced as tones of gray that satisfactorily represent the color brightnesses in the specimen. It is usually necessary to use specific light filters, either to provide correct rendition of colors on color film, or to record the colors as appropriate gray tones with suitable contrast on a regular film or plate. (*See:* FILTERS.)

Light Balancing Filters. All daylight-type color films can be used in photomicrography,

Photomicrography

1951

Hippuric crystals photographed with polarized lighting. Magnification: 150×.

Light Source	Tungsten, Type B, or Type L Film (3200 K) Filter No.	Type A Film (3400 K) Filter No.	Daylight-Type Film Filter No.
FILTERS FOR COLOR FILMS*			
6-volt ribbon-filament (average C.T.=3000 K)	82A	82C	80A+82A
6-volt coil-filament (average C.T.=3100 K)	82	82B	80A+82
100-watt coil-filament (average C.T.=3100 K)	82	82B	80A+82
300- to 750-watt coil-filament (3200 K)	None	82A	80A
Zirconium arc (3200 K)	None†	82A	80A
Photoflood lamp (3400 K)	81A	None	80B
Carbon arc (3700 K)	81D†	81B	80C
Xenon arc (5500 K)	85B	85	None†

*The filters suggested are considered to give approximate color-temperature compensation. Color test exposures are often necessary to obtain best color balance.

†A No. 2B filter is often used to absorb unwanted ultraviolet from arc illumination.

regardless of the type of illumination, if the correct filters are placed in the *light beam* to adjust the illumination to daylight quality. Light-balancing filters should be placed between the illuminator and the condenser of the microscope. Separate illuminators usually contain filter receptacles for this purpose.

Color Compensating Filters. Undesirable color effects are caused by several factors in color photomicrography in addition to exposing a color film to illumination other than that for which the film was designed. These effects can usually be corrected with color compensating filters—available in various densities in red, green, blue, cyan, magenta, and yellow.

Neutral Density Filters. Neutral density filters can be used in photomicrography to reduce image brightness as a means of controlling exposure time. A neutral filter will absorb a specific amount of light, depending on its density, without affecting the color quality of the illumination. The principal application of such filters is in the exposure of color films. They can also be used with black-and-white films to prevent overexposure. (*See:* NEUTRAL DENSITY and FILTERS.)

Neutral density filters are also used to reduce visual image brightness. A very dense filter is placed in the light path when image brightness is too high for comfortable viewing. A density of 1.00 or more will usually suffice for this purpose, but it

COLOR-BALANCE CORRECTIONS IN PHOTOMICROGRAPHY

Appearance of Photomicrograph	Possible Cause	Remedy
Slightly yellow	Emulsion variance Colored mounting medium Low color temperature of light source	Use CC10B filter. Use blue CC filter (CC10B or more). Use light-balancing filter of 82 series.
Slightly magenta (reddish blue)	Emulsion variance	Use CC10G filter.
Slightly cyan (bluish green)	Emulsion variance Heat-absorbing filter in light beam	Use CC10R filter. Use CC10R, or possibly CC20R, filter.
Slightly blue	Emulsion variance Abbé condenser not focused correctly	Use CC10Y filter. Adjust condenser for Köhler illumination.
Definitely blue	Ultraviolet radiation present during exposure with arc lamp High color temperature of light source	Use No. 2B filter to remove ultraviolet radiation. Use appropriate light-balancing filter of 81 series.
Slightly green	Emulsion variance Heat-absorbing filter in light beam	Use CC10M filter. Use CC10M, or possibly CC20M, filter.
Slightly red	Emulsion variance Condenser not focused correctly	Use CC10C filter. Adjust focus of condenser for Köhler illumination.
Slightly yellow-red	Low color temperature of light source	Use light-balancing filter of 82 series.
Definitely reddish yellow	Daylight film with tungsten source—no correction	Use No. 80A filter, plus light-balancing filter of 82 series.

should be removed for photography because it may prolong exposure time too much.

Black-and-White Photomicrography

In black-and-white photomicrography, filters are used primarily for control of image contrast. An increase in contrast is often desired in order to make a specimen stand out against the background or to differentiate between colored elements, which may appear to have equal brightness on black-and-white film.

Filters are often used to increase contrast in photomicrography of blood smears. In the United States, blood smears are commonly stained with Wright's Stain, a combination of methylene-blue and eosin stains. The first stain usually appears deep blue and the second light red. A green filter, such as a Kodak Wratten filter No. 58, will show more absorption for the eosin color and will render it with good contrast against the background. Another common stain combination, hematoxylin

and eosin, usually requires a green filter also. The particular green filter depends on stain concentrations. The No. 58 filter applies if the eosin color is pale; a lighter green, such as a No. 11 or No. 13, when the color is more intense.

CONTRAST FILTER COLORS*

Specimen Color	Contrast Filter Color
Blue	Red
Blue-green	Red
Green	Red
Red	Green
Yellow	Blue
Brown	Blue
Purple	Green
Magenta (blue-red)	Green
Violet	Yellow

*To increase contrast in black-and-white by recording a specimen color darker than normal, use a filter of the indicated color.

When a specimen color is moderately dense, detail within the specimen can be recorded if the filter color is the same as, or similar to, the specimen color.

Exposure Methods

As in other forms of photography, exposure in photomicrography is influenced by light intensity (image brightness) and by exposure time. Exposure time can be determined either by using a sensitive exposure meter or by making an exposure test series. Because image brightness in photomicrography can be quite low, particularly at high magnification, the exposure meter should be sensitive to very low light levels. To determine exposures with a hand-held meter, hold the meter above the eyepiece at a distance such that the diameter of the emerging light-beam will be slightly greater than the diameter of the photocell. Make the meter reading with the meter in this position in a dimly-lighted room. Some professional exposure meters have special microscope attachments. The manufacturer's manual gives instruction for these attachments.

When making an exposure test series, place any necessary filters in the light beam.

Exposure Tests. When exposing a 35 mm test film, include several frames, each exposed for a different length of time. Image brightness, of course, should remain constant. Process the exposed film and examine the individual frames over an illuminator to determine which one has received the correct exposure.

When a camera accepts sheet films, a series of test exposures can be made on one film sheet by the following procedure:

1. Pull out the dark slide of the film holder until the entire sheet is uncovered in the camera. Make an exposure for 1 unit of time; for example, 1 sec., 1/2 sec., 1/125 sec., or whatever initial time may be indicated by the image brightness level.
2. Push in the slide about 3 cm (about 1 inch) and *repeat* the exposure for the same unit of time.
3. Push in the slide another 3 cm and give an exposure for 2 units of time.
4. Continue to push in the slide to cover approximately 3 cm steps, exposing each step for twice as long as the previous one. The successive steps will then have received exposures of 1, 2, 4, 8 times the initial time unit.

Develop, fix, and wash the film as recommended in the instruction sheet. Examine the resulting negative to select the step that shows the best reproduction of the subject.

Exposure Calculation. Once the correct exposure time has been found for a particular set of optical conditions, the correct times for new conditions *with the same microscope and illumination* can be calculated. The factors that affect image brightness are changes in magnification or in numerical aperture. Magnification, of course, will change if a different eyepiece, a different objective, or a new eyepiece-to-film distance is involved. Also, if the objective is changed to one of higher or lower magnifying power, the numerical aperture will be different.

If the optical conditions for which the exposure time was originally determined by test are called standard, they can be compared mathematically with the new conditions to calculate the new exposure time, according to the following formula:

$$\frac{\text{New Exposure Time}}{\text{Standard Time}} = \left(\frac{\text{Standard N.A.}}{\text{New N.A.}}\right)^2 \times \left(\frac{\text{New Magnification}}{\text{Standard Magnification}}\right)^2$$

In this way, exposure time can be calculated when any of the optical exposure factors are changed.

Exposure Meters. Some types of exposure meters are made specifically for photomicrography and are sensitive enough to respond to light through a wide range, from very low to very high brightness. A meter scale may be precalibrated by the manufacturer to give a direct reading of exposure time, with various settings for film speed.

If a meter reads brightness, but no device is provided for correlating brightness and exposure time, the meter must be calibrated.

One type of meter is equipped with a "probe" containing a photocell. The probe is placed in the microscope eyepiece tube, with the eyepiece removed, in order to read image brightness. When

Many current photomicroscopes are equipped with photo-cells or photoresistors that integrate and measure the brightness of the image. A wide range of brightness can be accomodated; allowances for filter factors and other variables are included in the automatic exposure system.

a probe type of meter is used, the *same* eyepiece should always be used in the microscope for photography. Otherwise, the meter readings will not always be valid.

When an eyepiece-camera with a beam splitter is used over the microscope, light readings can be made from the light emitted from the eyepiece of the beam splitter. However, image brightness here will often be *less* than that seen by the film because the division of light varies with different beam splitters. In some systems, 90 percent of the light goes to the camera and only 10 percent is seen visually through the observation eyepiece. The actual division, however, may be 80-20, 70-30, or even 50-50, depending on the specific eyepiece camera in use. Hence, the amount of light division will influence the calibration of a light meter.

Making Exposure Readings. Exposure readings can be made in various positions: at the film plane of the camera, anywhere between the eyepoint of the ocular and the film plane, in the eyepiece tube of the microscope with the eyepiece removed, or from the light emitted from the observation eyepiece of a beam splitter. The best position, of course, is at the film plane, since the image brightness there is the same as would be recorded on the film. This position, however, is not always

accessible because the camera may be closed during photography. The ground-glass screen of a sheet-film camera allows this type of reading.

If the exposure reading is made at some position above the microscope eyepiece, the image brightness will always be *greater* than that at the film plane. This fact must be considered in calibrating an exposure meter. Also, the light reading should always be made at the same distance above the eyepoint.

Wherever the reading is made, there are two methods of measuring brightness, or exposure time. One method is to read just the background brightness with the specimen slide moved aside on the stage. This system provides a large area of uniform brightness on which to make a reading. The method is especially useful with reversal color film, where exposure time is dependent on the brightest part of the specimen—which is essentially the same as the background brightness.

The second method of measuring brightness is to read the actual brightness of the specimen image. This system also works efficiently for color films, as long as the specimen image has average brightness. If dense areas predominate the field, overexposure may occasionally be encountered, and the bright, highlight areas may appear washed out. This method should always be used, however, when negative films, either color or black-and-white, are to be exposed. The result is good rendition of detail in the darker areas of the subject.

Exposure Record. When photomicrographs are made often, it is advisable to keep a record of the conditions involved. A detailed record will permit duplication of a setup for future use, either in rephotographing a particular specimen, or for photography of similar specimens.

• *See also:* BRIGHT-FIELD ILLUMINATION; CLOSE-UP PHOTOGRAPHY; DARK-FIELD ILLUMINATION; ELECTRON MICROSCOPE; KOHLER ILLUMINATION; PHOTOMACROGRAPHY; SCIENTIFIC PHOTOGRAPHY.

Further Reading: Gander, Ralph. *Photomicrographic Technique for Medical and Biological Scientists.* Riverside, NJ: Hafner Press, 1969; Lawson, D. *Photomicrography.* New York, NY: Academic Press, 1972; Loveland, Roger P. *Photomicrography: A Comprehensive Treatise,* 2 vols. New York, NY: John Wiley & Sons, Inc., 1970; Walker, M. I. *Amateur Photomicrography.* Garden City, NY: Amphoto, 1972; Wolberg, Lewis R. *Art Forms from Photomicrography.* New York, NY: Dover Publications, Inc., 1974.

Photoresist

Photosensitive resists are organic resinous materials. When the photoresist in liquid or dry-laminate form is coated on a metal or semiconductor substrate, the dry coating is sensitive to ultraviolet and visible radiation. Exposure through a high-contrast film mask causes a change in the polymer structure of the resist, so that parts of the resist image are soluble while others are not. A suitable solvent is used to "develop" (wash away) the soluble resist. The result is a stencil pattern of hardened polymer with clear areas through which an etchant can penetrate, a metal can be plated, or a semiconductor material can be diffused. In modern technology the photoresist has become indispensable for production of microelectronic devices, printed circuits, and small metal parts.

Basically, photoresists are either negative working or positive working. In the negative-working system, the exposed areas of the resist are hardened by radiation and remain on the surface after development. With the positive-working photoresist, exposure renders the resist soluble, so that unexposed areas are the ones that remain after development.

Photoresists have low photographic speed so that exposure is usually made with the film mask in contact. Only in some microelectronic applications involving very small image areas is projection printing possible.

Most photoresists are sensitive only to ultraviolet or blue radiation; however, the sensitivity of at least one material has been extended to include the green wavelengths. This has the effect of increasing the photographic speed of the photoresist when it is exposed with tungsten light sources.

A fundamental advantage of the photoresist is that the resolving power is potentially higher than any comparable silver-halide material. Resolution is limited in practice by the coating thickness. Microelectronic devices are made with photoresists that resolve line widths on the order of 1 or 2 micrometres.

• *See also:* NAMEPLATES, PHOTOGRAPHIC; PHOTOFABRICATION; PRINTED CIRCUITS.

Phototypesetting

For nearly 500 years after the invention of movable type by Johann Gutenberg, the setting and composition of type was essentially mechanical. In the last few decades, photographic methods of producing pages of type have rapidly evolved. Phototypesetting uses a variety of mechanical, optical, and electronic methods of projecting the image of a type character onto a photosensitive film, paper, or printing plate.

In a basic form of phototypesetter, the type is contained in a font in the form of clear images in a black surround or a negative. This font can be in the shape of a grid, a disk, or a drum. To set type, the character is selected, the font is positioned, and the image of the character is projected onto a photosensitive material by an optical system using an intense light source (frequently a powerful flash lamp). Optical and mechanical methods are provided to index characters one after another to justify or adjust the width of lines and to produce succeeding lines. By introducing optical components that enlarge or reduce the character image, type can be set in a variety of sizes.

More sophisticated systems may use a cathode-ray tube to generate the character from a computer memory. Since this system does not require mechanical positioning of a type matrix, it is potentially much faster. With computer control, type can be set, combined with line and halftone graphics, and displayed on the face of a cathode-ray tube for projection onto photographic material. Advanced exposing methods, such as laser-beam recording, can scan copy, set type, compose pages, insert drawings and halftones, create tabular material, and expose all those images directly onto printing plates or phototypeset films and papers.

Photographic Materials

Photographic paper is the most commonly used phototypesetting material because of its low cost. Stabilization-processed papers are widely used. Paper-type galleys can be pasted down with line art, display type, and screened paper prints to form "mechanicals" for reproduction.

Phototypesetting film is used where a transparent base is desirable and the dimensional stabil-

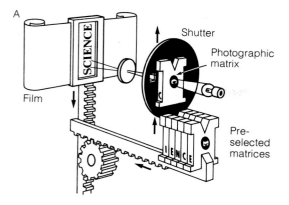

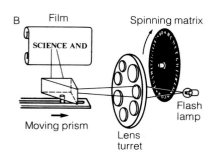

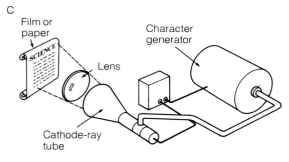

the typesetter. Any cleaning standard set for a camera or enlarger, however, must be much more stringent for a typesetter because generated images are usually quite small and difficult to repair.

Housekeeping is essential to quality control. Beyond the careful maintenance of the optics, mirrors, prisms, and so on, a careful check of possible voltage fluctuations must be made.

An area of potential difficulty with typesetter output is a difference in character thickness or line color from day to day. To reduce problems, it is important to use only high-quality photographic materials that have consistent speed, uniform emulsion characteristics, and excellent image stability. Processing should always be in fresh, properly replenished chemicals. Processors should be designed for processing phototypesetting output and should be adjusted properly.

Corrections and Makeup

In hot-metal typesetting, corrections are generally made by removing and replacing charac-ters or whole lines of type. In cold-type composi-tion the same principle is applied to a paper or film galley. Lines of type are cut out of a galley with a knife or a razor blade, and the corrected line is stripped in or mortised into the galley.

Corrections on Phototypesetting Paper. Cor-rections on paper galleys are most often made right over the original error. This is the quickest and simplest way of applying corrections. There are two drawbacks to this technique, however. When you lay down a piece of phototypesetting paper over a galley that is already down on a board or layout sheet, you are building up the mechanical. This layering can produce edge shadows when the final negative is shot.

ity of film is required. Film is often used in multiple-step processes for combination with half-tones and other art, especially with multicolor printing. Phototypesetting films that will produce negative images after exposure and reversal processing are available.

Some sophisticated typesetting systems will compose all the type and art and expose whole pages directly onto phototypesetting film or paper or metal lithographic printing plates.

Type Quality

A typesetter is an enlarger through which a photographic image is produced to variable sizes. The same housekeeping requirements that are maintained for enlarger equipment are fitting for

One of the easiest ways to eliminate edge shadows is to mortise the correction right into the galley. In this technique, the corrected piece of paper is laid down over the error. Next, cut around the perimeter of the new section and remove the old piece of galley. The correction is then placed in the opening and is held in place by wax, cement, or other adhesive.

Corrections on Phototypesetting Film. Film galleys are usually corrected by either running another galley or by stripping in the corrections on the existing galley. Usually, corrections on film galleys are stripped or mortised with the aid of mechanical devices that help in cutting straight lines and in aligning the pieces of the galley. Some of these devices can be set up for the point size at hand, which permits the cutting of slugs of type to allow a more accurate piecing together of the corrected galley.

Makeup. There are two basic ways to make up the galleys from phototypesetters. Traditionally, paper galleys are cut apart and pasted up onto pieces of cardboard (called boards), forming complete page mechanicals with windows put in place for halftones, or with pre-screened paper halftone prints put in place on the board. The so-called pasting is usually done with hot wax or special liquid adhesive solutions. Secondly, film galleys are cut apart and positioned on a stripping base with tape or adhesive.

• *See also:* Graphic Arts Photography; Screened Negatives and Prints.

Further Reading: Graham, Walter B. *Complete Guide to Paste Up.* Philadelphia, PA: North America Publishing Co., 1974; Romano, Frank J. *Photocomposition and You.* Salem, NH: GAMA Communications, 1974; White, Jan V. *Editing by Design.* New York, NY: R. R. Bowker Company, 1974.

Pictorial Photography

Throughout the development of photography there have been two major approaches to the expressive use of the medium: the straight, and the pictorial. In the simplest terms, the straight approach is concerned with making the subject appear real, thus speaking for and about itself. The pictorial approach is concerned with making the image

Pictorial photography is more concerned with interpretation and the presentation of beauty than with literal truth. Here, the photographer waited for fog and the rowers, seeking a particular mood. Photo by Michael Fairchild.

Sometimes the difference between straight and pictorial photography may depend upon the viewer. While this is a perfectly straightforward close-up photograph of a dandelion gone to seed, it has a certain abstract quality that puts it in the category of pictorial photography. Photo by Stephen Douthat.

In pictorial photography, the subject itself is of secondary importance; the emphasis is not on what the subject is, but rather on how it is presented. Photo by Irma Vitalis.

appear beautiful, thus speaking primarily about the interpretation and the mode of presentation, rather than about literal truth. The emergence and parallel growth of these two aesthetic attitudes is discussed in the article HISTORY OF PHOTOGRAPHY. Some aspects of the intent and the methods of pictorialism are covered here.

The Pictorial Approach

In pictorial photography, the function of subject matter is to serve as a vehicle for the photographer to display his or her emotional response, creative interpretation, and technical mastery. A straight photograph asks the viewer to have a direct experience with the subject; the medium—the fact of the photograph as a physical object itself—is meant to be essentially invisible. A pictorial photograph asks the viewer for an aesthetic reaction to the formal presentation—the finished photograph itself; any direct subject-viewer experience is of secondary importance.

As with other high art forms such as grand opera and classical ballet, pictorial photography offers the performance as the major aesthetic factor. A sincere display of virtuoso mastery and the use of creative variations in the handling of familiar or established subjects is the goal, not the revelation of new subjects, or of newly discovered aspects of known subject matter. Given this intention, it is not surprising that pictorialism aims at presenting perfection, which is synonymous with beauty, and thus concentrates on subjects that are physically and emotionally pleasing.

In the hands of an unimaginative or insensitive photographer, the pictorial approach can easily lead to imitation and artificiality. It is easy to produce pictures that are only slight—and meaningless—variations of other pictures, or to use color shifts, tonal simplification, texture effects, and other devices without regard to whether they are appropriate to the emotional qualities of the image. Such results are often merely academic exercises or clichés; they form part of the body of work to which detractors point as evidence that pictorialism is a hollow mode of expression.

However, there is a large number of photographs that demonstrate that any such failings are those of the individual, not of the pictorial approach. In addition, the current resurgence of interest in alternate methods of printing, image modification, and mixed-media imagery has brought new life and imagination to pictorialism. As the formal aspects of photography are being explored anew, a highly interesting "new pictorialism" is emerging.

Modern Pictorialism

Since the 1860's pictorialism has been the approach most widely used by serious amateurs. It is dominant in camera clubs and nontechnical photographic organizations, and comprises the kind of work both expected and submitted for the salons, exhibitions, and competitions organized by such groups. In the United States, the Photographic Society of America (PSA) authorizes pictorial exhibitions and competitions among its chapters each year and promulgates standards of judging and classes of awards. Monthly camera-club competitions in pictorial photography serve as training grounds for a great many aspiring pictorial photographers.

Some pictorial images are only partially created in the camera; final modifications may be made in the darkroom. This forest scene was posterized to give an autumnal quality not apparent in the original image. Photo by R. Scott Perry.

Pictorialism is the fundamental approach of advertising and editorial illustration, in which the intent is to dramatize a product of service; project a mood or emotion; or make visible a situation, idea, or abstract concept. Some of the most complex and technically dazzling pictorial images are created for these purposes.

A great many photographers who consider themselves artists and are concerned with the potentials of photography as a medium of aesthetic self-expression are pictorialists, whether they use the term to describe themselves or not. Since the artistic approach embraces an interest in both the formal and the decorative aspects of photography, all kinds of abstraction are pictorial. The great majority of new pictorial images in artistic photography are abstract in one sense or another. (*See:* HISTORY OF PHOTOGRAPHY.)

Methods of Pictorial Photography

Two of the major working considerations in pictorialism are technical excellence and composition. Since pictorial images are to a large extent

(Right) By choosing to photograph the reflection rather than the temple itself, the photographer used the surface of the water to break up the image, in the manner of an impressionist painter. (Below) Silhouetted against a dramatic sky, an ancient seacoast castle sits brooding atop a rocky promontory. By manipulation of lighting and camera angle, the photographer created a mood piece from an otherwise straightforward subject. Photos by Michael Fairchild.

Pictorial Photography

1961

Clarence White's "In the Orchard" (1902) is an example of early pictorial photography. The dreamy quality is a result of the soft-focus, painterly photographic style popular in that era. Photo from Camera Work; *reproduced courtesy of Aperture, Inc.*

A grain texture screen, placed directly on the paper during printing, resulted in the impressionistic appearance of this tranquil forest scene. Photo by Don Maggio.

preconceived, a photographer can devote maximum attention to these factors. That is seldom the case for a photographer taking documentary, journalistic, or other kinds of record pictures.

Some pictorial photographs are completely visualized and designed at the outset; the photographer's task then is to assemble and arrange all the necessary elements, photograph them, and carry through the printing or finishing stages in a way that will realize the original concept to the fullest extent. Other images may be only partially created in the camera. Until the negative or transparency has been processed and the photographer confronts the problem of how to modify or emphasize certain visual qualities for expressive effect, the final creative effect cannot be achieved.

Often the conception of the final image grows as various printing or duplicating stages are carried out. The full range of conventional and unconventional methods, and special effects, is at the photographer's disposal. The choice of what to do is based on the photographer's interpretation of the subject and the kind of visual mood or feeling that seems appropriate.

To the degree that an essentially unmodified presentation of a classic subject—a landscape or a nude study, for example—is intended, the pictorial approach tends to rely on the established conventions of composition, especially with regard to the location of a center of interest, balance, and color or tonal harmony. Lighting, pose, angle of view, placement of focus, filtration, and other factors are all selected and controlled with the final result in mind.

When images are essentially created at the darkroom stage by such techniques as combination or multiple printing, use of the Sabattier effect, and other methods of control, classical composition frequently gives way to approaches that originate in graphic design and illustration. Although the composition of such images may be less formal, it must provide as firm a visual structure for the picture as that of any work of fine art.

Because the ultimate aim of a pictorial photograph is to convey a response of aesthetic pleasure, its technical qualities must be as nearly perfect as it is possible for the photographer to make them. No matter how imaginative the visual concept may be, even small flaws in the execution will under-

mine its effectiveness. The methods used in the production of the final image are often complex. Because carelessness can undo a great deal of effort, the artistic growth of a pictorialist is generally slow. Each new technique must be thoroughly explored and painstakingly mastered before it can be considered part of the expressive vocabulary of the photographer.

It is not possible to specify pictorial subjects, techniques, or working methods in detail. Any subject matter can be approached with the idea of making a subjective interpretation, and of producing an image that presents personal feeling in a manner that is emotionally and aesthetically pleasing to the viewer. As in all art, the success of the final result depends on how sensitively the artist makes creative decisions within the limits—or freedom—of his or her technical mastery.

Forms of Pictorial Photographs

Historically, most pictorial photographs have been black-and-white prints. In recent years, slides and color prints have served as media for pictorialism. Even stereo slides serve a small number of pictorial photographers. Larger transparencies that are difficult to project have been one form of photography not widely used as a pictorial medium.

However, when the pictorial photograph is to be reproduced, large-size color transparencies are a widely used original material. There are periodicals and books published whose emphasis is on pictorial photography; and in these, it is the printed reproduction that becomes the object to be viewed. Large-size color transparencies work very well as originals from which such reproductions are made.

Exhibition of Pictorial Photographs

Since one of the major purposes of pictorial photographs is to give aesthetic pleasure to viewers, it is important that they be exhibited at a place where viewers can see them. Camera clubs hold local exhibitions, often called salons, where selected pictures made by members are exhibited. These are often hung in art galleries, bank lobbies, or other exhibition areas where the public can see, and hopefully enjoy, the photographs.

Concentration on one detail, such as this series of painted stripes on a building wall, can result in an interesting, abstract effect. Photo by Shelden Berdé.

Art museums, universities, and photographic museums often put together exhibitions of photographs—usually with a common theme. Such an exhibition may show one photographer's work, or it may be a representative show of several photographers whose work has something in common.

• *See also:* CAMERA CLUBS; COLLAGE; COMBINATION PRINTING; COMPOSITION; DECORATING WITH PHOTOGRAPHS; DOCUMENTARY PHOTOGRAPHY; GUM BICHROMATE PRINTING PROCESS; HISTORY OF PHOTOGRAPHY; LANDSCAPE PHOTOGRAPHY; MONTAGE; MULTIPLE-EXPOSURE TECHNIQUES; MULTIPLE PRINTING; NONSILVER PROCESSES; PLATINUM PRINT PROCESS; POSTERIZATION; SABATTIER EFFECT; SILK-SCREEN PROCESS; SOFT-FOCUS EFFECTS; SPECIAL EFFECTS; TONE-LINE PROCESS; VIGNETTING.

Pinakryptol

Pinakryptol green: 1:3-diamino-phenyldiazonium hydrochloride
Pinakryptol yellow: 1-methyl-2 (3-nitrostyryl)
-6-ethoxyquinoline methylsulfate
Pina-white: anthraquinone 1:7 disodium sulfonate

Dye compounds used as desensitizers and fog suppressants. The proprietary name Pinakryptol (or -cryptol) was given by the Pina Corporation to these dye substances when they were introduced in the 1920's. They have the property of desensitizing an exposed emulsion without destroying the latent image, making it possible to develop a film by inspection in a fairly bright light.

Pinakryptol green could be used either as a prebath or as a component of some developers; however, in highly alkaline developers of the type often used for automatic processing, it tended to produce irregular gray-green stains. In addition, in solution form, it could not be exposed to daylight. Pinakryptol yellow, a more powerful desensitizer, avoided staining but could not be added to most developers because it was decomposed by sodium sulfite. Pina-white neither stained nor decomposed under most conditions, but was less powerful than the other two substances.

The Pina- compounds are little used today. Modern automatic processing equipment does not require that films be desensitized, and other substances are more effective for controlling aerial fog. The high speeds and dye sensitization of modern emulsions generally make dye desensitization an impractical procedure for the individual photographer; also, Pina- compounds are not readily available.

• *See also:* ANTIFOGGANT; DESENSITIZING; DEVELOPERS AND DEVELOPING.

Pincushion Distortion

Pincushion distortion is a lens aberration in which the magnification of the image is greater at the margins of the field than at the center. As a result, the image of a square centered in the field is pulled outward at the corners, causing the sides to curve concavely. The size of the image of the subject is

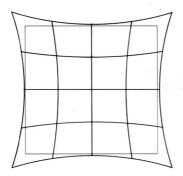

With pincushion distortion, lines parallel to a picture edge stretch outward at the corners, pulling subject area into a larger scale.

Pinhole Camera

A pinhole camera is the most basic image-forming device in photography. It is a direct descendant of the original cameras obscura used by artists from the sixteenth to the nineteenth centuries as aids to drawing perspective correctly. (*See:* CAMERAS; HISTORY OF PHOTOGRAPHY.) Instead of a lens, the camera has a small hole that admits light. As the accompanying illustrations of pinhole principles explain, an image is formed because light rays pass through the hole in straight lines. The angle of view is determined by the pinhole-to-film distance, while—for a camera of given dimensions—the image size is determined by pinhole-to-subject distance. Although the image is not as sharp as can be formed by a lens, all objects within the field of view are imaged with an equal degree of sharpness; in other words, a pinhole camera has infinite depth of field.

Because the pinhole is so small, exposures are usually several seconds or even minutes in length; this requires absolutely steady support for the camera. These factors and the reduced sharpness of the image are the main drawbacks of pinhole photography. However, the softness of detail and the extreme depth of field can be used expressively with subjects that are suitable for time exposures.

greater in the field than it would be in a lens without distortion. A lens with distortion, therefore, images straight subject lines as curved lines.

Pincushion distortion occurs because various rays of light are insufficiently refracted toward the lens axis. Mathematically, pincushion distortion is negative, because the rays place the image points outside their rectilinearly correct positions. In positive, or barrel, distortion, rays place the image points closer to the center than their correct positions. Changing the lens aperture setting has no effect on either kind of distortion.

• *See also:* ABERRATION; BARREL DISTORTION; LENSES; OPTICS.

A pinhole camera is the most basic image-forming device in photography. It is a direct descendant of the camera obscura, used by artists in earlier days to study and draw perspective. Although the image has an overall softness, all objects within the field of view are imaged with an equal degree of sharpness.

Pinhole Principles

Image Formation

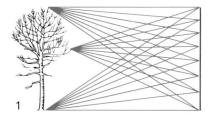 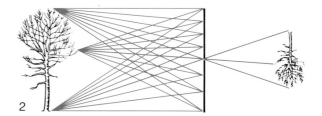

1. Light from various points on a subject follows multiple straight-line paths to a viewing screen or a film. No image is formed because light from one point falls on all parts of the film and is interfered with by light from all other subject points; everything is washed out.

2. A camera front with a small hole limits light reaching the film to a single path from each subject point; paths from other points are at different angles, so they cannot interfere. An image is formed because there is essentially a point-for-point correspondence between subject and image. Because paths are straight lines, the image is inverted.

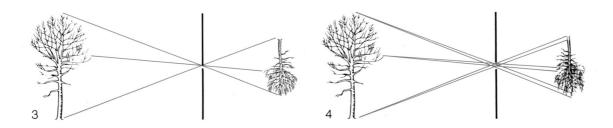

3. If the front plate could be infinitely thin and the hole infinitely small, each path would be limited to a single light ray and the image would be perfectly sharp, except for diffraction.

4. Actual diameter of the pinhole passes a bundle of rays from each point. Because rays diverge, subject points are imaged as small circles, reducing sharpness. Decreasing the hole size will increase image sharpness (until diffraction effects occur), but will greatly increase required exposure because there is less light to form the image.

Pinhole Principles (continued)

Angle of View

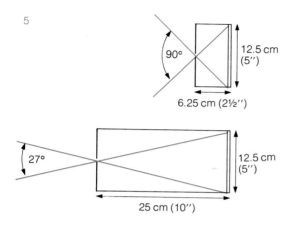

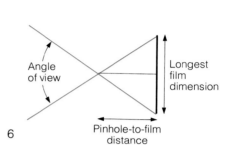

Angle of view is determined by film size and distance from pinhole.

5. As the distance between pinhole and film increases, the angle of view is reduced.

6. To determine angle of view for any pinhole setup, draw a T to scale, using the factors shown; connect the extreme points (colored lines) and measure the angle formed.

Image Size

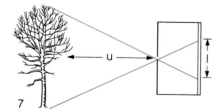

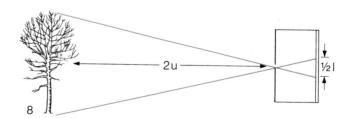

7. For a camera of given size, the distance (u) from a subject determines the size of its image (I).

8. If the distance is doubled, the image size is reduced to one-half. Similarly, if the distance were tripled, the image would be one-third of the original size.

Pinhole Principles (continued)

In overall terms, image size is related to subject size and distance from pinhole to subject and to film as follows:

$$\text{Subject size} \div \text{Image size} = \text{Subject distance} \div \text{Film distance}$$

For a given camera with a known pinhole-to-film distance, the formula is most useful in the form:

$$\text{Image size} = (\text{Subject size} \times \text{Film distance}) \div \text{Subject distance}$$

Example: Using a camera with a 12.5 cm (5-inch) pinhole-to-film distance, the image of a child 90 cm (36 inches) tall at a distance of 210 cm (7 feet) is:

$$(90 \times 12.5) \div 210 = 5.4 \text{ cm } (2\tfrac{3}{16} \text{ inches})$$

If the calculated image size is larger than the film size, only a portion of the subject can be included.

Exposure

The pinhole forms a stop of fixed size; exposure is controlled by time. The *f*-value of a pinhole is calculated:

$$f\text{-number} = \text{Pinhole-to-film distance} \div \text{Pinhole diameter}$$

Use the following diameters to determine pinhole *f*-values:

Standard needle size	Drill number	Hole diameter Millimetres	Inches
7	74	0.66	0.026
8	75	0.58	0.023
9	76	0.51	0.020
10	77	0.46	0.018
11	78	0.40	0.015
12	80	0.35	0.014
14	—	0.30	0.012
16	—	0.25	0.010

The optimum size of the pinhole (D_o) is a compromise between the "circle of confusion" created by the pinhole of each subject point and the enlargement of the image of each point caused by diffraction. The general equation used to find D_o is:

$$D_o = \sqrt{K\lambda l}$$

where K is a constant, λ is the wavelength light, and L is the camera length.

A more usable form is:

$$D = \sqrt{.0013\, L} \text{ or}$$
$$D = .036\sqrt{L} \text{ when D and L are in millimetres, or}$$
$$D = .007\sqrt{L} \text{ when D and L are in inches.}$$

Pinhole Principles (continued)

The following table shows optimum pinhole sizes for various camera lengths.

OPTIMUM PINHOLE SIZES FOR CAMERA LENGTHS

Camera Length		50 mm (2″)	75 mm (3″)	101 mm (4″)	152 mm (6″)	254 mm (10″)
Optimum pinhole size CD	mm	.26	.31	.36	.44	.57
	inches	.010	.012	.014	.017	.022
f-number		190	243	282	346	450
Nearest whole f-number		180	256	256	360	512
Film Speeds		Suggested exposure times for bright, sunlit scenes (seconds)*				
ASA 32		15	36	36	80	200
ASA 64		5	15	15	36	80
ASA 100–125		2	5	5	15	36
ASA 400		1/2	1	1	2	5
ASA 1250		1/8	1/2	1/2	1	2

*Black-and-white films corrected for reciprocity.

If a bellows camera is equipped with a pinhole, the *f*-value will change each time the bellows is moved. It may be useful to calculate the *f*-value at a marked position, and then to mark a few other positions. The *f*-value varies directly with the change in pinhole-to-film distance. If the distance is doubled, the *f*-value doubles; if the distance is halved, the *f*-value is halved.

Once the *f*-value of a pinhole is known, basic exposure can be determined from a normal meter reading of the subject. Exposure meters do not have *f*-numbers on them as large as those of pinholes. To find the exposure, count the number of stops from a convenient meter-indicated *f*-number to the *f*-value of the pinhole; double the meter-indicated time for each stop counted.

Since many meter calculators do not go beyond about *f*/32, the following reference scale may be useful. To extend the scale further, note that the numbers double at every other step.

f/ 8 11 16 22 32 45 64 90 128 180 256 360 512

Example: A No. 6 needle hole (0.74 mm diameter) used 12.5 cm (125 mm) from the film has a value of: $125 \div 0.74 = f/169$. The meter reading is 1/60 sec. at *f*/16. To determine exposure, figure: There are 7 stops from *f*/16 to the *f*-number closest to the pinhole *f*-value (16 to 180). So, the meter-indicated exposure time must be doubled seven times, or a total of $2^7 = 256\times$. The correct basic exposure is: $1/60 \times 256 = 256/60 = 4$ sec. (rounded off). Note that the calculated exposure may also have to be increased to compensate for reciprocity effect. Check the film instruction sheet. (*See:* RECIPROCITY EFFECT.)

Camera Construction

A pinhole camera may be made from any small, lighttight box or can. The major limitation in using such a container is that a darkroom or changing bag must be available for reloading after each exposure. A camera constructed from a self-contained film cartridge offers the convenience of several exposures without reloading. The same advantage is obtained by using a conventional camera body with a pinhole in place of a lens. Extension tubes can be used with rigid-body cameras to obtain various angles of view.

The two ends of a homemade camera are parallel. The end opposite the pinhole is flat so that the film is held in a flat plane. The pinhole itself has a cover to prevent light from entering the camera when you are not taking a picture.

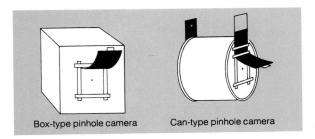

Box-type pinhole camera   Can-type pinhole camera

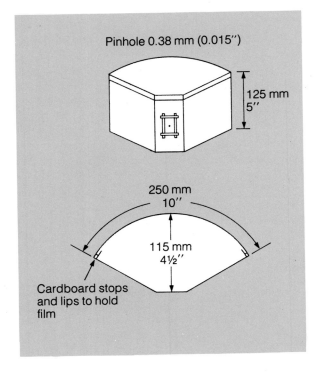

Pinhole 0.38 mm (0.015″)

125 mm
5″

250 mm
10″

115 mm
4½″

Cardboard stops
and lips to hold
film

(Above) Construction of box- or can-type camera is self-evident. The lid or cover must fit tightly over the end opposite the pinhole, and the interior must be black. Cardboard boxes can be reinforced with tape inside and out to add rigidity. Image quality of pictures depends primarily on how well the pinhole is made. (Right) Panorama pinhole camera uses 10×24 cm or 4″×10″ sheet film (20×24 cm or 8″×10″ sheet cut in two). It is made of cardboard cut and taped together with black masking tape. Spray the outside and inside with black matte paint before attaching aluminum foil with pinhole. This camera produces negatives large enough to produce acceptable definition in contact prints. Angular edge-to-edge coverage is 125 to 130 degrees. The center must be somewhat overexposed to get adequate edge exposure, and it will be necessary to dodge when making the contact print.

The interior of a can- or box-type camera must be painted flat black, or lined with matte black paper to prevent reflections. If a plastic lid is used on a can, it must be completely opaqued. Since paint flakes off plastic easily, a black cardboard insert is better; it will also add stiffness. A can-type camera is easier to reload if the lid forms the back; the film (or paper) can be taped to the inside. The lid should be secured with black (photographic) masking tape to eliminate light leaks and to prevent accidental opening. A cradle base or stubby "legs" taped to the outside of a can will prevent its rolling. The accompanying

---

Cartridge Pinhole Camera

Materials

1 cartridge of film, size 126.
1 piece of thin black cardboard, 32 × 146 mm (1¼″ × 5¾″).
1 piece of rigid black cardboard, 38 × 70 mm (1½″ × 2¾″), with a 13 mm (½-inch) square opening cut in the center.
1 piece of heavy aluminum foil 25 mm (1 inch) square.
1 piece of black paper, 25 mm (1 inch) square.
2 strong rubber bands.
1 No. 10 sewing needle.
Black masking tape.
A nickel or a dime.

Cartridge Pinhole Camera (continued)

Assembling the Camera

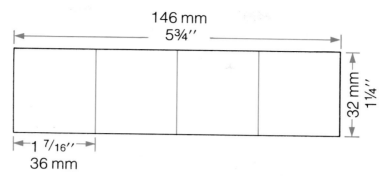

146 mm
5¾''

32 mm
1¼''

1 7/16''
36 mm

1. Measure and mark the large piece of black cardboard into four sections, each 36 mm (1⁷⁄₁₆ inches) wide.

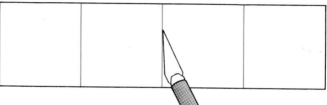

2. Using a knife, cut through only the top layer of cardboard along each of the lines. This will make it easier to fold the cardboard.

3. Fold the cardboard into a box and tape the edges together with the black tape. This is your camera box.

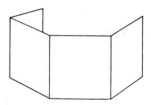

4. Using *only the point* of the sewing needle, make a very tiny pinhole in the center of the aluminum foil. When you make the hole, rest the foil on a hard, flat surface.

5. Center the pinhole in the foil over the square opening in the small piece of cardboard. Tape the foil to the cardboard on all four edges.

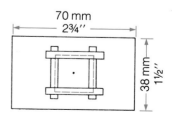

70 mm
2¾''

38 mm
1½''

6. Put the small piece of black paper over the pinhole and tape it along the top edge. Use a small piece of tape at the bottom of the black paper to hold it down between exposures.

7. Tape the cardboard with the pinhole to the box. Use plenty of tape, and make sure all the edges are taped together so that no light can get into the camera box.

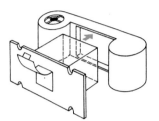

8. Put the camera box into the grooved recess in the square opening of the film cartridge. This should be a tight fit so that no light can get into the camera.

9. Use the two strong rubber bands to hold the camera in place.

10. Insert the edge of a nickel or dime in the round opening on the *top* of the film cartridge.

11. To advance the film in the cartridge, turn the coin *counterclockwise*. The backing paper (visible in the small window on the label side of the film cartridge) should move. The film has borders and numbers printed on it. Turn the coin slowly until the third and fourth numbers in each series on the backing paper show in the window. The film will then be in the proper position for picture-taking.

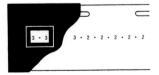

The angle of view of a pinhole camera is determined by the pinhole-to-film distance, and panoramic views are entirely possible with this type of camera. Photo by W. Arthur Young.

illustrations explain the construction of pinhole cameras.

Making the Pinhole. The pinhole must be a smooth circle; burrs or ragged edges will degrade image sharpness considerably. In addition, the hole can be too small, causing fuzzy pictures because of diffraction of the light rays and requiring extremely long exposures. However, exact size is not critical.

The pinhole can be made in the box or can material itself, but it is easier—and results are much better—to make the hole in a separate piece of material that is then taped in position over an opening in the camera body. Heavy-duty aluminum foil, the bottom of a disposable pie plate, or the backing paper from a roll of film are all suitable materials. For very best results, use aluminum or brass shim stock about 0.4 mm (⅟₆₄ inch) thick; some hardware and auto supply stores carry shim metal.

For a camera with the pinhole 75 to 150 mm (3 to 6 inches) from the film, the best results will be obtained with a pinhole about 0.34 mm (0.013 inch) in diameter. To make a hole this size, push a No. 10 sewing needle through the paper or metal to a point halfway up the needle's shank. For a smoother hole, rotate the needle as you push it through. If you are using aluminum foil or paper, sandwich it between two lightweight cards while you make the pinhole. This will help make a smoother, rounder hole.

You can also make a good pinhole in thin aluminum or brass sheet metal. Place the metal on a hard surface such as tempered hardboard. Make a small hole in the aluminum with an awl or an ice pick. Do not press too hard—the tip should just barely break through the surface. The hole will be ragged. Enlarge and smooth it by pushing a No. 10 needle into it from the indented side. Smooth the rough edges with very fine sandpaper and then open the hole with the tip of the needle. You can use the same method to make the pinhole directly in the metal of the can by working the hole through from inside the bottom of the can.

If you are adapting a conventional camera, make the pinhole in a separate piece of black paper or metal and make a hole 6 mm (¼ inch) or more in diameter in the center of one end of the camera body or the lens-board plate. Then tape the pinhole in position over the center of the hole.

Check the pinhole to make sure it is perfectly round by looking through the back of the camera. To see if the image is clearly visible, aim the camera

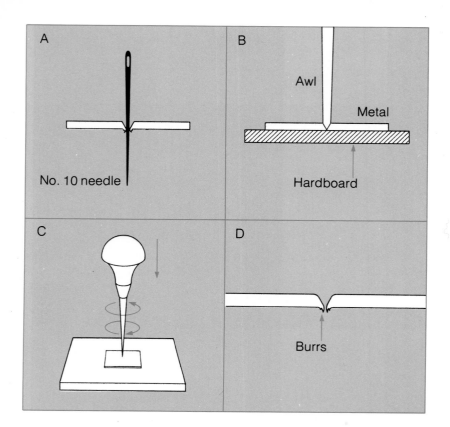

Making the pinhole. (A) Paper or foil can be punctured with a needle; sandwiching material between thin cards will prevent tearing and reduce burrs. (B) Shim metal should be supported on a firm surface, such as hardboard, as a dimple is pressed into it. (C) Rotating an awl or prick punch will help make a smoother, rounder hole. (D) Burrs must be removed with very fine (No. 0000) sandpaper or crocus cloth.

A

No. 10 needle

B

Awl

Metal

Hardboard

C

D

Burrs

toward a printed page and see if the letters show clearly.

The Shutter and Viewfinder. The shutter for the camera can be a flap of opaque dark paper hinged with a piece of tape. Use a small piece of tape to hold the shutter closed while you are not taking a picture.

A viewfinder for a pinhole camera, while usually not necessary, can be made of cardboard or wire. The larger frame should be slightly smaller than the film size and located directly above the pinhole at the front of the camera. If the film is not square, the viewfinder should have its longer dimension parallel to the longer dimension of the film. The small frame is a sighting peephole directly above the film and squarely behind the center of the large frame.

When aiming the camera at subjects closer than 1.5 metres (5 feet), tip it up slightly to allow for parallax—the difference between the view you see through the viewfinder and the image recorded on the film. This effect is caused by the separation between the viewfinder and the pinhole.

Loading a Can- or Box-Type Pinhole Camera

The "film" for the camera can be either film or fast photographic paper. Paper is easier to handle because it can be loaded into the camera under a safelight. Most film, on the other hand, must be handled in total darkness. The choice of film or paper may depend in part on the exposure times. Paper, because it is less sensitive to light than film, will probably require an exposure of about 2 minutes for sunlit subjects. Film may require only 1 or 2 seconds for subjects in sunlight.

If you decide to use paper, try a medium-contrast enlarging paper. You can obtain such a paper in the 4″ × 5″ or 5″ × 7″ size (corners may have to be trimmed to fit a cylindrical camera). If you use film, you can cut up a roll of medium- or high-speed negative film, 120 or 620 size, into suitably sized pieces. This must be done in total darkness, of course. Sheet film is easier to use because it is flat.

A camera made from a 2-pound coffee can will take a 2¼″ × 3¼″ piece of film or photographic paper. You can use a 3¼″ × 4¼″ piece if about ½ inch is clipped from each corner of the film or paper. A camera made from a 1-gallon paint can will take a 4″ × 5″ piece of film or paper.

When you have the required size of paper or film, tape it firmly to the inside of the end of the camera opposite the pinhole. The emulsion should face the pinhole. The emulsion on roll film is on the inside of the curl. Sheet film is identified by notches cut into one of the shorter sides. When you hold the film in a vertical position and with the notches in the top edge toward the right side, the emulsion is facing you. Another way to determine the emulsion side of either paper or film is to touch both sides with a moistened finger. The emulsion side will feel slightly tacky. (Test near the edge to avoid a fingerprint in the center of the picture.) You will need to tape down the four corners if you use cut-up roll film or paper. Taping two diagonal corners will work for sheet film. Close the camera, making sure the shutter is closed, too.

Taking Pinhole Pictures

Because time exposures are required, the camera must be absolutely steady. Tape it to a table, windowsill, chair, rock, or other rigid surface. Or use a lump of modeling clay or putty to mount the camera firmly on a steady support, such as a kitchen stool. Aim the camera by sighting over the top surface.

Use the small piece of tape on the black-paper shutter to hold the paper down over the pinhole after each exposure. This prevents light from entering the camera and spoiling the picture between exposures or reloading.

The following exposure tables give *approximate* recommendations. It is a good idea to make three different exposures, at different lengths of time, for each scene to be sure of getting a good picture. Take pictures at the recommended time, twice as long, and one-half as long.

CARTRIDGE PINHOLE CAMERA EXPOSURES		
Film Exposure Index	Bright Sun	Cloudy Bright
400	½ to 1 second	2 to 4 seconds
125	2 seconds	8 seconds
100	3 seconds	12 to 15 seconds

CAN- OR BOX-TYPE PINHOLE CAMERA EXPOSURES		
Exposure Index	Bright Sun	Cloudy Bright
Film, 400	1 to 2 seconds	4 to 8 seconds
Film, 125	2 to 4 seconds	8 to 16 seconds
Enlarging paper	2 minutes	8 minutes

Processing and Printing

Process film and paper in trays, or in plastic or glass dishes; film from cartridge-type cameras can be processed on reels in tanks. Use normal chemical solutions and processing procedures.

Print film negatives in the usual way. If you use paper to make your picture, make the camera exposure long enough to allow the resulting paper negative to be a little darker than an ordinary photographic print. Dry the paper negative and make a contact print from it in the normal way, with the emulsion (picture) side of the paper negative toward the emulsion (shiny) side of the printing paper. (*See:* PAPER NEGATIVE.)

• *See also:* CAMERAS; HISTORY OF PHOTOGRAPHY; LENSES; RECIPROCITY EFFECT.

Platinum Print Process

Prints in pure metallic platinum have great richness in the blacks, a long scale of gradations, and absolute permanence. The sensitivity of the platinum paper is low—all platinum prints are therefore contact prints. The process is based upon the light sensitiveness of iron salts that are used with platinum. A platinum salt is reduced, in the presence of a suitable developer, by the ferrous oxalate to which ferric oxalate in the emulsion has been reduced by the action of light.

The action of light upon a platinum salt was observed by Gehlen in 1804, and commented upon by Herschel in 1832. The first workable printing process was patented by William Willis in 1873 and subsequent years, and commercially coated paper was available until 1937, at which time the process was taken from the market, having been almost en-

The platinum printing process is based on the light-sensitiveness of iron salts used with platinum. A platinum salt is reduced in the presence of a suitable developer by ferrous oxalate, which was produced from ferric oxalate in the emulsion by the reducing action of light. Photo by Bill Crawford.

tirely superseded by other processes that were less expensive and that did not require the large negatives necessary for contact printing. Paper can be coated with platinum emulsion by hand.

The best results are obtained with pure rag papers; cheap wood-pulp papers will not give good results. Three papers currently available that have been used successfully for platinum prints are:

Rives BFK etching paper;
Crescent Bristol, Vellum surface (100 percent rag);
Crane's writing paper, kid finish (ecru white or white).

Although it is not absolutely essential with good papers, a preliminary sizing is desirable, and for this purpose gelatin, arrowroot, or tragacanth can be used. The disadvantage of gelatin is that it is very prone to form air bubbles, and arrowroot is preferable. To prepare the gelatin size, make a 2 percent solution of gelatin in water, and add 1 percent of alum. To make the arrowroot, rub 20 grams (308 grains) into a thin cream with water, then add to 1000 millilitres (32 fluidounces) boiling water with constant stirring, and continue boiling for 5 minutes. Allow to cool, and remove the skin that forms on top. The gelatin size must be used warm.

To apply the size, the paper should be pinned to a drawing board or other flat surface at the corners and the size applied with a broad flat brush in straight strokes, first across and then up and down the paper, until the surface is uniformly wet. Then a round soft brush (a perfectly clean shaving brush is excellent) should be worked all over the surface until it appears even and begins to lose its gloss. It can then be hung up to dry. For rough drawing papers the sheets should be immersed in the size for from 5 to 30 minutes, according to the thickness of the paper and the roughness of the surface. The paper should be drawn over the edge of the dish, so as to wipe off as much solution as possible, and then hung up to dry with the end that leaves the dish last at the top.

The platinotype process is a very old one and a great many formulas have been published for its use. The one below, by Paul Anderson, is probably the most modern; it has been presented in many books, magazine articles, and research papers. This is an edited version with quantities and conversions corrected as nearly as possible.

Solution No. 1
Water	62.5 ml
Oxalic acid	1.1 g
Ferric oxalate	16.4 g

Solution No. 2
Water	62.5 ml
Oxalic acid	1.1 g
Ferric oxalate	16.4 g
Potassium chlorate (10% solution*)	2.8 ml

Solution No. 3
Water	70.0 ml
Potassium chloro-platinite	15.0 g

These stock solutions, which keep indefinitely if stored in the dark, are mixed in varying proportions to give different degrees of contrast. The formulas are given in parts, which in practice will usually be drops; they are most convenient for measuring such

*To make a 10 percent solution of potassium chlorate, dissolve 10 grams of potassium chlorate in about 90 ml of water, then add water to make a final volume of 100 ml.

small quantities as will be used, because the working solution should be mixed only at the time of use. The minimum amount of sensitizer with which a 20 × 24 cm (8″ × 10″) sheet can be coated is about 46 drops. This should be doubled and allowed to soak in if the richest blacks are desired. With hard papers on which it is difficult to handle the larger volumes of solution, one minimum coating can be applied and allowed to dry, and then another coating applied over it. Or multiple printing can be resorted to, re-sensitizing the developed print and printing again.

It is essential that the ferric oxalate be pure; it tends to decompose with age and on exposure to air, producing ferrous oxalate, which causes foggy highlights in the prints. Pure ferric oxalate can be prepared by the user in the form of a 20 percent solution.

Prepare such a solution of ferric ammonium sulfate as follows:

Ferric ammonium sulfate	480.0 g
Hot water	500.0 ml

Heat until dissolved completely, then cool and add:

Ammonia (Sp. G. .880)	200.0 ml

This will produce a heavy precipitate of ferric hydroxide. Stir thoroughly, and filter through filter paper in a funnel; discard the clear liquid that comes through and pour plain water into the funnel several times, until the liquid that comes through tests neutral to litmus paper. Prepare the following solution:

Oxalic acid	215.0 g
Hot water	800.0 ml

When this is fully dissolved, pour it over the precipitate in the filter funnel, catching the liquid that flows through in a large beaker. This will dissolve the precipitate in the funnel. If any is left, take the solution just caught in the beaker and pour it over the filter again, and again catch the solution; repeat if necessary until the precipitate is completely dissolved. Then pour plain water through the filter, allowing the wash to add to the liquid in the beaker until the required volume is reached. This is a 20 percent solution of ferric oxalate; it must be stored in tightly closed brown bottles, away from light.

Working Solutions of Sensitizer

For very soft prints
Solution 1 . . . . 22 parts
Solution 2 . . . . 0 parts
Solution 3 . . . . 24 parts

For soft prints
Solution 1 . . . . 18 parts
Solution 2 . . . . 4 parts
Solution 3 . . . . 24 parts

For average prints
Solution 1 . . . . 14 parts
Solution 2 . . . . 8 parts
Solution 3 . . . . 24 parts

For strong prints
Solution 1 . . . . 10 parts
Solution 2 . . . . 12 parts
Solution 3 . . . . 24 parts

For extreme contrast
Solution 1 . . . . 0 parts
Solution 2 . . . . 22 parts
Solution 3 . . . . 24 parts

The paper is not sensitive to light until it is dry, so it can be coated in ordinary light. Pin or clip the paper horizontally on a firm support and pour the sensitizer onto it in a pool and spread it quickly with a brush, alternating the brush strokes at right angles, and continue the brushing until the paper surface is dry. Hang up the paper in the dark to complete the drying, which will take 5 or 10 minutes.

The sensitized paper can be printed as soon as it is dry, or it can be kept, with suitable precautions against the effect of dampness, up to about 3 months. It should be kept in a glass or metal container sealed with waterproof tape, with a preservative made of a small roll of asbestos that has been soaked in a saturated solution of calcium chloride, then desiccated over a stove and wrapped in cotton and a thin, porous paper.

Printing. Printing is done in sunlight, or with arc light, and the time depends upon the density of the negative, strength of the sunlight, or strength and nearness of the arc. For a general idea of the time, it will probably be between 3 and 10 minutes at 1.2 metres (4 feet) from an arc light. The image prints out in a light brown color, which is sufficient indication to the worker after a little practice in judging the depth.

If the print is not to be developed at once after printing, it should be returned to the container, as it readily absorbs moisture from the air, and this will result in degraded highlights.

Enlarged Negatives. Because platinum prints are made by contact printing, enlarged negatives are often desirable. Such negatives can be made in one step using a black-and-white direct-duplicating film, or in two stages on a copy-type black-and-white film. (*See:* DUPLICATE BLACK-AND-WHITE NEGATIVES.)

Developing. The developer keeps indefinitely, and improves with age, being kept up to volume by the addition of fresh developer to the old, which is decanted from the sludge that is likely to form in the bottom of the bottle.

Platinum Developers

Three formulas are commonly used for developing platinum prints, producing, respectively, cold-black, neutral-black, and warm-black tones. They are as follows:

Cold-black developer
Water (50 C or 120 F) . . . . 1.0 litre
Potassium oxalate . . . . 180.0 g
Monobasic potassium
phosphate . . . . 60.0 g

Neutral-black developer
Water (50 C or 120 F) . . . . 1.0 litre
Potassium oxalate . . . . 330.0 g

Warm-black developer
Water (50 C or 120 F) . . . . . . 1.0 litre
Potassium oxalate . . . . 330.0 g
Mercuric chloride* . . . . 4.0 g

---

*The exact amount of mercuric chloride depends upon the worker's preference for color. The above quantity is a good starting point, but more or less can be used, producing increasingly warm tones with greater additions.

The solutions are used at room temperature, between 15 and 27 C (60 to 80 F). Be sure there are no air bubbles on the print. Carry development to completion (about 2 minutes); there is no danger of overdevelopment, and conversely, it is not possible to secure additional density by forcing.

The developer may be used either hot or cold. Hot developer (up to 65.5 C or 150 F) gives warmer tones and decreases contrast.

Clearing. The standard treatment is to give the print, following development, three successive baths of 5 minutes each in a 1:60 solution of hydrochloric acid, followed by 20 minutes washing in running water. Weaker solutions of the acid are sometimes recommended because they give warmer prints, but such prints are likely to darken with age because of imperfect elimination of the iron salts in the weaker bath. If the iron salts are completely eliminated, as they will be in the 1:60 bath, the print consists of only pure metallic platinum and is absolutely permanent.

The print can be dried between blotters, before a fan, or by heat.

Multiple Printing. Depth can be added to the shadows of a platinum print, and the contrasts increased, by multiple printing. The print is sensitized as though it were plain paper. When dry, the negative is registered upon it, and printing, developing, and clearing proceed as in the usual process. This printing can be timed for the full scale of the negative, or only for the shadows. Any number of additional printings can be given.

Sepia Tones on Hot-Bath Papers

Sepia tones can be produced on the above paper by the use of a developer containing a mercury salt. There is some controversy about this process, some workers claiming that the mercury diminishes the permanence of the prints. Von Hübl gives the following formula for a sepia-tone developer.

Potassium oxalate	100.0 g
Potassium phosphate	50.0 g
Citric acid	20.0 g
Potassium chloride	10.0 g
Mercuric chloride	10.0 g
Water to make	1.0 litre

Develop at 80 C (176 F).

Prints in pure metallic platinum have great richness in the blacks, a long scale of gradations, and absolute permanence. Photo by Bill Crawford.

Most people think, however, that the real beauty of a platinum print lies in the neutral gray-blacks it produces, and there does not seem to be any real reason for a sepia platinum print, especially as it is considered less permanent.

The Cold-Bath Process

There is a general impression that the so-called "cold-bath" platinum papers were invented by William Willis and perfected by him in the 1890's. It is claimed that the process was a secret, and that the secret died with him. Be that as it may, a set of formulas for "cold-bath" platinum printing was published in the first edition of Prof. E. J. Wall's *Photographic Facts and Formulas* (1924). The directions given are quite confusing, and unfortunately, the whole process was reprinted without change in the current edition of that book.

A simplified and edited version of Wall's instructions is given below. It has *not* been tried in practice and is offered only for use as a basis for personal experiments.

The coating is mixed from a number of stock solutions that are prepared as follows:

Lead-iron solution

Lead acetate .... 10.0 g
Water .... 100.0 ml

Dissolve by the aid of heat, and add:

Oxalic acid .... 4.0 g
Water .... 50.0 ml

A white precipitate of lead oxalate is formed that should be collected on filter paper, well washed, and dried. For use, take:

Ferric oxalate .... 20.0 g
Lead oxalate precipitate, dried 1.0 g
Water to make .... 100.0 ml

Sodium ferric oxalate solution

Sodium ferric oxalate .... 50.0 g
Water to make .... 100.0 ml

Oxalic-gelatin solution

Gelatin (pure) .... 10.0 g
Water .... 100.0 ml

Allow gelatin to soak in the water for about 15 minutes and heat gently until the gelatin dissolves, then add:

Oxalic acid .... 2.5 g

This solution only keeps for a few days; it should be mixed freshly as required.

Sodium chloroplatinate solution

Sodium platinum chloride .... 1.0 g
Water .... 10.0 ml

Potassium chloroplatinite solution

Potassium chloroplatinite ..... 1.0 g
Water .... 6.0 ml

These last two solutions are light-sensitive and must be kept in brown bottles or in the dark.

To sensitize the paper, it should be fastened by glass-headed push pins to a flat surface with a sheet of blotting paper underneath. As it is important that the sensitizing solution should not come in contact with the pins, it is advisable to provide the latter with guards, which can easily be prepared by cutting small squares of cardboard, turning up the edges, and passing the pins through the middle. As the paper expands and crinkles on application of the liquid, the pins can be removed, and the paper restretched and again pinned down. The sensitizer is either *A, B,* or *C*:

A. Potassium chloropla-
tinite solution .... 3.0 ml
Lead-iron solution .... 4.5 ml
Sodium chloroplatinate
solution .... 7.5 drops
Water .... 3 to 8.0 ml

B. Potassium chloropla-
tinite solution .... 3.0 ml
Lead-iron solution .... 4.5 ml
Oxalic-gelatin solution .... 1.0 cc
Sodium chloroplatinate ...... 7.5 drops
Water .... 3 to 8.0 ml

C. Potassium chloropla-
tinite solution .... 3.0 ml
Lead-iron solution .... 3.0 ml
Sodium ferric oxalate
solution .... 2.0 ml
Sodium chloropla-
tinate solution .... 7.5 drops
Water .... 3 to 8.0 ml

The quantity of water in each formula is dependent on the surface of the paper; smooth surfaces require less, rough ones the greater quantity. Increase of the water to 2 to 14 times that specified above gives gray prints. The above quantity of sensitizer is sufficient for 3750 square cm (580 square inches) of paper. Increase of the sodium chloroplatinate gives increased contrasts, or an equal volume of a 10 percent solution of potassium bichromate can be used instead. Omission of these naturally gives softer effects. Sensitizer *A* with arrowroot sizing tends to brownish-black tones, but with plain, not arrowroot-sized, drawing papers, it produces black tones; with gelatin-sized papers, blue-blacks are given. *A* and *B* give too hard prints with contrasty negatives; then *C* should be used, as this gives softer results.

After printing until the image is faintly visible in grayish-violet against the pure yellow unprinted parts, the print should be rapidly and evenly immersed in either of the following developers:

Neutral potassium oxalate ..	250.0 g
Water to make	1.0 litre

Neutral potassium oxalate ..	100.0 g
Potassium phosphate	50.0 g
Water to make	1.0 litre

Take hold of both ends of the paper, immerse one end in the developer, face down, draw the paper through the solution, and then turn it face up. Development takes about 2 minutes. The tray should be gently rocked during development. When the print is dark enough, transfer it, without any intermediate rinse, to the clearing bath.

Clearing bath

Hydrochloric acid (concentrated)	20.0 ml
Water	1.0 litre

The tray should be rocked. After 5 minutes, remove the print and immerse it in a second tray of water acidulated as above, and after 15 minutes remove it to a third tray of half the above strength of acid. At the end of 15 minutes, place the print in running water for 30 minutes, then blot off between blotting papers and dry. Dilution of the developer gives more brilliant prints; or the same result can be obtained by adding 2 to 5 percent of a 1 percent solution of potassium bichromate, but in this case printing must be carried further than usual. In place of the bichromate, 0.5 to 1 percent of ammonium persulfate can be used, which shortens the scale of gradation, and this is particularly useful in the case of over-printing or when thin, flat negatives are used.

Platinum Toning

In the normal platinum process, what actually happens is that exposure to light forms an image of iron in the paper coating. During development, this reacts with the platinum salt in the paper to form an image of metallic platinum, the iron image being converted to a soluble iron salt that is removed in the clearing bath.

It is equally practical to produce a silver image first and transform it to platinum. In this case, though, the platinum salt is in the developer, which can thus be considered to be a toning bath. The method is to expose the negative on a silver printing-out paper; the exposure must be sufficient to produce a very dark image, as it will lose density in the toning.

After exposure, the print is thoroughly washed, then toned in a bath of potassium chloroplatinite. In this bath, the silver is converted largely to silver chloride, and platinum deposits upon and, to some extent, in place of the silver image. Following toning, the print is fixed in plain hypo, which removes the silver chloride and leaves an image largely composed of platinum.

This process was exceedingly popular during the early part of the present century, and a silver-chloride-collodion printing-out paper known as Aristo Platino was widely used; one writer estimates that around the turn of the century more than half of all photographic prints made in the United States were Aristo Platino prints, toned with platinum.

Aristo Platino has long since disappeared from the market, and at the present time no printing-out papers with collodion emulsions are being made anywhere in the world. Thus, the process is one of theoretical interest only. It is also possible to apply a platinum toner to a plain salted paper. (*See:* CALOTYPE.)

The toner is made up as follows:

Potassium chloroplatinite	0.3 g
Sodium chloride	3.4 g
Citric acid	3.4 g
Water to make	1.0 litre

This bath keeps indefinitely, but must be replenished to allow for loss of platinum salt to the prints. About 0.033 gram (½ grain) is added for each six 8″ × 10″ prints toned.

The paper is printed until a very heavy image is obtained, with some tint over the whites. It is then washed to remove excess silver nitrate, after which it is toned in the above bath. Progress of toning is judged by holding the print up and examining it by transmitted light. When all the red color is gone from the deepest shadows, the print must be washed in several changes of water; the first rinse is made alkaline with about 15 grams of sodium carbonate in a litre (½ ounce in a quart) of water. This is followed by three or four rinses in plain water. The print is then fixed for about 10 minutes in the following fixing bath.

Sodium thiosulfate	100.0 g
Sodium sulfite	50.0 g
Sodium carbonate	12.5 g
Water to make	1.0 litre

After fixing, the prints must be thoroughly washed; at least 1 hour in running water is the recommended time. Permanence of the print will depend upon the thoroughness of both fixing and washing.

• *See also:* CALOTYPE; PRINTING-OUT PAPERS.

Polarized-Light Photography

The wave motion of ordinary, unpolarized light vibrates in all directions perpendicular to the path of the waves. When light is reflected from smooth, non-metallic surfaces or is refracted by certain crystals or compounds, the direction of vibration is reduced primarily to a single plane—the light thereby becomes polarized.

Polarization occurs naturally by light scattering in blue sky, and by reflection, when light is reflected by water, glass, polished wood, and similar surfaces.

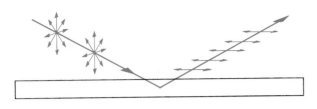

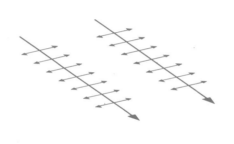

Polarization also occurs when light is passed through a polarizing substance, such as some natural crystals, and polarizing filters. In general photography it is a common practice to screen out the polarized component of light from a subject in order to render skies a deeper blue, to reduce reflections and glare in natural scenes both to "see" into water and increase the saturation of colors, and to eliminate reflections in copying. Techniques for these purposes are covered in the articles FILTERS, GLARE AND REFLECTION CONTROL, and COPYING.

In technical and scientific photography, polarized light is used to determine stress in materials subjected to tension or compression loads. (*See:* PHOTOELASTICITY.) It is also used to investigate the structure of crystalline compounds and to identify substances that have characteristic polarizing properties. Because these applications reveal fascinating colors, shapes, and patterns, they are often used to produce abstract pictorial images. Techniques for photographing crystal patterns by polarized light are explained in this article.

Controlling Polarization

The polarizing screens or "filters" commonly used in photography consist of millions of microscopic polarizing crystals suspended in plastic or coated on glass. The crystal axes are aligned so that they all refract energy fields in the same plane. In effect, the polarizer is a sieve with parallel slits. The direction of the slits determines the plane of polarization of the screen.

When the planes of polarized light and a polarizing screen are parallel, the light can pass through the "slits" of this "sieve." As the polarizer is rotated, less and less light is transmitted until the polarization plane of the screen is at 90 degrees to the plane of the light; in that position, no polarized light is transmitted.

(Above left) Unpolarized light vibrates in all directions perpendicular to the line of travel. When reflected at an angle from a smooth, nonmetallic surface, only light vibrating in a single plane is totally reflected; as a result, the light is polarized in that plane. (Left) Skylight becomes polarized when light from the sun is scattered by molecules of air in the atmosphere. Polarized skylight travels at right angles to the direction of the sun.

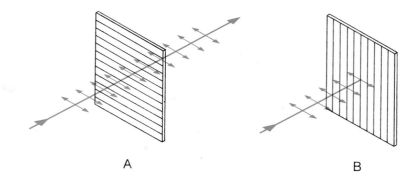

(A) A screen of polarizing crystals (a polarizing filter) will pass light polarized in the same plane as the screen. (B) When the screen is rotated 90 degrees, no polarized light is passed. Intermediate screen positions transmit varying amounts of the polarized light.

A

B

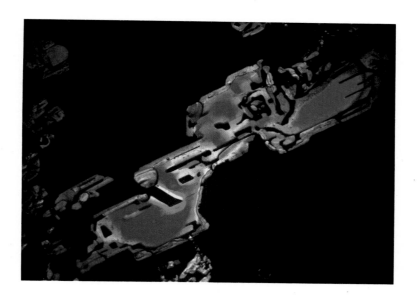

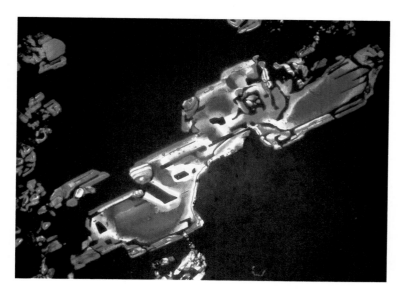

The top photograph was made with paired polarizing filters, rotated for maximum effect. The same crystals, in the photo below, show the result of another orientation of the polarizers at an angle other than 90 degrees. Note the absence of rich colors in the image and the drastic change in background density.

Polarized-Light Photography

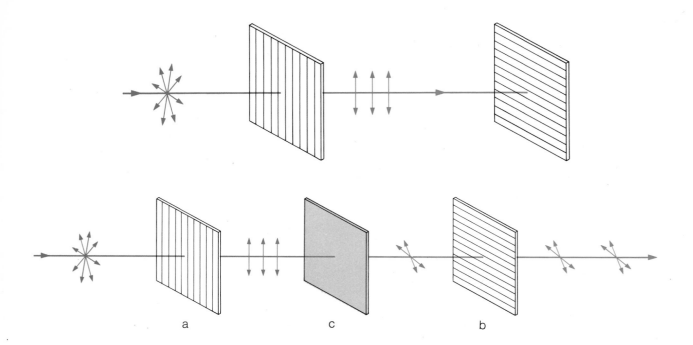

(Top) A screen will polarize light by passing energy in only one plane. Orientation of a second screen can determine how much of this light is transmitted. Screens are sometimes sandwiched together to provide intensity control of a light source. (Bottom) This two-screen setup used for analysis and to obtain color patterns consists of a polarizer (a) to provide polarized light, and an analyzer (b). The specimen (c) placed between screens changes polarization of light according to composition or structure of the substance being examined. As a result, some light is passed by the analyzer in distinctive patterns of colors and shapes.

If unpolarized light strikes the screen, only the energy that is vibrating parallel to the screen direction will be passed; thus polarized light emerges. A second screen placed in the path of the light can be used to control transmission by rotating its polarization plane in relation to that of the light. When the planes are at right angles, no light will be transmitted. The two-screen system is used for visual analysis (and to obtain "abstract" images) of substances that can affect polarized light. The first screen is called the polarizer, the second the analyzer; the specimen to be examined is placed between the screens. Interference effects in the light passed by the specimen produce light and dark color patterns.

Birefringent Color

When polarized light passes through various crystalline substances, it produces a variety of pulsating colors by a process known as *birefringence*.* Both experienced photographers and beginners are astonished when shown how easy it is to create these variegated patterns and record them on film—just a few simple chemicals are needed.

The brilliant colors and beautiful patterns originate in the following way. When light rays strike the first polarizer of a two-screen setup, the only rays to

---

*Not all crystalline substances produce this phenomenon; for example, sodium chloride (table salt) is unsuitable.

A light overall effect can be produced by rotating the polarizers at angles slightly less, or greater, than 90 degrees.

pass are those that are vibrating parallel to the favored direction of the polarizer. When the second screen—the analyzer—is oriented in its favored direction at right angles to the first polarizer, no light rays can penetrate the pair. When the crystal sample is inserted between the two polarizers, the light traveling through the first polarizer is intercepted by individual crystals in the pattern and split into separate components (birefringence). One of the components now vibrates in a new direction that differs 90 degrees from the original rays and therefore possesses the ability to pass through the second polarizer.

The color seen (actually the wavelength of the rays beaming through the second polarizer) depends on the unique structure of the crystalline material and the alignment of the crystal axes with respect to the vibrating rays. This is partly verified by rotating the glass sandwich while keeping the polarizers on each side fixed relative to each other. You can watch the colors change and move along various directions corresponding to crystal alignment.

A rather imperfect example of polarized light, in which portions of both ray components are mixed, becomes apparent when you hold the specimen and one polarizer in a fixed position while rotating the other polarizer. Continuous rotation of the polarizer produces an almost psychedelic effect. It is this phenomenon that is apparent in abstract pictorial images.

Creating Crystals

To begin, obtain some inexpensive compounds from a well-stocked drugstore or a local chemical-supply firm. The following table suggests a number of suitable compounds. You will also need two small squares of polarizing material, and some thin 50 × 50 mm (2″ × 2″) slide cover glass of the type used for binding 35 mm and other small transparencies. Polarizing material is available at many large photo stores, or from such firms as Edmund Scientific Company (Barrington, NJ); Bausch & Lomb, Inc., Scientific Optical Products Division (Rochester, NY); or Sargent Welch Co. (branches in many large cities). Two polarizing filters work well.

Crystals by Melting. The easiest way to get successful patterns is to select compounds that melt easily, such as dextrose, benzoic acid, urea, or citric acid.

Sprinkle one or two 3 to 6 mm (⅛″ to ¼″) grains, or the equivalent in smaller grains, onto the center of a glass slide and heat the underside of the glass with a hot iron. Use a tacking iron such as is used for dry-mounting photos, a clothes iron, or even a warming tray that has an imbedded metallic heating element. Keep the glass moving on top of the heat source for even heating, or the glass may crack. Moderate heat is best for most substances. Although this slow melting operation may take a while, it avoids boiling of low-melting-point chemicals that can produce excessive noxious vapor and numerous bubbles in the finished pattern. Some bubbles are unavoidable.

When melting is completed, place another piece of glass on top, squeezing the solution between the glass plates. Align the edges of the two glasses and fasten the resultant sandwich into a fixed position with spring paper clips (Boston type) or some spring

SOME CHEMICALS SUITABLE FOR MAKING CRYSTAL PATTERNS

Chemical	Melting Process	Evaporation Process	Comments
Ascorbic acid (vitamin C)		X	Soluble in water; partly soluble in alcohol. Recommended: rubbing alcohol (70% ethyl).
Benzoic acid	X		Melting point: 121.7 C (251 F).
Bromo Seltzer		X	Soluble in water.
Citric acid	X	Less effective	Melting point: 153 C (307 F); evaporation difficult.
Kodak Dektol developer		X	Tricky; sometimes helpful to make sandwich by adding second glass after partial evaporation. WARNING*
Dextrose (glucose)	X	Less effective	Melting point: 146 C (295 F).
Kodak developer *D-76*		X	WARNING*
Epsomite (Epsom salts)		X	Crystals tend to be thick, so experiment with concentration; also try sandwich.
Hydroquinone		X	Variable results; helpful not to dissolve entirely. WARNING*
Tartaric acid		X	WARNING: Causes eye irritation on contact.
Urea	X	X	Melting point: 132.7 C (271 F). Both processes excellent.
Vanillin		X	Soluble in mixture of 12 parts water, 2 parts glycerol, and 2 parts 95 percent alcohol.

*WARNING: Repeated contact may cause skin irritation and allergic skin reaction. Avoid breathing dust. May be harmful if swallowed. If swallowed, induce vomiting. Call a physician at once. Keep out of the reach of children.

clothespins while the liquid cools to room temperature and crystallizes. Squeezing the sandwich during cooling tends to keep the crystals thin, which is essential to success and adds a directional flow to the forming pattern. Clips can be placed onto two, three, or all four sides for different stresses.

The crystal image should have a waxy, translucent appearance. If it appears whitish, the crystals are probably too thick for satisfactory color. Use less chemical or remelt the compound in the glass sandwich with the clips in place. Some patterns are visually poor, requiring patience and repeated efforts. Variables that affect the final result are the amount of chemical used, rate of melting and cooling, type of stress placed on the sandwich, and even slight irregularities in the glass. It is never possible to duplicate results exactly.

The cooling and crystallization that return the chemical to a solid or semisolid state may take seconds or minutes, depending on the nature of the substance and the room temperature. To watch the crystals grow during cooling, place one of the polarizing films, commonly called polarizers, on top of the sandwich and one underneath.

For best viewing and greatest color saturation, orient the polarizers so that the direction of polarization in the upper film is perpendicular to the direction of polarization in the lower one. To determine this direction with polarizers that are not marked with arrows, take the two polarizers and hold them together in front of a light. Rotate one polarizer until the light is blocked out. Now slip the crystal sandwich between the polarizers. Where crystals have formed, there occurs a dazzling array of colors, varying with the compound and its properties. Portions of the sandwich will be black where the chemical is absent or still liquid.

When all the solution has crystallized, some small black spots may remain where the chemical is absent or because of trapped air bubbles or irregularities in the glass. If there are only a few bubbles, you may still be able to locate a portion of the crystal pattern containing a suitable composition unmarred by these spots. Heating the slide slowly with one or two grains, as suggested, seems to keep the bubbles to a minimum. When you obtain an interesting pattern, bind the edges of the crystal sandwich with slide-binding tape to preserve the pattern for days or weeks, but do not wait too long to record the best patterns on color film since some substances tend to deteriorate more rapidly than others.

Summary of Melt Procedure

1. Assemble necessary materials: 50 × 50 mm (2″ × 2″) cover glass, vial of chemical, tweezers or chemical spoon, and a tacking iron or suitable heat source for melting.

2. In a well-ventilated area, deposit a very small amount of chemical onto the center of a cover glass and heat evenly, holding the glass with clips or clothespins.

3. Do not boil—slow heating is best. As soon as liquid forms, place a second glass on top and squeeze the liquid into a thin film by attaching clothespins or clips.
   WARNING: Avoid breathing fumes by keeping your face away from the hot melt.

4. Insert the crystal sandwich, which appears colorless, between the two polarizers to watch the crystals form. Crystallization occurs almost instantaneously with most substances.

5. If you do not plan to photograph the crystals immediately, bind the edges of the sandwich with tape for semipermanence. Some substances evaporate or absorb water from the air with time, requiring a seal of clear nail polish (lacquer) around the edges of the sandwich. Even this precaution does not always prevent deterioration of the crystal pattern.

Two examples of crystals produced by the melt process. (Top) Benzoic acid spears are at 4½× magnification and (bottom) citric acid crystals at 4× magnification. All magnifications cited refer to the image size on the film.

Crystals by Evaporation. Evaporation is not as popular as the melt process because it requires more time and patience. Some compounds, such as urea, give consistent results, while others require persistent effort and trial and error with this method. Ascorbic acid, tartaric acid, Epsom salts, salicylic acid, and Bromo Seltzer are water-soluble substances suitable for making crystals. Various photographic chemical compounds such as hydroquinone and some powdered developers will also give good results.

Preliminary application of a wetting agent such as Kodak Photo-Flo 200 solution permits water solutions to spread more evenly for evaporation. Wipe a glass slide cover with the wetting agent or even add a drop to the chemical solution if it seems to help. Some photographers sprinkle a few drops of water onto a cover glass, dissolve a small-spatula measure of chemicals into the drops, and evaporate the solution. This works sometimes, but many compounds require a more exact concentration to obtain the crystal thickness that gives optimum color.

It is better to be methodical. A chemical balance is not necessary; merely measure enough chemical to

(Left) Ascorbic acid (vitamin C) crystals formed by evaporation from a rubbing alcohol (70% ethyl) solution. Magnification is 4×. (Right) These urea crystals were produced by the water-solution evaporation process. Magnification is approximately 1×.

cover an object such as a quarter or a half-dollar, and stir it into a half ounce of water. If crystals are too thin, increase the amount the next time. Since evaporation may take several hours or more, place the glass slide, coated with solution, onto a shelf or in some other out-of-the-way place.

The goal is to get relatively thin crystals that tend to do most of their growing parallel to the glass surface. For better results with some chemicals, place a cover glass on top (as in the melt process) with or without clips after partial evaporation has produced a few crystals. This procedure may delay the completion of the crystallization process a week or more.

Handling Chemicals

Many of the chemical compounds suitable for making crystal patterns are used in small amounts as food additives. These include benzoic acid, dextrose, citric acid, and vanillin. Since even quite common chemicals can be harmful in large doses, make it a rule to handle all chemicals carefully and store them out of the reach of children.

In addition to the hazard of ingestion, some chemicals can irritate the skin and eyes. Others will decompose from excessive heat into harmful vapors. For this reason it is important to prepare materials by the melt process in a well-ventilated area and to keep your face away from the melt. Using the evaporation process avoids any problems with vapors.

Photographing the Crystal Pattern

You can copy the crystal pattern immediately with camera and color film, or set it aside until several fine patterns have developed. Many different color films are adequate; Kodak Ektachrome 64 film and Kodachrome 25 film (daylight) both have given excellent rendition.

Popular Setups. The most popular way to record the crystals on film is to use a 35 mm single-lens reflex (SLR) camera and (1) a macro lens, one especially designed for close-ups, (2) the normal 50 mm camera lens or a wide-angle lens with extension tubes, or (3) the camera with a bellows attachment plus the normal or wide-angle lens. Most macro lenses give sharp images but are limited to a maximum of 1× magnification—whereas extension tubes permit 2× or better magnification. A bellows attachment allows a film image that is 5× that of the original crystal with a 35 mm lens or 7× with a 28 mm lens.

To provide a diffused-light source for copying with color film, try a slide sorter. Place a blue photo bulb or an electronic flash unit behind the plastic viewing panel to get light compatible with daylight-type color film. Position the crystal sandwich, with properly oriented polarizers on each side, on the slide sorter in front of the tripod-mounted camera. Rather than focus or move the camera with a macro lens or extension tubes, it is easier to move the slide sorter back and forth along the edge of the table until the crystal image is sharp in the camera viewfinder. Always use a cable release to avoid camera movement.

If the crystals are extremely small or you desire to photograph only a small portion of the total crystal pattern (perhaps a 13 mm [½″] segment), you will need to work with a bellows attachment. If the bellows has a slide-copying attachment, simply slip the crystal sandwich into the slot provided for the color transparency that you would normally copy with this attachment. A plastic diffusing screen behind the slot allows you to aim the camera and bellows-copier setup directly at a light source such as the sun, a photoflood, or an electronic flash unit.

To shield both the camera lens and the glass sandwich from reflections or stray light, use a makeshift lens shade. A curved sheet of black paper or a dark cloth will do. You can fashion a loose-fitting tube between the lens and the crystal sandwich. Reflections and lens flare can ruin copying attempts.

Exposure. If the camera has through-the-lens metering, you can make nonflash exposure calculations easily—right in the viewfinder. When using electronic flash or an adjustable camera having no built-in meter, you will have to do some experimenting for correct exposure. Whatever the light source and method of determining exposure, bracket each setup by taking at least three pictures at three different *f*-stops, and keep records to be sure of getting optimum results at later times. For additional information, see the articles CLOSE-UP PHOTOGRAPHY, EXPOSURE, and PHOTOMACROGRAPHY.

Other Setups. If a bellows or extension tube is not available, try a high-power supplementary lens in combination with a long-focal-length camera lens. A +10 supplementary lens used on a 90 mm or 135 mm lens should give acceptable results.

Another procedure involves using a slide projector to project the crystal image for copying. Low-wattage, cool-running projectors are best. Compounds must have melting points equal to or higher than urea, or heat from the lamp will decompose the crystal. Place a sandwich of urea crystals (or a comparable substance) with polarizers on each side into the slide gate of the projector. Copy the image on the screen or a white wall with almost any camera having adjustable shutter and aperture controls. For details about how to copy a projected image, see the article DUPLICATE SLIDES AND TRANSPARENCIES.

Photograph of a thin section of rock—about $\frac{1}{1000}$ of an inch. Subject is a section of Manhattan schist seen at $5\times$ magnification.

Greater magnification of very small sample sections can be obtained by photographing through a microscope. A petrographic microscope has built-in polarizers for convenience, and very high-quality optics. But it is easy to improvise with any kind of microscope. One polarizer is placed below the substage condenser, the other (the analyzer) above the stage, usually just below the eyepiece, or in front of the camera lens (if the lens is used). Various methods of making camera-microscope setups are covered in the article PHOTOMICROGRAPHY.

Photographing Minerals and Rocks by Polarized Light

One of the most interesting applications of polarized-light photography is the photographing of min-

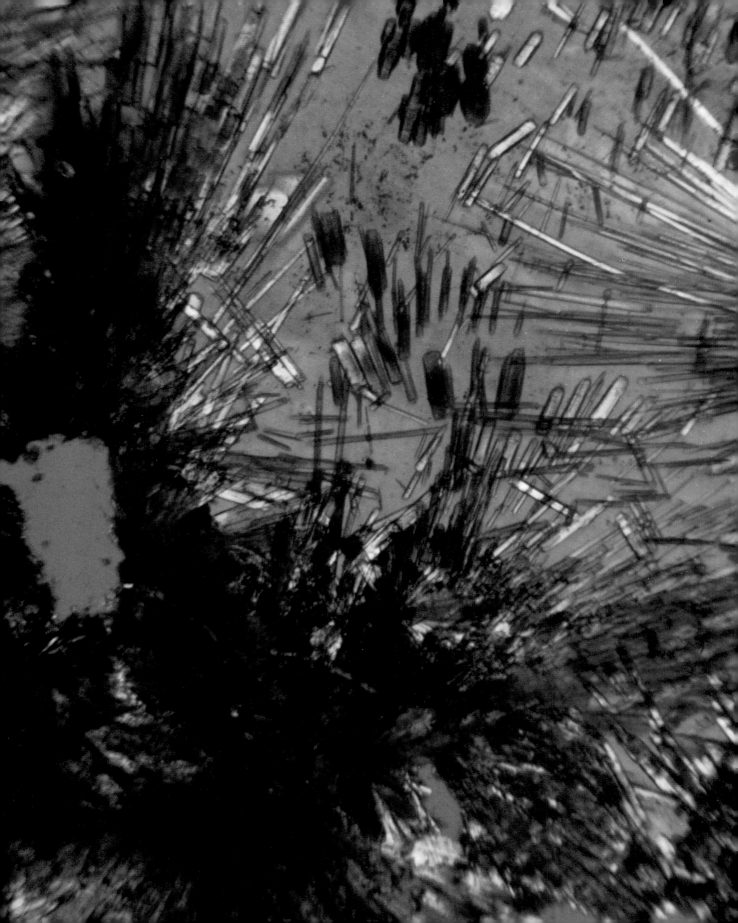

erals and rocks. When examined by polarized light, these specimens reveal great natural beauty.

In addition, thin sections of ancient crystals provide important geological information to a trained observer. A vesicular basalt might supply data about a previously unrecorded period of volcanism; a garnet gneiss may yield facts about an epoch of mountain-building; and a third rock thin section could show evidence indicating a time of meteorite impact. In the case of sedimentary rocks, many limestones reveal mysteries from ancient seafloors where the soft sediment once trapped the remains of creatures that are now extinct.

The technique of cutting and grinding thin slabs of rock to .025 mm (.001″) thickness is routine for rock technicians but presents a problem for most photographers. Fortunately, prepared thin sections are available from various suppliers. Glass-mounted mineral and rock sections usually measure 25 × 45 mm (1″ × 1¾″), but the rock slides cemented to the glass with epoxy are somewhat smaller. You will need the higher magnification of a bellows attachment to get suitable image size of the mineral crystals, although thin sections featuring large mineral fragments can often be recorded satisfactorily by using extension tubes.

Order thin sections composed of the larger mineral grains (hornblende, pyroxene, mica cleavage pieces) or the coarse-grained rocks (granite, dunite, schist). Coarse limestones and marble are also suitable, but avoid clastic rocks such as siltstone, sandstone, and shale. Basalt and rhyolite are fine-grained rocks that need a microscope capable of 20× magnification or better.

• *See also:* CLOSE-UP PHOTOGRAPHY; COPYING; DUPLICATE SLIDES AND TRANSPARENCIES; EXPOSURE; FILTERS; GLARE AND REFLECTION CONTROL; PHOTOELASTICITY; PHOTOMACROGRAPHY; PHOTOMICROGRAPHY.

Further Reading: Cooke, Robert W. *Designing with Light on Paper and Film.* Worcester, PA: Davis Publications, Inc., 1969; Croy, Otto R. *Croy's Creative Photomicrography.* Garden City, NY: Amphoto, 1968; Karsten, Kenneth. *Abstract Photography Techniques.* Garden City, NY: Amphoto, 1970; Langford, M.J. *Advanced Photography: A Grammar of Techniques.* New York, NY: Focal Press, 1972.

Portfolio

The portfolio is an organized collection of a photographer's work, designed for a specific purpose. Although the fine-arts or non-commercial portfolio may be of interest to the reader, its form and style are much less structured than those of the sales portfolio. Therefore, the fine-arts portfolio is described only briefly while the sales portfolio is examined in detail. The methods used for a commercial portfolio are equally valuable for the fine-arts presentation.

Fine-Arts Portfolio

This kind of portfolio is prepared primarily by photographer-artists to be shown to photo galleries, art museums, and collectors. Its purpose is to increase the recognition and stature of the photographer, as well as to sell photographs individually or in a group. Fine-arts portfolios differ widely in shape, size, and style, depending upon the taste and sensibilities of the photographer. They may range from a limited edition of booklets to an elaborately produced collection of matted, numbered prints.

Sales Portfolio

The sales portfolio, in contrast, is designed by freelance photographers as a showcase of their best work for presentation to prospective clients. It is the photographer's single most important selling tool. In order to succeed, it must follow certain definite principles of salesmanship in both form and content. It usually consists of prints, and published work, if available, in the form of tear sheets. A selection of transparencies as well as color prints may be included. Photographers who are beginning their careers and have no published samples often initially show a judicious selection of prints and color transparencies.

Defining Markets. As a selling vehicle, the sales portfolio must show work that is geared to the interests and needs of the markets for which it is intended. Two major market areas are *editorial* and *advertising,* each of which has different require-

◄ *The technique of cutting and grinding thin rock sections, while routine to rock technicians, presents a problem for most photographers. Fortunately, prepared thin sections are commercially available. This is a polarized light image of tourmaline crystals at 15×.*

ments. Other markets include public-relations and industrial or corporate work such as brochures and annual reports. There is some overlapping in the type of photographs used by these various markets, but each has its own basic approach to photography.

A sales portfolio can be geared to only one market area, or it can be general, showing a variety of types of work. The portfolio that is too general, however, may leave prospective clients with no clear impression of the photographer's talents and is therefore to be avoided.

The Successful Portfolio. Every successful portfolio, whether that of a top-level professional or a semipro, embodies these characteristics:

The subjects shown are relevant to the interests of the clients to whom they are presented.

Subjects are grouped together logically to emphasize the various types of work shown.

The portfolio is neat, compact, and easy to view.

The quality of work selected for showing is consistently high and equals or surpasses that of competitors.

Portfolio Format

An initial requirement for assembly of a portfolio is the determination of the basic format. The sizes and shapes of the primary elements—photographs, transparencies, and tear sheets—will be the determining factors. Most photographers choose a high-quality case, binder, or box for their portfolios.

Cases. The flexible zippered case with handle is preferred by most professional freelance photographers for the editorial portfolio. It is also excellent for the general portfolio. With ring binder and acetate sleeve protectors, its pages hold both prints and tear sheets in compact, organized form. Since the pages are all the same size, the problem of using material consisting of different sizes is minimized. Prints or clippings of any size or proportion are framed uniformly.

Cases are available at art- and camera-supply stores in a choice of plastic, leather, or canvas. The 11″ × 14″ and 14″ × 17″ sizes* are recommended

---

*These are print measurements. Outside case measurements run slightly larger.

because anything smaller allows no flexibility in print sizes and tends to appear insignificant as well. An advantage of the 14″ × 17″ size is that it can accommodate 11″ × 14″ horizontal prints, so that the case need not be turned around in order to view them.

The ring binder is also used for the editorial or general portfolio, but is less popular than the zippered case with handle. It is more cumbersome to carry and, without closure, its contents are less protected from the weather. Also, it cannot carry as much extra material in front and back flaps as the case. However, the book is less expensive, and it is possible to have a cover made for it.

For the advertising portfolio, the hard-cover box is the most professional and practical choice. It carries a selection of prints and tear sheets that have been mounted or laminated and can be handled separately. Art directors like this presentation because they can take out individual samples to examine at will. Photographers find it easy to group and regroup samples for different clients and also convenient to pull out individual samples for specific requests.

Fiberboard cases, and aluminum or other types of travel cases, are acceptable although perhaps less modish. They must, however, be in prime condition and the contents must be simplified in form and very well organized in order to present a professional image. Numerous envelopes, folders, and boxes are to be avoided.

Prints and Tear Sheets. It is important to keep all prints and tear sheets, with the exception of those used in books with sleeved pages, to one or two uniform sizes. This can be achieved in the size of the print itself or with borders or mounts. Editors and art directors find it distracting to handle assorted sizes.

Mounts should be lightweight. Heavy mounts make a presentation appear forbiddingly large, require more time for examination, and are burdensome for the photographer to carry.

Exhibition prints are rarely suitable for the portfolio. They have been designed for a different purpose—to be seen on the wall rather than in the hand. They seldom fit either in size or style with other samples.

Laminating. This is accomplished professionally by sandwiching or clipping a print between plastic sheets. A lamination, which is lightweight and easy to handle, protects the work and enhances its appearance. Laminations can be had in mat or glossy finish, with a fine edge or border of white, black, or clear plastic. By ordering borders, all material can be made to a uniform size.

Laminations are used for color prints as well as for black-and-white work. They wear well, usually until a particular sample is replaced with something else. It may be a good idea, however, to keep an extra tear sheet of important samples on hand in case a new lamination should be needed.

Some surfaces are seen with an overall blistered effect. These are not true laminations but are produced by sealing the edges of two sheets of plastic. This method is best avoided.

Acetate Sleeves. The use of acetate sleeves is desirable for many formats. Sleeves tend to dull and become scratched, and must be replaced frequently. Although photographers complain about this feature, they should realize that the sales portfolio is their most vital selling vehicle. The relatively small cost and bother are minor when compared with the great advantages of making an attractive showing.

Slides and Transparencies. It is important to display slides and transparencies so that they appear as impressive as possible and are easy to handle.

Mounted 35 mm Color Slides. Slotted to hold 20 or more slides, plastic sheets or pages are the most convenient way to show 35 mm slides. Placed on a light box, a number of sheets can be looked over quickly. The slightly frosted plastic is preferable to the clear type for both appearance and wear.

Black mat mountings are elegant and impressive. They are especially suitable for advertising portfolios in which graphic effect counts. Matted sheets cut to hold twelve 35 mm slides are available at art-supply stores. Acetate should be attached to front and back of mats to protect the slides.

Nothing shows up color slides as dramatically as projecting them onto a screen or a white wall. Just as films become more lifelike when projected onto a movie screen, the larger size achieved by projection intensifies the effect of a slide. Subtle nuances of color and detail that might otherwise be missed reveal themselves clearly.

Projecting color slides is not always possible, however, because many editors and art directors object to the time taken in setting up the projector.

In other cases the proper facilities are not available —the room is too light, or the space too cramped. The best solution is to have a projector and mounted color slides in a tray ready for use when the situation permits.

Projection trays need not be filled to capacity. Anywhere from 50 to 100 or more slides can be used, although the quantity is optional. Showing too many slides should be avoided; the number you use depends on how good the photographs are and the skill with which they have been both selected and arranged.

Stamp your name in the same place on the mount of every 35 mm slide. This enables you to see whether the slide is right side up without holding it up to the light and examining it. When you have many slides, this small time-saver can be important. If matted sheets are used, your name can be embossed on them, or a printed label can be attached.

Larger Transparencies. You can show 2¼″ × 2¼″ transparencies in mounts on a light box or by projection. Black matted sheets can be used to mount several images. It is preferable to use these sheets to mount all color transparencies larger than 2¼″ × 2¼″. For those 8″ × 10″, the matting is optional. In every case the transparencies should be protected with acetate sleeves or sheets attached to front and back.

Assembling the Portfolio

Before starting to select the photographs for a sales portfolio, decide clearly what markets it will be intended for. Your portfolio will necessarily emphasize the type of photographs used by these markets. The portfolio designed to reach editorial clients will differ greatly from the one prepared for advertising agencies or public-relations organizations. To be successful, it must present work that is relevant to the needs of clients, not only in terms of subject matter but in photographic style as well.

The best way to determine market requirements is to look through the pages of various magazines. If your intended market is advertising, look at the ads. The larger-circulation women's magazines are a source for ads covering a wide assortment of products and services. If your markets are primarily editorial, pay particular attention to the pictures shown in feature spreads and article illustrations. Note especially those similar to your own work. Developing a keen sense of what the markets are using will help you choose the best samples for your portfolio. If you lack needed samples or are missing those on subjects you are interested in pursuing, make some through self-assignments before completing the portfolio.

Organization. As clients look through portfolios, they pay particular attention to the subjects that interest them. When organizing a portfolio, it is best to show all pictures in groups. Photographs might fall into categories such as candid portraiture, travel, children, nature, and industry. An additional advantage of grouping subjects in this fashion is that it helps make sure your strongest subjects are emphasized. Should you have too many samples of a subject to include all in one group, divide them into two parts and place the second part in another section of the portfolio.

Prospective clients have no other way of judging a photographer's abilities than by what is shown them. Present only work that will make a favorable impression. You should not show photographs for which excuses must be made; this tends to create doubt in the client's mind. It is difficult to be objective in criticizing one's own pictures, but it is essential to eliminate all but the best.

In arranging the portfolio, a good rule to follow is to place four or five striking images at the beginning and end. This helps to capture the client's initial attention and create a lasting final impression.

General and Specialized Portfolios

Many professional photographers specialize in either advertising or editorial work. This is particularly true if they reside in a metropolitan area having a concentration of large-magazine offices and picture agencies. If you are located in an area of smaller markets, however, you may have to show a more varied or general portfolio in order to survive economically. If this is so, do not try to show "a little of everything" in your portfolio. Your portfolio will make a stronger impression, and you will obtain better assignments, by concentrating on the types of work in which you have the greatest competence.

The Editorial Portfolio. The editorial portfolio is designed for presentation to editors of magazines and newspapers. It consists primarily of photojournalistic photographs and tear sheets of published work. Many publications use some posed photographs as illustrations for articles, and a few may be included in the editorial portfolio.

Editors look for candid shots that capture the mood of an instant, portray the essence of a personality, or tell a story. Other criteria are good composition, well-handled lighting, and content that is clearly recognizable at a glance. Photographs that show the photographer's imagination and his or her ability to use the camera to give a situation visual impact should be emphasized.

With a good portfolio it is usually unnecessary to change photographs constantly to conform to the subject matter of each publication, but it is important to study one or two issues beforehand. Knowing the general tone and subject matter of a publication helps the photographer decide which aspects of the portfolio to emphasize when presenting it. Avoid the common editorial complaint that photographers "don't do their homework" and arrive in total ignorance of what the publication's concerns are.

Try to make it easy for your viewer to go through the portfolio with transitions that lead smoothly from one group of photographs to another or from one idea to another. Transitions can consist of related visual relationships or themes. For example, a visual transition might be made between a picture of a farm worker in a wheat field and one of an airplane in flight because they both contain a broad open sky. A thematic transition might relate photographs of one sport with activity in another sport.

Sequences. Sequences help make a portfolio interesting. They may include a part of a picture story or may be images connected by a related theme. Examples include such themes as children playing, street scenes, or a series of facial expressions, or technical effects such as multiple exposures, or unusual action pictures.

Long picture stories may slow the movement of a portfolio. Generally it is best to include a few of the pictures and to place the rest in a folder in the back flap, or to show the entire picture story from the folder. Most editors want to see how a photographer handles a picture story, but this can be demonstrated with contact sheets in many cases.

Prints and Contact Sheets. Show only first-rate prints. Dust or fingerprints from the negative make a poor impression, as do prints that have been carelessly spotted.

A set of contact sheets allows editors to judge not only the photographer's ability to cover a story but how well he or she crops with the camera, understands lighting, and knows lenses. Contacts must be of high quality so that they can be scanned easily. It is helpful to mark the images you prefer with red grease pencil.

The Advertising Portfolio. This type of portfolio basically involves three categories of photographic illustration: (1) people, or people using products; (2) fashion and beauty; and (3) still life. The portfolio may present one category, or all three, depending upon the degree of specialization.

Many advertising illustrations appear to be candid, as if taken by an editorial photographer, but in reality are not. They have been carefully planned and set up in advance to give this effect while communicating a specific message for the advertiser. The editorial look is achieved by using professional models, selected props or accessories, and backgrounds created in the studio or searched out and arranged for beforehand.

The bulk of an advertising portfolio must demonstrate to the advertising art director that the photographer is capable of producing a variety of lighting and technical effects, of using models effectively, and of handling the often complicated logistics of arranging shots that must be correct in every detail. To be successful, the portfolio should also show the photographer's ability to think through ideas or to translate a sales message into visual terms.

To be sure, art directors in agencies sometimes require purely editorial photography, although the percentage of such illustrations is relatively small. Subjects such as candid portraits, travel scenes, and beautiful landscapes may be effectively included in the portfolio.

People. Illustrations of people include a great variety of subject matter: people doing things, going places, or using products; head close-ups showing different expressions; people buying, looking at, or making use of products. Typical of the latter group are photographs of a woman buying groceries, a couple watching television, or a man polishing an automobile.

Fashions include clothing and accessories for men, women, and children, photographed indoors and outdoors. They must be highly contemporary, not only in styling but in feeling or treatment. A separate category of fashion samples covers cosmetics and beauty products, ranging from hair shampoos to lipsticks, body oils, and shaving products.

Most fashion photography is done by photographers who either specialize in this area or make it a sub-specialty. This type of photography requires paying close attention to current fashions, having a knowledge of many tricks of the trade, and possessing special talent. The photographer must have a feeling for the way in which people move, sit, or stand. Those who merely dabble in fashion photography rarely are able to produce sufficiently good samples to impress discriminating art directors.

Products. The term *still life* applies to photographs of inanimate objects of small or medium size. Typical examples are household items such as blankets, dishes, flatware, soap, or decorative accessories for the home. Still-life illustrations cover a wide range of products, from perfume and liquor bottles to radios and television sets.

Food photography is in the same category. Some photographers specialize in this area exclusively. To take good food photographs for advertising, you need a high degree of expertise in lighting and special technical effects.

Other Portfolios. In addition to editorial and advertising markets there are a number of others to which the portfolio may be addressed. As stated earlier, there is considerable overlapping in the types of photography used by each market.

Public Relations. The public-relations field is a wide and growing market. It includes public-relations agencies and the public-relations divisions of many large institutions, organizations, and commercial firms. The portfolio, or the parts of it intended for this market, should be primarily editorial in content. However, since many brochures and mailing pieces also use illustrations, some advertising samples can be included.

Industrial and Corporate. The industrial portfolio should show in-plant machinery and workers, executive portraits, still life, and architecture (photographs of office or reception areas). Architectural samples should demonstrate a photographer's ability to deal with either interior or exterior photography. A well-rounded industrial portfolio carries photographs showing a variety of lighting techniques, effective images of large and small pieces of machinery, and illustrations of special techniques such as infrared, close-up, or high-speed photography.

Annual reports come under this heading. The portfolio designed to obtain annual-report work should include a few good candid executive portraits.

Industrial portfolios must show competence in handling difficult lighting situations. Especially important are photographs showing work with fluorescent lighting, self-luminous objects, and lighting of large areas.

Market Diversity. There are no absolute rules governing the contents of a portfolio. The single essential factor is that it must be directed to a viable market and contain samples of work suitable for that market. Beyond the subjects described here are specialty areas such as architecture, medicine and science, travel, and sports.

• *See also:* LAMINATING; PRINT MOUNTING; SLIDE PRESENTATION.

Portraiture

From the earliest times, human beings have depicted themselves graphically for many reasons, in many ways. The style of portraying the human likeness has changed constantly throughout history. During the early part of the nineteenth century, however, the art of the portrait had reached a zenith of realism. The technique of oil-painting a mirror-likeness (often with some mechanical help from the *camera obscura*) was in the height of fashion. If this had not been so, perhaps the advent of photography would not have caused such a furor, and its progress would not have been so rapid.

Today, electronic flash, multi-element coated lenses, and color negative film—technological miracles in themselves—are combined so that one photographer can produce lifelike and natural photographs of more sitters in a single day than the earliest photographers captured in a lifetime.

In the photographic medium, the style of posing the portrait subject has changed constantly through the years, just as it has in painting.

However, the problem has not changed; the challenge is still to make a portrait more than a

Daguerreotype portrait of Asher B. Durand by an anonymous U.S. photographer, c. 1855. The ability to capture intensely lifelike images has been the most important feature of photography from its very beginning.

record, to let it reveal some of those intangible qualities that are recognized as being part of the uniqueness—the individuality—of a human being.

The Nature of a Portrait

In a sense, the epitome of portraiture is capturing on film the likeness that matches the sitter's self image. But that does not mean a picture that denies actuality and simply flatters the subject by presenting idealized perfection—an image of fantasy and dream. The truly masterful portrait is one that evokes from the subject the response: "Yes, that is who I am. At my very best, that is me, and I am proud to be seen this way."

This kind of picture can only be made by a photographer who has a perceptive understanding of people, coupled with technical and expressive mastery of the medium.

The Subject's Feelings

The carefully controlled lighting and posing of a portrait can convey the intelligence, sensitivity, and strength of the subject, as well as a likeness. However, the candid approach to portraiture is helpful to characterization through association with familiar objects and places; the subject is at ease in familiar surroundings and thus is more natural in expression and pose.

The ordeal of having a formal portrait done is, to most people, one of the most agonizing of experiences. The photographer must do everything possible to eliminate this feeling of camera-shyness. One method is to place sitters in the roles of host or hostess in their own homes, or among familiar objects from home or work. The least a studio photographer can do to relieve the sitter's tension is to remove him or her mentally to familiar territory by finding a subject of conversation that the sitter can elaborate upon until the proper expression is captured. The sitter's state of mind is reflected in his or her face. The photographer must be more concerned about the subject's feelings than about anything else.

All have a mental image of their own appearance, usually rather idealized. When the subject is at ease, in comfortable surroundings, and interested in conversation, the photographic image approaches the appearance of the mental image.

Technical Excellence

A good photographic portrait is the sum of a number of different qualities. Lighting, composition, posing, photographic style, and technical excellence are all parts of the whole. Good technical quality makes the difference between a drab portrait and one that "lives"—conveys the personality of the subject, or tells the story it is intended to tell.

Technical quality produces expressive quality. delicate gradation in highlights, a muted range of colors and tones in deep shadows, a rich scale of hues and values between light and shade, as well as the contrast, density, and color balance appropriate to the subject.

Quality in a portrait is usually obvious only when it is poor. If it is very good, then the observer sees only the subject and is not conscious of the technicalities of photography. This is as it should be. People are interested in the subject of the portrait, not how the picture was obtained.

Negative Quality. No matter how imaginative or delicate the lighting for a portrait may be, it will not carry over into the print unless attention is given to the factors in negative-making that influence image quality. These factors are (1) the camera lens and (2) the choice of film, exposure, and development.

Lenses. The choice of lens focal length will make the difference between a natural-appearing portrait perspective and a distortion of the subject's features. In addition, a soft-focus lens may improve the attractive quality of the portrait.

Lens Focal Length. To avoid unnatural size relationships in pictures of people, choose a lens of a longer focal length than you would normally use. A focal length of about one-and-one-half or two times the diagonal of the negative is about right for a head-and-shoulders portrait, while a somewhat shorter focal length is adequate for three-quarter-length and full-length figures. The chart "Working Distances," in this article, gives suggested lens focal lengths and minimum working distances for various kinds of portraits taken in the studio.

Soft-Focus Lenses. Although the question of whether or not to use a soft-focus lens may be a matter of personal preference, most portraits are not made with sharp commercial lenses. Such lenses record every wrinkle, line, and blemish. As a result, the portrait is somewhat crude unless the sitter has practically flawless skin. Otherwise, an inordinate amount of skillful retouching may be needed to make the picture presentable.

Soft-focus lenses are specially designed to leave a moderate residue of spherical aberration. The effect of such aberration is to image a point, not sharply as with an ordinary lens, but with a halo of decreasing intensity around it thus diffusing and reducing the contrast of the fine detail in the image. Putting the lens out of focus does not achieve this effect; it is a built-in characteristic. With most soft-focus lenses, the amount of spherical aberration, and therefore the degree of softness, can be controlled either by stopping the lens down or by altering the separation between the component elements. If a soft-focus lens is not available, diffusing disks placed over the camera lens can be used to give a similar effect.

Negative Exposure. Incorrect exposure of the negative is probably one of the main causes of poor

Portraits can be enhanced by special techniques for great expressiveness. Soft focus and diffusion effects can be impressive, but they should be used sparingly and with care.

quality in portrait photography. Too little exposure results in loss of shadow detail. In spite of increased development, in the case of black-and-white, the loss persists. A print from such a negative will almost certainly have shadow areas that are just plain black patches without detail to relieve them. A print from an underexposed color negative will not only be without detail in the shadows, but the shadows themselves usually will have an unpleasant green color that cannot be corrected in printing.

Overexposure produces several undesirable effects. The principal ones are a flattening, or a lack of gradation, in the highlights and a desaturation of color. The effect of overexposing the negative shows in the print as a single tone instead of gradation in the highlights. This is probably the most serious of all shortcomings in portrait photography. No matter how good the lighting is, overexposure destroys its effect.

Studio Portraiture

Traditionally, formal portrait sittings have taken place only in the studio. And today, the portraits produced in professional studios still dominate the field, both in quality and (except for school pictures) in quantity. There is a definite trend toward location and outdoor portraiture, but the portrait studio, if suitably arranged, still remains ideally suited to its original purpose.

The Studio. The studio is a place away from distraction, where photographer and subject can be in harmony. It is a familiar place, comfortable to be in, where the sitter is subjected to no unnecessary noises or surprises and can maintain composure and privacy.

Studio Size. The camera room should be spacious enough to move around in, with sufficient working space completely surrounding the posing bench.

An important dimension is the distance from the posing bench to the background. It should be enough so that no shadow from the subject will fall on the background, no matter how tall the subject is. This distance should also allow the background to fall out of sharp focus when the lens is stopped down to the working aperture.

There should be foreground room enough to use a lens of fairly long focal length and still cover a half-figure. And there should be plenty of room behind the camera to allow the photographer to move about freely.

The width of the studio should be such that both the main and the fill lights can move, in an arc around the subject to the background, without having to change the light-to-subject distances.

The floor space around the posing bench should be the most constantly used space in the studio. A

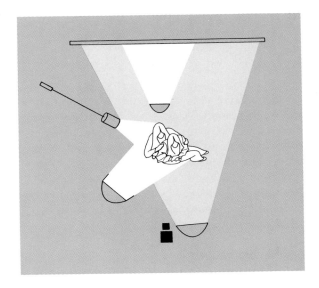

Group portraits present problems of pose and arrangement. Here, mother and daughters are posed in a classical triangular composition. An 80 mm lens was used to take in the entire setting without foreshortening. The main light is a spotlight far to the left; fill light on the subject is provided by a floodlight beside the camera. General light on the animals and the background comes from a floodlight on the left; the intense light directly behind the subjects is from a spotlight of the right.

This double portrait was made using a fill light beside the camera and a main light to the left for a lighting ratio of approximately 4-to-1. A hair light on a boom and a weak background light completed the set-up.

Portraiture

WORKING DISTANCES

Film Size	Type of Portrait	Suggested Focal Length*	Minimum Working Space† (in metres)	(in feet)
35 mm	Head and shoulders	75 mm	4.9	16
	Full-length figure	50 mm	5.2	17
	Groups 3 metres (10 feet) wide	35 mm	5.2	17
70 mm or 2¼" × 2¼"	Head and shoulders	120 mm	4.9	16
	Full-length figure	80 mm	5.5	18
	Groups 3 metres (10 feet) wide	50 mm	5.8	19
6 × 7 cm or 2¼" × 2¾"	Head and shoulders	135 mm	4.9	16
	Full-length figure	90 mm	4.6	15
	Groups 3 metres (10 feet) wide	60 mm	5.5	18
9 × 12 cm or 4" × 5"	Head and shoulders	215 to 250 mm or 8½ to 10 inches	4.6	15
	Full-length figure	150 mm or 6 inches	4.9	16
	Groups 3 metres (10 feet) wide	100 mm or 4 inches (wide field)	5.5	18
13 × 17 cm or 5" × 7"	Head and shoulders	300 to 350 mm or 12 to 14 inches	4.6	15
	Full-length figure	200 to 215 mm or 8 to 8½ inches	4.6	15
	Groups 3 metres (10 feet) wide	135 mm or 5½ inches (wide field)	4.9*	16
18 × 24 cm or 8" × 10"	Head and shoulders	350 to 400 mm or 14 to 16 inches	4.6	15
	Full-length figure	300 mm or 12 inches	5.2	17
	Groups 3 metres (10 feet) wide	190 mm or 8 inches (wide field)	5.5	18

*Not using camera swings.
†These values assume the image occupies 90 percent of the negative dimension and includes an allowance of about 2 metres (7 feet) for lights, background, and camera working room.

portrait-lighting setup should not be static; that is, with lights placed in one spot, unmoved for sitting after sitting. Move the main and fill lights back and forth, as well as up and down, to create patterns and ratios of highlight and shadow on the contours of the subject's face until the effect is most enhancing. It follows that, since no two subjects are alike, no two lighting situations should be exactly the same.

Working Distances. The accompanying chart was compiled to give the *minimum* studio working space needed to take three particular kinds of portraits. Note that, with certain wide-field lenses, this minimum camera-to-subject distance can cause some subject distortion at the edges of the picture.

The final dimension to consider in the portrait studio is the ceiling height. It should be high enough to clear the hair-light boom and provide vertical space for a background adequate for a standing figure, but low enough to be painted white and used as a bounce-light reflector for skylight effects. The consensus of portrait photographers is that a flat, white ceiling, free from beams and ductwork, is ideally located at a 3.6-metre (12-foot) height.

Camera Height for Normal Perspective. One of the most important decisions you make at the outset of a portrait sitting is at what height to place the camera in relation to the subject. A series of factors influences this decision. The first factor is the amount of the figure you are going to include in the photograph: For normal perspective in a head-and-shoulders portrait, place the camera level, with the optical axis of the lens at the height of the subject's lips and tip of the nose. For a three-quarter figure, lower the camera until the center of the lens is level with the upper chest. For a full-length figure, lower the camera again until it is level with, or a little below, the waist. This low position will produce an increased feeling of grace and composure.

A

Effects of Camera Height on Portrait Perspective and Lighting

(A) Camera at eye level; (B) 9 cm (3½ inches) below; (C) 18 cm (7 inches) below; (D) 25 cm (10 inches) below; (E) 35 cm (14 inches) below; (F) 9 cm (3½ inches) above; (G) 18 cm (7 inches) above; (H) 25 cm (10 inches) above; (I) 35 cm (14 inches) above.

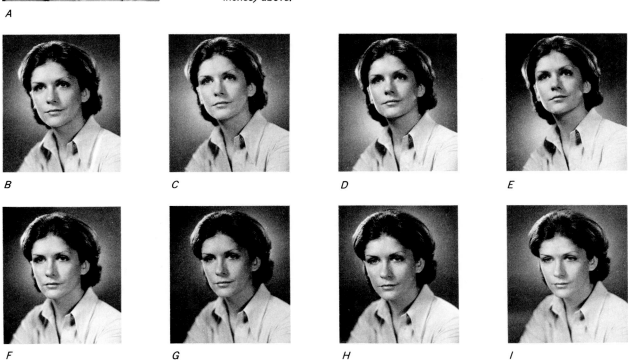

B   C   D   E

F   G   H   I

Another factor affecting the choice of camera height is the shape of the subject's face and how you would like to influence the way it is rendered. In a head-and-shoulders composition, raise the camera above the center of the face to help elongate the nose, narrow the chin, reduce fullness of the jaws, or broaden the forehead. Lower the camera below the center if you wish to shorten the nose, reduce the width and height of the forehead, or accentuate the chin and neck.

The accompanying illustrations were made with an 8″ × 10″ studio camera and a 14-inch lens. The electronic flash lighting was used throughout the series without any adjustment in position or height. The only changes were raising and lowering the camera and refocusing on the eyes.

As you compare the illustrations, pay particular attention to the shape of the head, length of the nose and neck, and general contour of the figure. Analysis of the series illustrates another factor in choosing the camera height in portraiture. Note the change in lighting effect as the angle of reflection is changed by raising or lowering the camera. Lighting is the means of creating form. Therefore, to produce the most effective portrait, the lighting must be balanced and adjusted in accordance with the camera height chosen for the sitting.

Backgrounds and Settings. A studio must have a variety of high- and low-key backgrounds to complement the character, skin and hair color, and clothes of a wide variety of subjects. The expedient of having only one or two colors of drapes, seamless paper, or painted flats is suitable only if you want everything to look the same—but a coin-operated photo booth can do that.

The function of a background is greater than just filling in around the subject. It should contribute to the mood and expressiveness of the picture without calling attention to itself. For practicality it should be economical and easy to handle.

Painted and photomural backgrounds are widely used because they can be changed quickly and easily and require little storage and setup space. The character of a background often can be changed dramatically by a few well-chosen foreground props. The functions, choice, and production of backgrounds for many kinds of pictures are covered in the article BACKGROUNDS.

On some occasions, an actual (or apparently) complete setting may be appropriate for a portrait. When it is not possible to use an actual location, the set must be constructed in the studio. This is a process that consumes a great deal of time and effort and ties up studio space. In addition, care is required to produce a setting that will photograph as "real." A studio that has a recurring need for a variety of realistic settings will probably find it worthwhile to invest in front-projection equipment. This provides the greatest versatility with little or no demand for additional studio space. (*See:* FRONT PROJECTION.)

The lighting is largely from the right side with only a weak fill at the camera and bounce light from a white wall at the left. Note that the light-costumed lady has been placed away from the main lights, while her partner stands closer to the lights, to compensate for both his dark suit and his darker complexion. The lighting ratio is approximately 5-to-1.

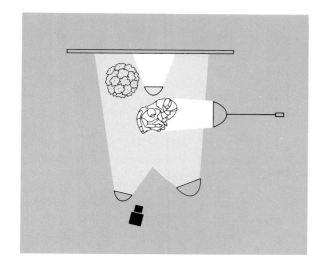

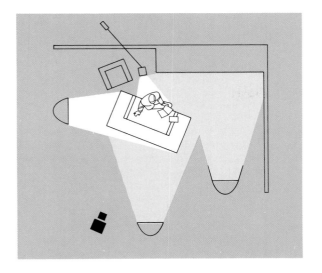

An executive studio portrait. For a formal portrait, pose and camera height can be used to form an impression of the individual. This subject is sitting in a relaxed position, but a low camera angle helps suggest that he is an important person. Because the subject has a slim face and excellent character lines, broad lighting was used at a 3-to-1 ratio. A single hair light was used with one additional light to brighten the corner.

Location Portraiture

Location portraiture is photography done in an indoor place other than the portrait studio.

The problems of location work are similar to those of studio portraiture, but they are compounded by unfamiliar conditions. Low ceilings, small rooms, and cluttered furniture are frustrating in many instances. The inability to make and evaluate test exposures in advance of the sitting adds immeasurably to the difficulty of the situation.

However, portraiture in the home, for all its inconveniences, produces very satisfying results. Since the subject is in familiar territory, expressions and attitudes are relatively more relaxed and natural. More importantly, the objects included in the photograph are not merely props but reflect the true personality of the sitter.

Location portraiture is not for the beginner. Full familiarity with equipment is essential, because seldom will it be used as conventionally as it is in the studio.

Because of the travel time and cost, as well as the outlay for specialized equipment, location portraiture may be an expensive undertaking for the photographer. Therefore, it must be relatively more expensive for the customer. Make sure that the quality of the resulting pictures is worth this extra expense. If possible, visit the location before the day of the sitting. Plan where the subject will be situated and what will be included in the picture. Mentally plan the position of the lights, or make a rough sketch of the floor plan. Locate electrical outlets. (It is better to have electronic flash units with their own power supply.) Investigate the possibility of using existing natural light. Insist that the sitter plan to devote the required time exclusively to the sitting, without distraction or interruption. You will find that extensive planning will pay off in better, more professional photographic results. Start the actual sitting with simple sets and basic lighting. Do not experiment at first. Gradually increase the complexity of the setup as the sitting progresses, and finish by recording the unusual situations that often present themselves. By proceeding in this deliberate manner, you will find that your subject will choose the photographs according to a personal degree of sophistication. Since all of the pictures contain familiar elements, the chances of immediate acceptance of more than one of the poses are greatly heightened.

Outdoor Portraiture

Although it might seem easy to pose a subject outside to take advantage of natural light and surroundings, outdoor portraiture requires all of the sensitivity and professional know-how of studio work. Success lies in selecting a relevant background, setting a mood by pose or activity, and finally, directing viewer attention by selective focus, print manipulation, and cropping.

Outdoor portrait lighting, necessarily, is quite fundamental. The sun usually backlights or sidelights the subject, with flash units or reflectors adding the proper fill-in illumination. One of the qualities that separates the professional portrait from the snapshot is the proper maintenance of a reasonable lighting ratio. This is particularly true in outdoor portraiture, where the main light—the sun or sky— is quite unadjustable.

A reasonable lighting ratio is something between 1 to 2 and 1 to 6; that is, where the light on the shadow side is from ½ to ⅙ that on the highlight side, as measured by a reflection light meter.

In general, the very best lighting for taking portraits outdoors occurs mid-morning or mid-afternoon under hazy sunlight conditions. There is just enough light cloud cover or atmospheric haze so that definite shadows are just barely discernible.

When you must shoot in the direct sunlight, try to schedule the shooting time in the morning or afternoon when the sun angle is about 30 degrees from the horizon. Try not to shoot around noon when the sun is high; this will cause nose and eye shadows to be very uncomplimentary. You can partially overcome the harsh lighting contrast of an overhead sun with a larger diffuser or "scrim." This is a gauze or mesh panel held over the subject's head by an assistant in order to diffuse the harsh light. Obviously, its use is largely limited to close-up work on windless days.

When you shoot in bright sunlight, turn your subject away from the sun so that his or her face is in shadow. This creates a rim or backlight effect that is very pleasing to the eye. To be sure you do not lose important shadow or highlight detail, compress the scene's brightness range by illuminating the shadows adequately.

Another solution to giving some direction to the light is with a technique known as *subtractive lighting*. Simply, this consists of shielding the side of the

A charming outdoor portrait can be created by the simplest of means. The sun serves as backlight; two flash units provide frontal illumination. A moderate aperture (f/5.6) offers a shallow depth of field at this close camera distance.

subject's face with a black umbrella or a head screen called a gobo. In a sense, this "subtracts" light from that side if positioned properly. You should not try to subtract light from the frontal planes of the subject's face.

There are two methods of providing the fill source with which to maintain the proper lighting ratio. The first and simplest is to use large reflectors. You can make adequate flat reflectors from 50 × 60 cm (20″ × 24″) double-weight mounting board, with one side white and the other covered with matte aluminum foil that has been crumpled and reflattened. Do not use mirror-finished foil, as it produces specular reflections and hot spots. Use the matte aluminum side when you need a fairly strong fill and the white side for a soft glow. Regardless of the reflector, base your exposure on the fill-light intensity.

The other method of fill-lighting is to use electronic flash, as explained briefly here and more fully in the article FLASH PHOTOGRAPHY. The fundamentals of portrait lighting arrangements and light ratios are explained in the following sections in this article. Valuable information for outdoor and location portraiture is also included in the article AVAILABLE-LIGHT PHOTOGRAPHY.

Fill-In Flash. The high contrast of back sunlighting and shadow on a person's face can be reduced with a flash used from the camera position. The main concern is to avoid too much flash illumination, which gives the appearance of unnatural lighting. Usually, the flash is simply too strong, which means that it would best be used at a 3.5- to 6-metre (12- to 20-foot) camera-to-subject distance. For closer use it should be heavily diffused.

The important thing is that the flash should lighten the shadows, not eliminate them. The degree of fill-in flash can and should be controlled. Use the accompanying table, which works for any film. (The camera settings are based on the ratio of flash to sunlight and not on the film speed.)

Assume that you have an interchangeable-lens camera that has a focal-plane shutter and X-synchronization for electronic flash. Locate the output of your unit on the table and read to the right to locate the distance range your subject should be within, for a good fill-in-flash shot. You will get full fill (2-to-1 lighting ratio) when your subject is at the near distance, average fill (3-to-1 lighting ratio) when your subject is at the middle distance, and slight fill (6-to-1 lighting ratio) when your subject is at the far distance.

Most flash units put out too much light to be used conveniently for fill-in flash outdoors. One answer is to use a second, small unit with a minimum output for fill-in work.

Portrait Lighting

Equipment. A wide variety of light sources can be used for portraits, so long as they have certain features. It must be possible to position the lights easily, and to control the direction, beam shape, and intensity of their outputs. This calls for units of moderate size and weight, sturdy but flexible stands, and a variety of barn doors, diffusers, and reflectors. The size and weight of the equipment are serious concerns for location work.

For color photography, all units should produce illumination of the same color temperature so that single filtration can be used at the camera if required. Ideally, the light and film should be matched so that filtration is not necessary.

Continuous light sources have the advantage of making the lighting arrangement visible at all times. However, they create heat and glare that can make the subject very uncomfortable. In addition, their power consumption may create problems on location. Electronic flash units are widely used because of their compactness, high output, and the daylight color temperature of their light. Low-wattage mod-

FLASH-TO-SUBJECT DISTANCES FOR FILL WITH ELECTRONIC FLASH
(Distance for Ratios—2:1–3:1–6:1)

Output of Unit BCPS	Shutter Speed with X-Synchronization					
	1/30 (in feet)	1/30 (in metres)	1/60 (in feet)	1/60 (in metres)	1/125 (in feet)	1/125 (in metres)
350	1½–2–3½	.45–.6–1.05	2–3–4½	.6–.9–1.35	3–4–7	.9–1.2–2.1
500	2–3–4	.6–.9–1.2	2½–3½–5½	.75–1.05–1.65	3½–5–8	1.05–1.5–2.4
700	2–3–4½	.6–.9–1.35	2½–3½–6	.75–1.05–1.8	4–5½–9	1.2–1.65–2.7
1000	2½–3½–5½	.75–1.05–1.65	3½–5–8	1.05–1.5–2.4	5–7–11	1.5–2.1–3.3
1400	3–4–7	.9–1.2–2.1	4–5½–9	1.2–1.65–2.7	6–8–13	1.8–2.4–3.9
2000	3½–5–8	1.05–1.5–2.4	5–7–11	1.5–2.1–3.3	7–10–15	2.1–3–4.5
2800	4–5½–10	1.2–1.65–3	6–8–13	1.8–2.4–3.9	8–11–18	2.4–3.3–5.4
4000	5–7–11	1.5–2.1–3.3	7–10–15	2.1–3–4.5	10–14–20	3–4.2–6
5600	6–8–13	1.8–2.4–3.9	8–11–18	2.4–3.3–5.4	12–17–25	3.6–5.1–7.5
8000	7–10–15	2.1–3–4.5	10–14–20	3–4.2–6	15–21–30	4.5–6.3–9

Note: Some focal-plane shutters will not synchronize at speeds faster than 1/60 sec.

eling lights can assist in arranging the electronic units, and test shots on instant-print material will show the actual results. In many studios, a combination of sources is used: continuous units for background lighting, flash units for subject lighting.

The Lighting Umbrella. One of the most useful innovations in portrait photography in recent years is the soft lighting technique produced by the use of umbrellas. The photographic umbrella consists of a metal shaft and a collapsible framework covered with cloth. The cloth covering is made of white or silvered material that is highly reflective. The light source—electronic flash, tungsten, or quartz lamp— is mounted on the shaft and aimed into the center of the underside of the parabolic framework. The quality of the light that is reflected from this surface is reminiscent of the soft, diffused, nondirectional light produced by the north skylight of early photographic studios.

The umbrella is a broad, natural-looking light source that is extremely portable. The quality of the light can be changed to match the mood of the subject. Umbrellas are available in a variety of shapes, sizes, and reflective qualities: 1 to 2 metres (3 to 6 feet) in size, square or round, flat or parabolic, matte or smooth, white or silvered. By changing the shape, reflective surface, or manner of mounting the light source, you can obtain a series of increasing contrasts.

1. The softest umbrella illumination is produced by a flat matte-white surface, with the light directed entirely toward the reflecting surface from as far down the shaft as possible.
2. You can achieve slightly more direction or contrast with a silvered, still flat umbrella.
3. More sparkle is added if the umbrella is a silver parabolic canopy, with light directed into it from the focal point on the shaft.
4. Still additional specularity can be created by using a bare bulb in the silver parabolic canopy. The effect here is toward a point source, softened by the additional light that is reflecting from the canopy.

Fill light is usually from another, more diffuse umbrella or from a flat reflector.

Do not mix white and silvered material in different umbrellas or reflectors when shooting color. The result of this type of mismatch is similar to mixing tungsten and daylight on the same negative—impossible to print. For additional information, see the article UMBRELLA LIGHTING.

Basic Portrait Lighting Techniques. Proper portrait lighting can create modeling and realism. Using the concept that light areas of a print project and dark areas recede, place highlights on the five frontal planes of the face (forehead, nose, chin, and both cheeks) with the neck and sides of the face in shadow. This helps lend a desirable third-dimensional effect to the subject.

The forehead, cheeks, nose, and chin are the five facial planes that should be lighted to dominate the portrait.

Equally important, the lighting can be used to idealize. Facial defects can be obscured in a shadow; a broad nose can be narrowed with a short lighting of the "split" variety.

Probably the most basic single principle governing portrait lighting is that there should be *one dominant light source,* with all other lights subordinate and subservient to it. Accordingly, the character and placement of the main, or key, light in relation to the position of the subject is of primary consideration to the portrait photographer. Its placement is used as a means of classifying the three main types of lighting: *broad lighting, short lighting,* and *butterfly lighting.* (See the accompanying illustrations.)

Lighting Variations. From these three basic lighting positions for the main light, any number of derivations can be achieved.

Bounce Light. Bounce light is derived from the broad lighting position. This is accomplished by aiming the main light *directly away* from the subject to a suitable reflector. The light that is reflected to the subject is soft, shadowless, and most flattering. Often no fill-in light is used, or perhaps only further bounce from another reflector on the far side of the subject to soften the shadows.

Direct Light. Another derivation from the broad lighting position is so-called direct light. The main light in direct lighting is a high, reflectorless unit that throws an all-over sun-like illumination on the subject. Usually directed on the side of the subject turned toward the camera, the direct light is more directional than bounce light and gives more highlight separation. Fill-in is accomplished by an auxiliary light source or large reflectors.

(Left) Broad lighting: the main light illuminates the side of the face that is toward the camera. Broad lighting is primarily a corrective lighting technique used to widen thin or narrow faces. (Center) Short lighting: the main light illuminates the side of the face that is away from the camera. Short lighting tends to narrow the image of the face and is a useful corrective for round or plump faces. (Right) Butterfly lighting: the main light is directly in front of the face. This placement is successful with faces of average width. While it is considered very suitable for glamour photography of women, butterfly lighting is not recommended for male subjects because it tends to highlight the subject's ears and give them an unnatural prominence.

Window Light. A popular use of the short lighting position is window light. Usually a combination of daylight and auxiliary electronic flash, it produces a natural, soft, low-key portrait. The subject is placed beside a window lit by skylight, not direct sunlight. The fill-in unit is on or near the camera and is one-half or less the intensity of the window light. When using color film, be careful that the color temperature of the fill-in light agrees with the daylight coming in the window. (Photographic daylight is considered to be 5500 K.)

Split Light. The main light can be moved far enough behind the subject so that only half of the face is highlighted and there is no triangular patch of light on the nearest cheek. This variation of short lighting, known as "split" lighting, is used only rarely, and then to produce moderately dramatic low-key effects, conceal facial defects in the shadow side of the face, or slenderize a very broad nose.

Ceiling Bounce. One of the most widely used forms of bounce lighting, where the electronic flash unit is on camera and pointed directly up, automatically gives the results of a softened butterfly lighting position. Once again, fill-in can be accomplished by reflectors placed horizontally under the subject's chin, or by white floors.

Drawbacks to this form of butterfly lighting are the necessity for white ceilings and the lack of specular highlights in the photographic subject's eyes. (A 3″ × 5″ card, taped to the flash head, will reflect some light from a unit aimed at the ceiling, and this will add sparkle to eyes. It will also relieve shadows caused by eyeglasses.) However, used with a reflex-type camera, ceiling bounce is ideally portable lighting for following a small child in a high-key studio.

Setting Up Portrait Lighting Arrangements. While it is possible to make a professional portrait with only one light, a portrait photographer normally uses a number of lights to build a suitable lighting for the subject. No two photographers proceed in exactly the same way; you should follow an efficient, consistent operating method of adding lights to a portrait set. The list of individual lights might be the following:

1. Background light.
2. Main light.
3. Fill-in light.
4. Hair light.
5. Backlight, or "kicker."

The lights are usually set up in their numbered order.

The Background Light. Customarily, the background light is a small flood light on a short stand placed about midway between the subject and the background. Its purpose is to help provide tonal separation between the subject and the background and, when color film is used, to control the color and general rendition of the background. Although it is a matter of personal preference, some photographers start the lighting buildup by adjusting the position of the background light. Exact placement of this light can be achieved more easily when its effect can be observed by itself.

Placement of the background light is facilitated by first directing it *toward the subject,* watching the shadow the modeling light casts. The subject's shadow should completely cover the camera, thus making sure that the lens will not see any part of the background light itself. The background light is then rotated 180 degrees, and final placement adjustments are made.

For normal portraits, the light on the background should be about the same intensity as the main light on the subject. Tone and color should be achieved by proper selection of the background. Underlighting will only cause weak, hard-to-print tones that have an unpleasant greenishness in color.

White backgrounds for high-key portraits can be very effective. To produce them, use a background light of sufficient intensity to yield a background brightness four times that of the main subject. Employing the same white background and reducing the strength of the background light to that of the main light is apt to produce greenish or bluish gray tones around the subject in the fall-off areas of the background.

In using white backgrounds for high-key portraits, there is considerable danger that excessive flare may cause a loss of picture contrast. To minimize this problem, photograph the background at a slight angle and make sure that the background is no larger than necessary. Use an efficient lens hood and black screens, just out of camera range, to minimize this image-destroying flare.

The Main Light. Generally, this is a flood lamp or broad light source located higher than the subject's head and at approximately 45 degrees to one side of the camera-subject axis, usually in the short-

son for using the main light very high would be to emphasize forehead wrinkles as much as possible, as in character-study work.

Most photographers use a diffused main light because a sharp shadow from the main light is not so desirable in portraiture as it is in commercial product photography. Diffused lighting minimizes facial textures, helps to minimize retouching, and, accordingly, is used most often for conventional portraits of both men and women. As a matter of personal preference, a few photographers use an undiffused main light for men, to accentuate character lines in the face or to produce a brilliant glamour effect. But this lighting is more difficult to control and would be used more for a special effect or salon results than for normal portraits.

With regard to the question of short versus broad lighting, the subject's facial structure determines which way the main light should be arranged. The average oval face is presented most flatteringly with short lighting; the broad face, also with short lighting; and the narrow face, with broad lighting. The accompanying diagram illustrates these three basic situations.

A high-key background is achieved by letting the sun strike the surroundings, while keeping the light off the side of the subject's face that is closest to the camera. A reflector or fill-in flash may be called for to provide a proper ratio for exposure.

light position. One method of placing this light properly, using the modeling lights, is to watch the resultant catchlights in the eyes. As seen from the camera-lens position, these catchlights should be located at approximately the 1 o'clock or 11 o'clock position in the eyes, depending on whether broad or short lighting is used and on the direction the subject is facing. Obviously, the catchlight location will vary somewhat from subject to subject. For example, for a person with deep-set eyes or a person wearing a wide-brimmed hat, the main light will have to be lowered somewhat from the normal. However, the important point is that the main light must cause catchlights high in the eyes; otherwise (if it is too high, for instance), the eye sockets will appear to be excessively dark and recessed. About the only rea-

(Top) With a normal, oval face and conventional short lighting, the main light has been positioned laterally so that it places a triangular highlight on the cheek nearest the camera. (Center) In order to make a wider than normal face appear more normal, the main light has been moved farther to the left and the width of the triangular highlight reduced. (Bottom) Highlighting a comparatively greater area of a narrow face can make it appear somewhat wider. Thus, the width of the highlighted area of the face in any portrait should be about equal, regardless of the facial type.

Note that the width of the highlighted area for all three subjects is approximately the same. The lighting has been designed to idealize the narrow and the broad faces and present them as normal. The basic consideration is that the broader the face, the more it should be kept in shadow; and, conversely, the narrower the face, the more it needs to be highlighted. It is for this reason that the triangular highlight on the broad face is intentionally smaller than the equivalent area on the normal face. The reduction of this cheek highlight is accomplished, of course, by moving the main light slightly farther behind the subject. This is a delicate adjustment. Its effect can be judged accurately only from the camera-lens position.

Broad lighting, used less frequently than short lighting, requires additional care and skill. The broad position of the main light means that too great a portion of the near side of the subject's face, including the ear, will be highlighted excessively. To keep this area in shadow, some means of controlling the distribution of light must be used. Shading can be accomplished by means of feathering, barn doors, or head screens. Obviously, a combination of these methods can be used.

The Fill-In Light. Generally, the fill light is diffused, used close to the camera at lens height, and placed on the side of the lens opposite that of the main light. Some slight modification of this position may be necessary for people wearing glasses, to avoid reflections.

The lateral position of the fill light is determined to some extent by the specular facial highlights this light causes. The effect must be observed carefully from the lens position. If, for example, a person has a type of skin that reflects the image of the fill light too strongly when the light is right next to the camera, these specular highlights can be reduced by moving the fill light slightly away from the camera. Often, this lateral adjustment is critical in controlling the degree of highlight brilliance.

Another consideration in the lateral position of the fill light is that undesirable shadows caused by smile lines may be created by using this light too far from the camera.

Almost inevitably, the fill light will add a lower pair of catchlights to the eyes. These secondary catchlights are usually considered objectionable, not so much because they tend to belie the basic principle of one main light source, but because they often create the impression that the subject has a directionless stare (a starry-eyed effect). Consequently, this second pair of catchlights should be removed. This can be done either by etching them in the negative (if a black-and-white film was used) or, more easily, by spotting them on the print (which can be done on either black-and-white or color prints). Color negatives cannot be etched successfully, due to the color-layer structure of the emulsion. (*See:* RETOUCHING.)

The section in this article on lighting ratios contains additional information about exact placement of the fill-in light.

The Hair Light. This small lighting unit, generally used on a boom from above and behind the subject, is almost a necessity. It not only adds some detail to the reproduction of the hair but also provides a useful means of subject-background separation.

There are three general positions relative to the subject where the hair light can be used effectively: directly overhead, either to the right or the left of the subject's hair at head level, or above and to one side. In any case, the hair light should seldom be allowed to spill over onto the face, since this may cause small but distracting highlights and belie the basic principle of a single light source. A suggestion for placing the hair light properly is to bring it forward gradually until its illumination just strikes the forehead or the cheeks, as the case may be, and then move it back until the highlight on the skin disappears.

Aside from the photographer's personal preference as to the rendering, the color and, especially, the degree of sheen of the hair dictate the amount of hair illumination required. Brunette hair requires more intense illumination than blond; dull hair, regardless of color, requires a relatively intense hair light in order to restore a desirable sparkle. The actual intensity required can only be determined by recognizing an artistic visual balance within the studio.

The Backlight. Often referred to as a "kicker," the backlight finds most use in outlining the shoulders of men's dark suits, to separate them from dark backgrounds. It is also helpful in adding detail to hair and, in rare instances of dramatic portraits, as a facial backlight. This lighting unit, generally a spotlight, is used slightly above the height of the

Steps in Building a Short Lighting Setup

A

B

C

D

E

(A) Main light only; (B) fill light added; (C) background light added; (D) hair light added;
(E) kicker lights added on both sides.

Steps in Building a Broad Lighting Setup

A

B

C

D

E

(A) Main light only; (B) fill light added; (C) background light added; (D) hair light added; (E) kicker lights added on both sides.

subject's head and usually, but not always, on the same side of the subject as the main light. If used properly—better too little than too much—and from the same side of the subject as the main light, it can help add strength to a masculine face when it rims or grazes the extreme edge of the face. When the backlight is used on the opposite side from the main light, it often creates an undesirable effect by outlining the ear and making it appear to pull away from the head.

A precaution in using the backlight is that it usually should not be allowed to strike the tip of the subject's nose. If it does, it may give an abnormal appearance to the nose. Just a slight repositioning of either the light itself or the subject's head can prevent this lighting error. Be sure that both the hair light and the backlight are turned off when taking an exposure-meter reading. Not only do these lights have no effect on the basic exposure, but the danger is that they may influence the meter incorrectly. And, of course, no backlight should shine directly into the camera lens, since this might cause glare that would reduce the image contrast. A barn door or snoot can be used to shield the lens.

Lighting Ratio. Lighting ratio refers to the relative intensities at the subject position of the main light plus the fill-in light to the fill-in alone. Generally, for normal contrast in portraits, the ratio should be in the neighborhood of 3 to 1. This ratio will produce good, salable portraits for both black-and-white and color photography. In black-and-white portraiture, a high lighting ratio, say even 8 to 1, can be partially remedied by printing the negative on a low-contrast grade of paper. However, in color photography there is only one grade of paper available, and the principal method of contrast control is the establishment and maintenance of a consistent 3-to-1 lighting ratio by the photographer.

In general, a 3-to-1 ratio is achieved when, as measured at the subject, *the main light is twice as bright as the fill-in light when the fill-in light is used close to the camera lens.* This is because the fill light from the front places one unit of light over the entire face, while the main light from the side (being twice as intense) places two units of light only on the main-lighted areas of the face. Thus, there is only one unit of light in the shadows, but one plus two (that is, three) on the main-lighted areas.

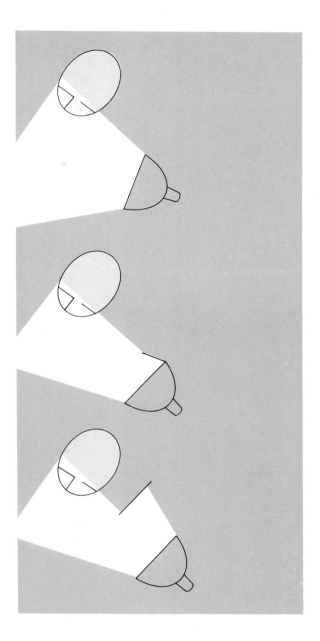

(Top) A "feathered" light refers to the fact that the subject is illuminated by the peripheral area of the light cone. Generally, the light is feathered in such a way that the reflector axis is in front of the subject. (Center) In a broad-lighting situation, an alternate method of shading the nearest ear is to use the barn-door baffle attached to the lamp reflector. Barn doors are also useful in shading white blouses or bald heads. (Bottom) A head screen has the advantage of more positive shading control, since it can be used independently of the subject. Two screens will be useful as studio accessories.

1-to-1 lighting ratio

2-to-1 lighting ratio

3-to-1 lighting ratio

6-to-1 lighting ratio

10-to-1 lighting ratio

Lighting Ratios. A 1-to-1 ratio appears flat because the main light and the fill light are reflected at equal intensity by the subject. A 10-to-1 ratio is contrasty and unflattering. Softer ratios of 2-to-1 or 3-to-1 are generally useful for either black-and-white or color portraits. Higher ratios require care in exposure and printing, and they are usually selected for male, rather than female subjects.

Establishing the Ratio. There are several simple methods of establishing a 3-to-1 ratio. These methods include using:

1. Both the main light and the fill light at equal distances from the subject, with the main light at twice the fill-light intensity. For example, with variable-power electronic flash units, the main light could be used at 200 watt-seconds, with the fill light at 100 watt-seconds.
2. Two identical lights, but with the main

light closer to the subject. The specific distance for each light can be determined quickly by thinking of the lens *f*-stop openings as a distance scale. With this system, a 3-to-1 ratio is achieved if the main light is "one stop" closer to the subject than the fill light. For example, if the main-light-to-subject distance is 4 feet (1.2 metres), the fill-in light should be placed 5.6 feet (1.7 metres) from the subject; if the main light is at 8 feet (2.4 metres), the fill light should be at 11 feet (3.4 metres), and so on.

3. Two identical lights equidistant from the subject, with a diffusing screen over the fill light to reduce its intensity by one-half. One thickness of spun glass approximately meets this requirement. An exposure meter can be used to check the amount of light absorbed by the diffusing screen. However, the disadvantage of this method is that the main light is usually undiffused—probably an undesirable situation for general portraiture.

4. An exposure meter. Flash meters adapted for measuring incident light can be used directly. Reflected-light meters can be used to read the light reflected from a test card, such as the Kodak neutral test card, held close to and in front of the subject. Either the gray side or the white side can be used, whichever gives more satisfactory readings at the particular level of illumination under consideration. When the main plus fill-in illumination is read, the incident-light meter or card should be turned to the position that gives the maximum reading. The actual reflectance is not important for this use, because the readings are only comparative and will not be used for exposure determination. All lights should be on if an incident-light meter is used. If a test card is used, any backlights or sidelights that might influence the meter directly should be turned off. When fill-in illumination is read, the incident-light meter or card should be turned toward the camera lens, and the main light should be turned off.

The exposure-meter method for establishing the desired lighting ratio is recommended, since the lights can be used feathered or baffled with barn doors or head screens, thus not inhibiting any desired technique of lighting control for the most artistic effect.

Highlight Brilliance. Highlight brilliance usually refers to the degree of specularity of facial highlights. The principles governing this important aspect of facial rendition should be very familiar to portrait photographers. Generally, most photographers strive for an artistic midpoint between the two extremes of rendering a face so that it appears perfectly matte and rendering it with such strong highlights that it appears excessively oily. Up to a point, the more brilliant the facial highlights, the more three-dimensional the rendition becomes. Of course, this effect can be overdone; if so, it is especially unfortunate in color portraiture, because the skin color will then be lost in resulting prints.

Most of the necessary control over highlight brilliance can be provided by a slight lateral movement of either or both the main and the fill-in light. It is absolutely necessary to appraise this effect from the position of the camera lens, however. If additional controls are needed for certain subjects, they can be furnished by either of the following means.

The first is applying makeup to the subject. Powder can be used to reduce excessive facial reflectivity; cold cream, applied judiciously, to increase highlight brilliance. (*See:* MAKEUP.)

The second lies in the lighting. The larger and more diffused the frontal light, the more matte the face will appear; conversely, small and undiffused lights cause the most pronounced highlight brilliance.

As an occasional technique, some photographers use, in addition, a small, undiffused light called a "highlighter," above and in front of the subject's face, to reinforce the highlights by adding to their specular appearance. This light should be fairly weak; it should cause no discernible shadows of its own when used in conjunction with conventional lighting; and it should not be used so far forward as to add additional catchlights to the eyes.

In either black-and-white or color portraiture, beware of obliterating delicate facial highlights by overexposing the negative.

Corrective Techniques

The successful portrait photographer realizes that the principal aim is to obtain characteristic likenesses of the subjects. At the same time, however, the photographer may have to temper reality a bit to prevent certain features from looking unpleasant or even grotesque. The portraitist does this by combining judicious posing, suitable lighting, and appropriate choice of camera angle. Although each situation in portraiture is different from all the others, the following suggestions for corrective treatment are generally accepted.

Other Approaches to Portraiture

This article has concentrated on traditional portraiture as a planned event. There are many special occasions that call for portraits of a special nature. Weddings and graduations are by far the most common such occasions, but there are many more in which the function of a portrait is to commemorate the event as well as the individuals involved.

Portraiture need not always be a planned activity. Spontaneous portraits occur repeatedly in the course of candid photography, especially during vacations and travel. The imaginative photographer should be sensitively alert for such opportunities.

Portraits can be enhanced by special techniques for great expressiveness. Soft-focus and diffusion effects are widely used. Double-exposure, multiple printing, and more extreme effects such as colored lighting or posterization must be used sparingly and with great care. It is very easy for a special effect to overwhelm an image so that the technique rather than the individual becomes the actual subject of the picture.

CORRECTIVE TREATMENT	
Difficulty	**Suggested Treatment**
Prominent forehead	Tilt chin upward
	Lower camera position
Long nose	Tilt chin upward
	Face directly toward lens
	Lower main light
	Lower camera position
Narrow chin	Tilt chin upward
Baldness	Lower camera position
	Screen to shield head
	Use no hair light
	Blend top of head with background tone
Angular nose	Minimize effect by turning face toward lens
Broad face	Raise camera position
	Use short lighting
	Turn face to three-quarter position
Narrow face	Lower main light
	Use broad lighting
Wrinkled face	Use diffuse lighting
	Lower main light
	Use three-quarter pose
Double chin	Raise main light
	Tilt chin upward
	Use high camera position
Facial defects	Keep on shadow side
Prominent ears	Hide far ear behind head
	Keep near ear in shadow
	Consider profile view
Glasses	Tilt downward by elevating bows slightly
	Adjust fill light laterally
	Have subject raise or lower chin slightly
	Use small light source and etch reflection from negative
Deep-set eyes	Lower main light
	Use lower lighting ratio
Protruding eyes	Have subject look downward
Heavy-set figure	Use short lighting
	Use low-key lighting
	Use dark clothing
	Vignette shoulders and body
	Blend body with background tone

Large sheets of colored theatrical gels were used to make this tasteful, yet theatrical, portrait. Spotlights gave the photographer better control than floods would have in creating the crosslighting with strongly contrasting colors. Where the colors overlap at the subject a third color is created.

The following list of cross-references will lead the interested photographer to many additional techniques and approaches to portraiture.

• *See also:* Available-Light Photography; Baby and Child Photography; Backgrounds; Barn Doors; Candid Pictures; Children, Photographing; Commencement-Day Pictures; Composition; Flash Photography; Front Projection; Glamour Photography; High Key; Lighting; Makeup; Models and Modeling; Proof; Retouching; School Photography; Soft-Focus Effects; Theatrical Photography; Umbrella Lighting; Wedding Photography; Yearbook Photography.

Further Reading: Allen, Mary. *Portrait Photography: How and Why.* Garden City, NY: Amphoto, 1973; Brooks, David. *Small Camera Portraiture.* Los Angeles, CA: Petersen Publishing Co., 1977; Castle, Paul. *Promotional Portrait Photography.* Upper Darby, PA: Studio Press, 1974; Croy, O.R. *The Photographic Portrait.* Garden City, NY: Amphoto, 1976; Editors of Time-Life Books. *Studio.* New York, NY: Time-Life Books, 1971; Eisenstaedt, Alfred. *People.* New York, NY: Viking Press, 1973; Manning, Jack. *The Fine 35 mm Portrait.* Garden City, NY: Amphoto, 1978; Mason, Reginald H. *Portraiture at Home.* Dobbs Ferry, NY: Morgan and Morgan, 1977; Nibbelink, Don D. *Picturing People.* Garden City, NY: Amphoto, 1975; Nurnberg, W. *Lighting for Portraiture,* 7th ed. Garden City, NY: Amphoto, 1969; Spitzing, G. *Photoguide to Taking Portraits.* Garden City, NY: Amphoto, 1974.

Posterization

Artists and designers usually represent subjects in pure line or in a full range of graduated tone. However, rich, broad effects can be produced by replacing full gradation with a limited number of flat tones. The most effective application of this technique is found in poster drawing.

A similar effect can be achieved photographically through the techniques of posterization. During posterization, the normal tones of a subject are separated into several distinct tones with the use of high-contrast films. These films are then printed in register and in combination to create a photograph that shows a sharp delineation of tones. Color posterizations often show unreal color combinations.

Posterization lies on the fringe of photography and graphic arts but is, nevertheless, a purely photographic technique. Posterized reproductions can be characterized by the number of tones of which they consist. For example, the simplest posterized print consists of two tones—black and white (see the following illustrations). Black-and-white posterization is easily achieved by limiting the process to a single-tone separation or a high-contrast negative. Reproductions of this type are suitable for newspaper advertisements.

More common are three- and four-tone posterization. A three-tone print consists of black (representing the shadows), gray (representing the middletones), and white (representing the highlights). A four-tone print consists of black, white, light gray, and dark gray. Posterized prints consisting of more than four tones are usually not successful, since the result looks too much like a continuous-tone image. In color posterizations, tones are represented as different colors, so that more "tones" can be used effectively.

For special effects, tint or texture screens can easily be included in the posterized print; screens can be attached to the tone separations at the second or third stage of the process. To eliminate interference between screens, a line screen can be printed vertically on one tone separation, and a similar screen printed horizontally on a second tone separation. The final reproduction will show a crosshatched effect from the combination of the two screens.

Although posterizing produces unique and dramatic results from appropriate photographs, not all photographs lend themselves to this process. Pictures with simple patterns and strong designs usually produce the best results. A little experimentation with some of the many possible variations in posterization technique indicates that results are limited only by the imagination.

Posterizing Technique

Both black-and-white and color posterizations can be made from an original black-and-white print, a black-and-white negative, a color negative, or a color transparency. In working from an original color negative or transparency, a high-contrast panchromatic film such as Kodalith pan film 2568 (Estar base) must be used for the tone separations. Ortho films, such as Kodalith ortho film and Kodak professional line copy film, are not sensitive to red. Selecting the proper materials is most important; use the following table as a guide.

Because this process requires that tone separations be made to the size of the final print, the high-

Original	High-Contrast Negatives	High-Contrast Positives
Black-and-white negative	*Kodalith* ortho film 4556, type 3 (*Estar* thick base) *Kodalith* ortho film 2556, type 3 (*Estar* base) *Kodak* professional line copy film 6573	
Color negative	*Kodalith* ortho film 4556, type 3 (*Estar* thick base) *Kodalith* ortho film 2556, type 3 (*Estar* base) *Kodak* professional line copy film 6573	*Kodalith* pan film 2568 (*Estar* base) (made first)
Color transparency	*Kodalith* pan film 2568 (*Estar* base) (made first)	*Kodalith* ortho film 4556, type 3 (*Estar* thick base) *Kodalith* ortho film 2556, type 3 (*Estar* base) *Kodak* professional line copy film 6573

(Above left) This high-contrast photograph illustrates the simplest form of posterization; it contains only two tones—black and white. Photo by Barbara Jean. (Above) A three-tone posterization combines a highlight negative and a shadow negative printed slightly out of register. Photo by Linda Campbell. (Left) This four-tone posterization was made from three high-contrast negatives. Photo by Carole G. Honigsfeld.

contrast films must be exposed in register and printed in register. For critical work, a pin-register printing frame and a register punch should be used. However, for some subjects, perfect register is not essential. Simply placing each sheet of film in the same corner of the printing easel provides satisfactory register for such subjects. For the production of contact-printed posterized prints 40 × 50 cm (16″ × 20″) or larger, a pin-register system is a necessity. It is practically impossible to stack masks of large dimensions in the corner of an easel. The density of these high-contrast masks precludes registering them visually. However, large prints enlarged from smaller negatives can be registered visually.

Tone Separation

Tone separation is a function of exposure. A series of exposures onto a high-contrast film, such as Kodalith ortho film 4556 or Kodalith pan film 2568, breaks the tone range of the continuous-tone original into shadow tones, middletones, and highlights. In working from an original negative, underexposing allows adequate exposure only through the thinnest areas of the negative, thus producing a shadow positive. The shadow areas are blocked up and the middletones and highlights remain clear. Overexposing allows adequate exposure through all densities of the negative except for specular highlights, thus producing a highlight positive. In other words, both shadow areas and middletones are blocked up and only the specular highlights remain clear. Obviously, normal exposure produces a middletone positive that falls between the shadow positive and the highlight positive. The three positives should be examined to be sure that they provide definite tone differences. The steps in making a tone separation are detailed in the accompanying box.

Making a Tone Separation

Use a Kodak safelight filter No. 1A (light red) and select the appropriate high-contrast film from the table "Selecting Materials."

1. Make a test strip with a wide range of exposures on high-contrast film.
2. From the test strip, select three different exposures.
3. Exposure No. 1 should be very light and record only the highlight areas. Make a film positive using this exposure.
4. Exposure No. 2 should be normal, showing detail through the middletones. Make a film positive using this exposure.
5. Exposure No. 3 should be very dark and have detail only in the shadow areas. Make a film positive using this exposure.

Exposures 1 (highlight), 2 (midtone), and 3 (shadow) are tone separations. If the original image was a negative, the tone separations will be positive images. To produce tone-separation negatives, contact-print the three films onto additional high-contrast film.

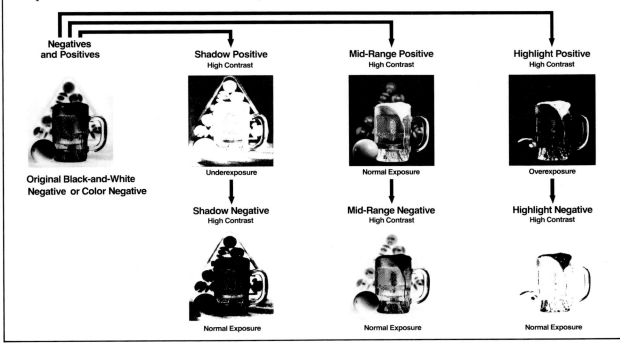

Negatives and Positives

Original Black-and-White Negative or Color Negative

Shadow Positive
High Contrast
Underexposure

Mid-Range Positive
High Contrast
Normal Exposure

Highlight Positive
High Contrast
Overexposure

Shadow Negative
High Contrast
Normal Exposure

Mid-Range Negative
High Contrast
Normal Exposure

Highlight Negative
High Contrast
Normal Exposure

Pictures with simple patterns and strong design elements usually make the best posterizations. This four-tone posterization was made from a photograph that had a broad tonal range.

Posterizing Black-and-White Prints

When making a black-and-white posterized print, print one high-contrast negative at a time. If you are not using a pin-register system, register the negatives as illustrated in the section on posterizing color slides.

Starting with the shadow negative (darkest overall), adjust the exposure time to obtain a light gray tone, and make an exposure. Remove the shadow negative from the paper, replace it with the midtone negative, and print again, using the same exposure as that used for the shadow negative. Since exposure is cumulative, each area becomes progressively darker with successive exposures. If the print were processed at this point, the shadow areas would be a dark gray; those areas exposed only with the midtone negative, during the second exposure, would be a light gray.

Now, make a third identical exposure using the highlight negative and finally, process the print. The shadow areas, which received all three exposures, will be dark gray; the highlight areas, which received only one exposure, will be light gray; and the specular highlights, which received no exposure, will remain paper-white.

For posterizing in black-and-white printing, use only high-contrast negatives. When working from an original negative, first prepare a black-and-white intermediate film positive. This intermediate positive should be full-scale with contrast somewhat higher than average. In working from an original print or transparency, the intermediate film positive is not necessary, since the positive original yields negative tone separations.

These procedures are summarized in the accompanying table.

Posterizing Black-and-White Prints

Use the appropriate safelight for the paper.

1. Make tone-separation negatives.
2. Register the negatives. If you do not have a pin-register system, you can tape the edge of the negatives to the baseboard so that you can flip them over the paper one at a time.
3. Starting with the shadow negative (darkest overall), adjust the exposure time to obtain a light-gray tone, and make an exposure.
4. Remove the shadow negative and replace it with the midtone negative. *Do not move the paper.* Print again using the same exposure.
5. Remove the midtone negative and replace it with the highlight negative. *Do not move the paper.* Print again using the same exposure.
6. Process the print normally.

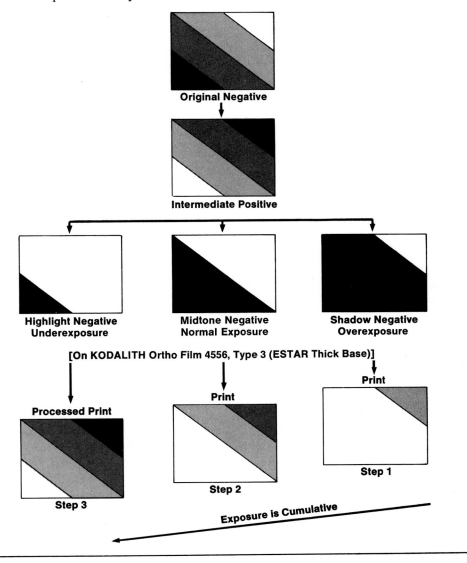

Original Negative

Intermediate Positive

Highlight Negative
Underexposure

Midtone Negative
Normal Exposure

Shadow Negative
Overexposure

[On KODALITH Ortho Film 4556, Type 3 (ESTAR Thick Base)]

Processed Print

Print

Print

Step 3

Step 2

Step 1

Exposure is Cumulative

Enlarging Posterized Prints. The instructions up to this point have referred to posterized prints produced by contact-printing. Large-size sheets of high-contrast film can be costly. This cost can be reduced by making the tone-separation positives and negatives in a size to fit your enlarger, and enlarging the negatives onto the paper.

The steps of preparing the negatives are identical to those used to prepare contact negatives.

When enlarging, put the most detailed negative in the enlarger and a sheet of blank paper in the easel. Then turn on the enlarger light, and with a pencil, draw a number of key registration lines on the paper. Be sure to include lines that will help locate the other two negatives.

Under safelight, replace the registration sheet with a sheet of photographic paper and expose the one image. Mark one corner of the paper so that you will be able to replace it in the easel in the same orientation. Put one of the other negatives in the enlarger and the registration sheet in the easel. With the enlarger light on, slide the easel around until the projected image lines up with the pencil lines. Replace the registration sheet with the paper (under safelight) in the same orientation and expose. Repeat with the third negative, and develop the print.

Posterizing Color Prints

For posterizing in color printing, you need both high-contrast negatives and high-contrast positives. You can use either Kodalith ortho film 4556, type 3 (Estar thick base), or Kodak professional line copy film 6573, to make both the negatives and positives. From an original negative, the tone separations are positives. Reverse them to obtain negatives by contact-printing them onto additional film. From an original slide, the tone separations are negatives. Reverse them to obtain positives by contact-printing onto additional film.

Register the positives and the negatives. The positives are used for masking during the color-printing operation. For example, if the first exposure is made with the shadow negative, then the second exposure is made with both the shadow positive and the midtone negative in register. The shadow positive masks the areas of the color paper that were exposed through the shadow negative, so that these areas are not affected during the second exposure with the midtone negative. When making the third

exposure with the highlight negative, use the midtone positive mask to cover the areas of the color paper that were exposed during the first exposure with the shadow negative and during the second exposure with the midtone negative.

The added dimension of color complicates posterizing. Deciding which color to reproduce in each tonal area is simply a matter of personal taste. You can save time and materials by trying to visualize the image in advance and planning the end result.

Printing Color Posterizations

Method 1: White-Light Printing with Subtractive Color Filters. The use of white-light printing to produce a posterized Ektacolor paper print is perhaps the most practical procedure for a beginner. In addition to a standard enlarger setup with a No. 2B filter, the Kodak Wratten filters in the accompanying table are recommended.

SUBTRACTIVE COLOR FILTERS		
Kodak Wratten Gelatin Filter No.	Color of Filter	Color Produced in Print
25 or 29	Deep red	Cyan
58 or 61	Deep green	Magenta
47 or 47B	Deep blue	Yellow
44	Cyan	Red
32	Magenta	Green
12	Deep yellow	Blue

Since these six filters are sharp-cutting, they allow for great control over the color in the reproduction. They are preferable to color compensating (CC) filters or color printing (CP) filters.

For best results, balance the color paper emulsion to produce a neutral color, using standard CC or CP filters in the enlarger with an unexposed, developed color negative in the negative carrier.

Once the emulsion is balanced in, make a test to determine the exposure time for printing through one of the six filters. For example, select the green filter and make a series of test exposures, using the midtone high-contrast negative. Evaluate the color rendition of the print by using each of the six filters

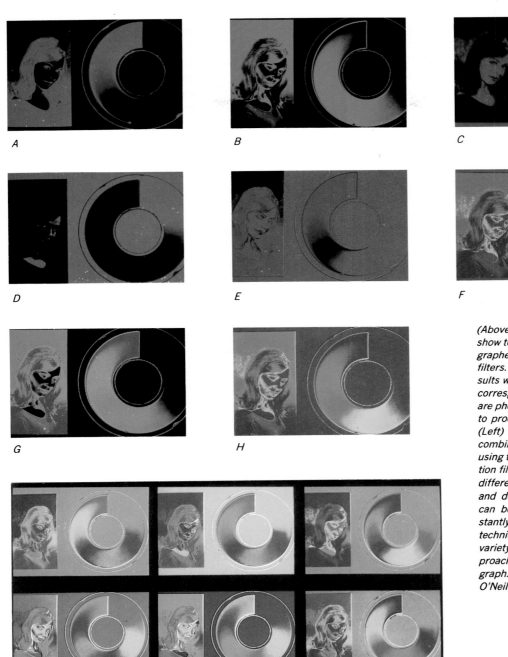

A

B

C

D

E

F

G

H

(Above) Illustrations A through D show tone-separation films photographed through different-color filters. E through H show the results when the positives and their corresponding mask negatives are photographed in combination, to produce a color posterization. (Left) These are some of the color combinations that are possible by using the same set of four separation films and exposing them with different color filters. As exciting and demanding as posterization can be, photographers are constantly working to extend the technique by an almost endless variety of new techniques and approaches to the posterized photograph. Photos by Jerome P. O'Neill, Jr.

to make separate prints at the same exposure time selected from the first exposure series. Simply change exposure to make the color lighter or darker.

Since this is a negative color system, the desired color is produced by printing through the complementary filter. For example, printing through a Kodak Wratten filter No. 25 (red) exposes the red-sensitive layer of the color paper. As a result, cyan dye is formed during processing; the final print is cyan. Similarly, printing through a Kodak Wratten filter No. 58 (green) exposes the green-sensitive layer of the paper, producing a magenta image. Printing through a blue filter produces a yellow image. Cyan produces red, magenta produces green, and yellow produces blue. For a more complete discussion of color negative-positive theory, see COLOR PRINTING FROM NEGATIVES.

To produce a posterized color print, use the

A

B

These color-slide variations were done in the camera; the colors visible in the pictures are the colors of the filters placed over the camera lens. (A) 25 red, 12 yellow, and 47 blue filters; (B) 25 red, 58 green, and 47 blue filters; (C) 47 blue, 58 green, and 12 yellow filters; (D) 25 red and 58 blue. The background received no exposure and so remained black. Photos by Barbara Jean.

C

D

This color posterization was made from a black-and-white original. Highlight, midrange, and shadow areas were photographed on three intermediate interpositives. Subsequently, highlight and shadow positives were made from their respective negatives. The films were registered and printed in combination by exposing through a 25 red filter to produce the cyan image, through a 44 cyan filter to produce the reddish-black image, and through a 47 blue filter to produce the yellow image. Photo by T. H. Grove.

filters listed in the following box and follow the procedure described.

Method 2: Tricolor Printing. The tricolor exposure method for color printing is perhaps the most difficult method to use. However, this system yields a wide variety of colors and shades for the posterized color print. As compared with the white-light exposure method, tricolor exposure allows greater flexibility in choosing a color and also allows greater control over the purity or saturation of a color.

Tricolor exposure is an additive printing method. Three separate exposures are made onto color paper through red, green, and blue separation filters. Because of the selective color sensitivity of the three emulsion layers of the color paper, the need to "fine tune" exposure and filter packs is eliminated. The primary filter recommendations for this type of printing are Kodak Wratten filters No. 25 (red), No. 99 (green), and No. 98 (blue). Color balance, as well as print density, depends entirely upon the exposure times through these filters. Additional instructions for tricolor-printing techniques are usually furnished by the manufacturers of tricolor-printing equipment.

Masking and Printing Color Posterizations

Tone Separation	Positives	Negatives	Masking	Filtration	Printing
Shadow	**Key** S: Shadow M: Mid-Tone H: Highlight	S		None	1
Low Mid-Tone	S +	M		Red	2
High Mid-Tone	M +	H		Blue	3
Highlight	H			Green	4

Method 3: Color Negatives of Colored Art Paper. One of the most predictable methods of producing a posterized print is with negatives of colors and textures. These negatives can be prepared by photographing various colored art papers on color-negative film. You will find ready-made texture patterns in woven fabrics, stucco walls, wood grain, reticulated film, and pressed glass. When copying these textures onto film, be sure to keep the lighting uniform and the exposure constant.

To print a posterization with the texture negative, first make a straight print of the texture negative and balance the color using CC or CP filters in your enlarger. When you have the correct color balance for the texture negative, you can print the posterization following the procedures already described.

Each color texture negative you use in the posterization process will have to be color balanced as described above. If you plan to use many color texture negatives, you may want to make a gang proof or contact print of a group of negatives and determine the color balance for the whole group at one time.

You can produce light and dark shades of one color with a single texture negative by changing the exposure.

Posterizing Color Slides

It is possible to create posterized slides using a 35 mm camera and an electronic flash unit. Make 4″ × 5″ high-contrast negatives and positives, just as you would to posterize a color print. Register the films on a sheet of opal glass or plastic so that they will flip in and out of the camera range as shown in the accompanying diagram. Place the electronic flash unit at least 30 cm (1 foot) below the glass and aimed directly at the glass. Mount the camera on a firm support, such as a tripod, and aim it down at the film on the glass. If you plan to do a lot of copying work using an electronic flash unit as the light source, you may want to build a copying box like the one illustrated.

Posterizing Color Prints

Use a Kodak safelight filter No. 10 or No. 13 (dark amber) with Ektacolor papers.

1. Make tone-separation negatives and positives, and register them.
2. Place a sheet of unexposed, developed color-negative film in the filter drawer of the enlarger. This is not necessary if the filters from which you are printing are incorporated in negatives. Balance the paper to produce a neutral color as described in the text.
3. Make separate test strips from the highlight positive and each of the three negatives (highlight, midtone, and shadow negatives), using the filter you have selected to use with each one. After processing the test strips, select and record the best exposure time for each negative and for the highlight positive.
4. Print the shadow negative using the exposure determined above.
5. Remove the shadow negative and replace it with the shadow positive and the midtone negative in register. *Do not move the paper.* Print this combination, using the exposure determined above for the midtone negative.
6. Remove the midtone negative and shadow positive, and replace them with the midtone positive and the highlight negative in register. *Do not move the paper.* Print this combination, using the exposure determined above for the highlight negative.
7. Remove the midtone positive and highlight negative and replace them with the highlight positive. *Do not move the paper.* Print this positive, using the exposure determined above for the highlight positive.
8. Process the paper in the normal way.

(Left) To register the film, first select the combination of negatives and positives required to produce a color posterization. Visually register the films over the picture-taking area on the opal glass. Tape the films along one edge so that you can flip them in and out of the picture-taking area. Make an exposure through a colored filter; then flip the film out of the picture-taking area. Make a second exposure through a different colored filter; then flip the film out of the picture-taking area. Continue exposing the films in this manner until all the stages of the posterization have been exposed.

(Right) This box has a sheet of opal glass or plastic on the top. The white cardboard set at an angle reflects the light from the flash up through the opal glass. The light bulb provides the light necessary for focusing the camera and registering films, but it should be turned off during the exposure. The electronic flash can be fired manually or by synchronization with the camera shutter. Use the sharp-cutting filters recommended for color printing in the text. The filter will reproduce its own color in the slide; so with this method of posterizing, it is easier to determine the color than with color printing.

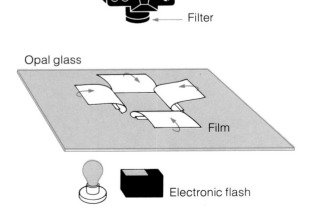

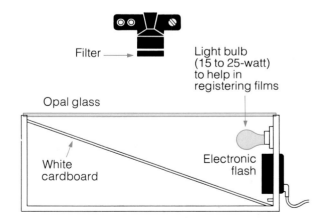

Posterizing Color Slides

Work in a dimly lighted room.

1. Make tone-separation negatives and positives and register them.
2. Use a slide copier or the copying method described in the text. Determine the exposure for your equipment by making a series of test posterizations at various lens openings. Keep good records and have the film processed, then select the best exposure. If you use the suggested CC or CP filters, you will not have to vary the exposure to compensate for different filter factors, so the exposure will be the same for the whole posterization. Once you have determined which lens opening produces a well-exposed slide, you can make all your slide posterizations at that exposure.
3. Copy the shadow positive with the appropriate filter over the camera lens.
4. Remove the shadow positive and replace it with the shadow negative and the midtone positive in register. *Do not move the camera.* Copy this combination onto the same frame of film with a different color filter over the camera lens.
5. Remove the midtone positive and the shadow negative and replace them with the midtone negative and the highlight positive in register. *Do not move the camera.* Copy this combination onto the same frame of film through a different color filter.
6. Process the film normally.

Review the procedure described previously for printing with high-contrast negatives and positives. Use the same method of combining the films, but instead of printing onto paper, copy them onto a single frame of film. Use a different colored filter over the camera lens during each exposure. An exposure of $f/22$ or $f/16$ will produce good results with medium-speed (ASA 64–80) film, but of course this depends on the output of the flash unit and the distance from the flash to the opal glass. Use the same exposure for each film and filter combination.

If your camera will not make multiple exposures, work in a darkened room. (You can have a very dim light in the far corner from the camera.) Set the shutter on "T" or hold it open on "B," and manually flash the electronic flash for each exposure. If you leave the filter over the lens or put the lens cap on while arranging the films between flashes, you should be able to produce the registered multiple exposures needed with this method.

You can produce 35 mm negatives with this system by using a color negative film. Printing these negatives as you would any color negative will eliminate the problem of registering at the easel. However, prints made in this manner usually are not as sharp as prints made directly from high-contrast films enlarged the same size as the paper.

The photo-posterization techniques described here are basic. By combining them with other photographic controls such as the tone-line process, bas-relief, and Sabattier Effect, or by using more than one negative, you can achieve many different and fascinating effects.

• *See also:* BAS-RELIEF; COLOR PRINTING FROM NEGATIVES; COLOR SEPARATION PHOTOGRAPHY; DUPLICATE SLIDES AND TRANSPARENCIES; FILTERS; HIGH CONTRAST; SABATTIER EFFECT; SPECIAL EFFECTS; TONE-LINE PROCESS.

Further Reading: Langford, M.J. *Advanced Photography: A Grammar of Techniques.* New York, NY: Focal Press, 1972; Ruggles, Joanne and Philip. *Darkroom Graphics.* Garden City, NY: Amphoto, 1975; Yule, John A. *Principles of Color Reproduction.* New York, NY: John Wiley and Sons, Inc., 1967.

Potassium Bichromate

Bichromate of potash, potassium dichromate

Sensitizer for gelatin in the carbon, carbro, and gum-bichromate processes. Bleach for black-and-white reversal films. Also, used in chromium intensifiers, and combined with sulfuric acid in tray cleaners.

Formula: $K_2Cr_2O_7$
Molecular Weight: 294.21

Bright orange-red crystals, soluble in water, insoluble in alcohol and ether.

CAUTION: Potassium bichromate is poisonous if taken internally. It may cause chromium dermatitis if allowed to remain on skin.

Potassium Bisulfite

Potassium hydrogen sulfite

Analogous to sodium bisulfite, but not commonly available. When the potassium salt is called for, potassium metabisulfite is usually substituted. (*See:* POTASSIUM METABISULFITE.)

Formula: $KHSO_3$
Molecular Weight: 120.17

Potassium Bromide

Most common restrainer and antifoggant in developers. It is also used in making photographic emulsions, and in bleaches used in toning.

Formula: KBr
Molecular Weight: 119.01

White crystalline granules or powder, somewhat hygroscopic, soluble in water, only slightly soluble in alcohol and ether.

Potassium Carbonate

Potash, Pearlash, salt of tartar, carbonate of potash

Used as an alkaline accelerator in developers, where a slightly higher pH is needed than can be obtained with sodium carbonate, as in glycin developers.

Formula: K_2CO_3
Molecular Weight: 138.20

White granular powder, quite hygroscopic. Very soluble in water, insoluble in alcohol and ether.

Potassium Chloride

Chloride of potash, muriate of potash

Used in making silver chloride emulsions in place of sodium chloride. It is sometimes used as a restrainer, in addition to potassium bromide, in special developers.

Formula: KCl
Molecular Weight: 74.55

Colorless or white crystals or powder, freely soluble in water and alkali solutions, insoluble in alcohol.

Potassium Citrate

Tribasic citrate of potash

Used in preparation of silver chloride emulsions, especially for printing-out papers. Potassium citrate is sometimes used as a restrainer in developers for positive films. It is also an ingredient in copper toning baths.

Formula: $K_3C_6H_5O_7 \cdot H_2O$
Molecular Weight: 324.34

White granular powder, deliquescent. It is very soluble in water, slightly soluble in alcohol.

Potassium Cyanide

Cyanide of potash

Used as fixing agent in certain collodion processes, bleach for certain intensifiers, local reducer in process work.
Formula: KCN
Molecular Weight: 65.11

White, deliquescent, granular powder, freely soluble in water, slightly soluble in alcohol. It is unstable in solution.

CAUTION: Deadly poison! Very dangerous to handle. Use only in well-ventilated areas; never pour used solution down sink drains, or into a waste container that may contain acid.

Potassium Ferricyanide

Red prussiate of potash

Combined with hypo to form Farmer's Reducer. It is also used in bleaches for removing silver image in color film processing, in toners, and in sensitizers for blueprint papers.
Formula: $K_3Fe(CN)_6$
Molecular Weight: 329.25

Ruby-red, lustrous crystals, freely soluble in water, slightly soluble in alcohol.

Potassium Hydroxide

Caustic potash, potassium hydrate, potassa

Strong alkali, used as an accelerator in some developers in place of sodium hydroxide.
Formula: KOH
Molecular Weight: 56.10

White or slightly yellow deliquescent lumps, pellets, or sticks. It is very soluble in water, and soluble in alcohol.

CAUTION: Caustic poison; causes severe burns if it comes in contact with eyes, skin, or mucous membranes.

Potassium Iodide

Iodide of potash

Used in emulsion making, in preparing solutions of iodine, in preparation of mercuric iodide intensifier, and as an auxiliary restrainer in certain developers.
Formula: KI
Molecular Weight: 166.02

Colorless or white crystals, white granules, or powder. It is soluble in water and alcohol.

Potassium Metabisulfite

Potassium pyrosulfite

Used in acid fixing baths for papers where no hardening is needed. Potassium metabisulfite is also used as a preservative in developers, particularly in formulas using pyrogallol as developing agent. It is interchangeable with sodium bisulfite in any formula where the latter is called for. Generally, sodium bisulfite is used because it is less expensive.
Formula: $K_2S_2O_5$
Molecular Weight: 222.32

Fine, needle-like crystals or crystalline powder, soluble in water. The dry chemical emits a noticeable odor of sulfur dioxide, and must be kept tightly covered; it deteriorates rapidly in moist air.

Potassium Oxalate

Neutral oxalate of potash

Used in ferrous oxalate developer, and in developers for platinum papers.
Formula: $K_2C_2O_4 \cdot H_2O$
Molecular Weight: 184.23

Colorless, transparent crystals, freely soluble in water, insoluble in alcohol and ether.

CAUTION: Poisonous if ingested.

Potassium Permanganate

Permanganate of potash

Oxidizing agent, used in reducers, bleaches, and stain removers. Its purple color is bleached by thiosulfates and sulfites, hence a solution of potassium permanganate is sometimes used as a test for residual hypo in negatives and prints.
Formula: $KMnO_4$
Molecular Weight: 158.03

Purple-black, needle-like crystals. Soluble in water, sulfuric acid, and acetic acid, but is decomposed by alcohol.

CAUTION: Poisonous if ingested.

Potassium Persulfate

Potassium peroxydisulfate, Anthion

Oxidizing agent, used in super-proportional reducers in the same way as ammonium persulfate. It has also been used as a hypo eliminator because of its ability to oxidize traces of sodium thiosulfate to sodium sulfate.
Formula: $K_2S_2O_8$
Molecular Weight: 270.32

Colorless or white crystals, no odor, soluble in water, insoluble in alcohol. Potassium persulfate decomposes in air, hence must be kept tightly closed in a cool, dry place.

CAUTION: Irritates skin. May cause dermatitis.

Potassium Sulfide

Potassium monosulfide

Do not confuse potassium sulfide with the crude form sometimes called "liver of sulfur," which is a mixture of various sulfides. The purified form is sometimes used in toning baths when sodium sulfide is unobtainable, but the latter is less expensive.
Formula: K_2S
Molecular Weight: 110.26

Yellow or reddish-yellow deliquescent crystals or fused masses.

CAUTION: Poisonous if ingested.

Potassium Thiocyanate

Potassium sulfocyanide, potassium sulfocyanate, potassium rhodanide

Used in toning baths, particularly with gold toners for both printing-out papers and enlarging papers. It is also used as a mordant in dye-toning baths. It is a silver halide solvent, and has been used as a fixing bath for low-temperature processing, but tends to attack gelatin at higher temperatures or in large concentrations. It is also used as a silver solvent in developers to produce finer grain by reducing the size of the individual silver grains, and also to attain clearer whites in reversal processing by removing trace densities.
Formula: KSCN
Molecular Weight: 97.18

Colorless, deliquescent crystals, very soluble in water, also soluble in alcohol and acetone.

Praxinoscope

Invented by Emile Reynaud (1844–1918), a French motion-picture pioneer, the praxinoscope was one of a number of devices for viewing or projecting images in motion that were predecessors of the photographic motion picture. The name was coined from Greek roots meaning "action-viewer."

The praxinoscope is a further development of the zoetrope. It consists of a series of motion-sequence images mounted around the circumference of a rotating cylinder or drum. The images face inward toward a mirrored reflector that has as many facets as there are images. As the device is rapidly revolved on its center post, a new image is seen each time a mirror comes into position to reflect it to the observer's eye. Viewing through a mask that cuts off the mirror segments on either side greatly improves the effect.

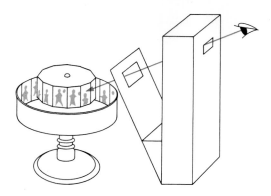

In a praxinoscope with a masking viewer, the inner window (on the slanted surface) was decorated with painted drapes to look like a tiny theater proscenium.

In a projecting praxinoscope, transparencies rather than opaque images are used. A light source outside the drum transilluminates the images as they revolve past; a lens picks up their reflections and projects them on a screen.

A praxinoscope is relatively simple to construct. It is interesting both as a toy, and as a practical demonstration of the principles of sequential motion and the persistence of vision.

• *See also:* MAREY, ETIENNE JULES; MOTION STUDY; MUYBRIDGE, EADWEARD JAMES; ZOETROPE; ZOOPRAXISCOPE.

Printed Circuits

The term "printed circuit" refers to that type of electronic circuitry in which conventional strands of wire are replaced by patterns of conductive material on an insulating base or substrate. The substrate may be glass or ceramic, but most often it is a solid or laminated plastic material.

In some printed circuits, additional components such as resistors and capacitors are added to the pattern during the manufacturing process. In any case, the basic steps for making the printed circuit board remain substantially the same.

Photographically Produced Printed Circuits

A typical example of the photographic printed-circuit process can be broken down into a number of steps, each of which has an important part in the general process.

1. Master artwork of the circuit is drawn or produced with plastic tapes so that it is 4 to 20 times the final size.
2. The master artwork is reduced to final size in a process camera. A master transparency is made on a high-contrast film or plate. Depending on the subsequent process, a negative or positive image may be made. In any case, it is common practice to refer to the final reduced image as a "transparency."

Originally, printed circuits were actually printed with conductive ink or paint, and fed into a printing press to create wiring patterns. Modern printed circuits are made utilizing photofabrication techniques.

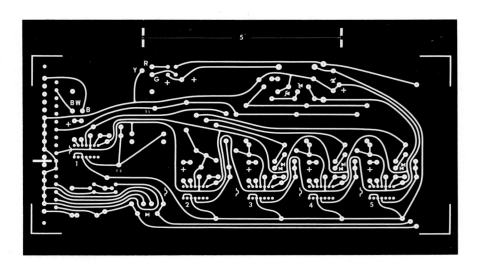

3. A printed-circuit blank or "laminate" with an unbroken copper-foil (or similar material) coating is cleaned and coated with photoresist.

4. The dry, resist-coated stock and the master-pattern transparency are placed in contact and exposed to ultraviolet radiation. The photoresist hardens wherever the radiation passes through clear areas of the transparency. Those areas under the opaque or black portions of the transparency receive no exposure and do not harden.

5. The exposed resist coating is next subjected to a solvent developer that dissolves the portions of resist that did not receive exposure. The exposed portions of resist remain tightly bonded to the copper surface and are relatively unaffected by the developing agent.

6. Following this treatment, the entire board is subjected to an etching bath. The etchant dissolves those portions of the copper surface that are not protected by the resist. Once etching is complete, discrete areas of conductors that are precisely positioned on the surface of the board will remain.

7. Finally, the resist is removed from the surface, and the board is ready for drilling and circuit-component mounting.

Many other photographic techniques are used for producing printed circuits. The process steps differ widely. Nevertheless, the process just described is still used in industry and can be used by an advanced electronics experimenter to produce prototype circuits.

• See also: PHOTOFABRICATION; PHOTORESIST.

Printing-Out Papers

Printing-out paper is a type of contact-printing paper that produces an image solely by the action of exposure; development is not required.

The first photographic papers were printing-out papers. They saved time and greatly reduced wasted paper in the era when the sun was the only practical printing light. By using a contact-printing frame with a hinged back, a photographer could periodically inspect the progress of a print and bring the process to a halt when the image had reached satisfactory strength. There was no need to make preliminary test strips to determine exposure, and printing could be accomplished without need for a darkroom.

The prints produced generally had a deep reddish-brown color that, when fixed, changed to a rather unpleasant yellowish-brown. This was commonly counteracted by treating a print first in a gold toning bath to improve the image color, followed by fixing in a plain hypo solution. A somewhat purplish-black image was the usual result, but it could be varied through blue-browns to a pinkish tone, depending on the solutions used and the character of the individual emulsion. The advent of developing-out papers, which did not need sunlight for printing, required far shorter exposures, and produced generally superior tones, eventually caused printing-out papers to become virtually obsolete.

The only printing-out papers intended for continuous-tone work currently available are Kodak studio proof paper and similar papers of other manufacturers. They are commonly used for portrait proofs and left unfixed, so that they will turn deep black or red all over upon repeated exposure to light. They are not intended for permanent prints and may not react well to either gold toning or fixing baths.

A special type of printing-out paper is made for use in oscillographs and other types of scientific recording instruments. These papers are of very high contrast and produce only line, rather than continuous-tone, images. They vary in type. Some produce a visible image upon exposure, others require an auxiliary exposure to ultraviolet radiation to "photodevelop" the image to a visible state. Like other printing-out papers, they will eventually turn dark all over or fade with continued exposure to light; they can be made permanent by processing in a special developer. These papers have no use in ordinary photography and are not generally available in camera stores.

Because modern continuous-tone printing-out (proof) papers are different from their predecessors, their response to toning and fixing cannot be predicted. The following procedures and formulas were in use into the 1930's. They can form a base for experimentation with present-day products, if desired.

Printing-Out Toning and Fixing Procedures

1. Make a deep, rich print by contact exposure to sunlight (or other source of strong ultraviolet radiation).
2. Wash the print 15 to 20 minutes, until the water ceases to show milkiness when poured into a clear glass container.
3. Treat 5 to 10 minutes in the following bath, with frequent agitation.

Gold toning bath

Gold chloride	0.23 g
Ammonium thiocyanate . . .	3.50 g
Water	1.00 litre

(Either dissolve the chemicals in separate quantities of hot water and mix together for immediate use, or dissolve them in cold water and let stand 10 to 12 hours before use.)

4. Rinse briefly in plain water, then immerse in a stop bath of 0.45 gram of sodium sulfite per 30 millilitres of water.
5. Wash the print thoroughly, about 15 minutes.
6. Fix in a 10 to 15 percent plain hypo solution (100 to 150 grams sodium thiosulfate in water to make 1 litre).
7. Wash and dry as with a conventional print.

• *See also:* CALOTYPE; HISTORY OF PHOTOGRAPHY; PAPERS, PHOTOGRAPHIC.

 **Printing, Photographic**

This article outlines the methods of making photographic prints. A photographic print is usually a positive image, generally on a paper base, but sometimes on film.

In the negative-positive photographic process, the film exposed in the camera is processed to produce negative images. The negatives are then printed to produce positive prints.

In the reversal process, the camera film is processed to produce positive images, known as transparencies or slides. These can be printed on reversal-print material—either reversal paper or reversal duplication film to make prints or duplicate transparencies. An alternative to making prints is to print the original transparency on a color-internegative film to make color negatives, which are then printed on regular paper to make prints.

There are basically two types of photographic printing: contact printing, and optical printing. The latter is also known as projection printing.

Contact Printing

In contact printing, the original image is placed in close contact with the printing paper or film. The sensitized material is then exposed to light through the original image. The sensitive emulsion receives more or less exposure depending on the densities in the film original.

Commercial contact printers usually are designed to make contact prints from fairly large negatives. They consist of a box that houses lights for exposure. The top of the box has a glass sheet in which the film is placed, emulsion-side up. A platen, molded with a soft material, such as rubber, plastic foam, or felt, is pressed down on the sensitized material and film to achieve contact.

Another method of contact printing is to use a printing frame. This is a frame with a sheet of glass and a hinged back that serves as a platen. When the original film is placed in contact with the sensitized material and held in close contact with the platen, an enlarger is often used as the light source for exposing the print. Some contact-printing frames use vacuums to insure good contact. (*See:* CONTACT PRINTING.)

Optical Printing

In optical or projection printing, light from a bulb is distributed over the area of the original image by condenser lenses or by a diffusing material. A lens is used to form an image of the negative or transparency on the sensitive surface of the printing material.

The most common optical printer is an enlarger. (*See:* ENLARGERS AND ENLARGING.) Photofinishers use automated or semi-automated printers (other forms of optical printers) to produce enlarged prints, duplicate transparencies, or transparency prints. Motion pictures are printed on special optical printers that have automated transport mechanisms for the original film as well as for the film-print material.

Printing Techniques

Most printing is "straight"; that is, the print is made with a single, overall exposure to the image of the original film. However, the printing process lends itself readily to modifications either to improve the quality of the image or for artistic purposes. Dodging, or holding back, and burning-in during exposure are common procedures for improving the photographic tones of an enlarged print. Combination printing is the process of making a single print from more than one original image.

Normal printing materials have silver halide emulsions. There are, however, a number of special printing processes that do not utilize silver halide emulsions, or that use a silver halide emulsion in conjunction with other materials. Examples are gum-bichromate prints, carbon and carbro prints, cyanotypes, platinotypes, vesicular prints, diazotypes, and paper-negative prints.

Original negatives or transparencies are often printed in special ways to produce derivations. Unusual materials and procedures, such as extreme alterations in printing and processing, produce images that are photographic in nature, but do not appear to be straight photographs. Solarization, Sabattier effect, bas-relief, posterization, and tone-line processes are examples.

• *See also:* BLACK-AND-WHITE PRINTING; BLACK-AND-WHITE PRINTS FROM COLOR FILMS; BURNING-IN; COLOR PRINTING FROM NEGATIVES; COLOR PRINTING FROM TRANSPARENCIES; COMBINATION PRINTING; CONTACT PRINTING; DIRECT POSITIVE PROCESSING; DODGING; DUPLICATE SLIDES AND TRANSPARENCIES; ENLARGERS AND ENLARGING; LARGE COLOR PRINTS AND TRANSPARENCIES; NON-SILVER PROCESSES; PAPERS, PHOTOGRAPHIC; PRINTING-OUT PAPERS; SPECIAL EFFECTS.

Prints, Mounting

Mounting a photograph means attaching it to a stiff support. The mounting material can be cardboard, wood, plywood, plastic foam-core mounting board, tempered hardboard, or other material.

Mounting can enhance the visual effect of a picture. Some pictures look attractive when mounted on a white mat and put into a frame; other pictures look their best if they are flush-mounted and displayed without a frame. A mounted print not only looks better than an unmounted print, it also lasts longer, because the mount acts as a stiffener and thereby helps to keep prints from becoming bent or torn.

The substance for attaching the print to the mount comes in several forms. Photographers generally use dry-mounting tissue for a smooth, long-lasting application. This is a sheet of material that is sandwiched between the photo and backing, sealing one to the other under heat and pressure by a dry-mounting press.

If you do not have access to a dry-mounting press, you can find a variety of mounting cements in liquid and spray form. Double-stick papers and tapes also give good results.

Photographs that are only to be mounted and not framed usually do not have the protection of glass over the surface. For this reason, it is a good idea to use a protective spray on the print surface. With the emulsion sealed in this way, the print can be cleaned without fear of marring the surface. If the mounted print is hung in a public place, you may wish to laminate it for additional protection. This plastic material is laid over the print, sealing it from the air and offering protection from scratches and finger marks. *(See:* LAMINATING.)

Pictures that are to be framed should be mounted on triple-weight matboard. Cut the matboard a little smaller than the frame channel so it will fit in easily without binding.

For a simple, modern look, flush-mount a print on ¼-inch-thick cardboard. Cut the print a little larger than the mount, and then use a sharp knife, razor blade, or paper cutter to trim off the excess print after mounting. Finish the edges of the mount with a black felt marking pen.

When a picture is to be displayed without a frame, you may wish to try a stiffer material than cardboard. Tempered hardboard is generally used for this purpose, as it is relatively inexpensive and easy to cut to any size or shape. Depending upon the application, however, wood, plastic, or even metal can be used. Be sure to test to see that the sealant will stick to the backing material. In addition, there are products available that have a plastic foam core covered either by cardboard or a hard resin veneer. Their low weight and high strength make them particularly suitable for transportable photo display situations.

Displaying pictures on mounting materials alone lends a more direct, graphic look to the photograph. Without a matting and frame, attention is drawn directly to the image. The effect is clean and contemporary, with particular application for business-oriented environments. Mounted photographs can be cut into interlocking shapes or cut out along lines within the photo to lend a three-dimensional feeling to a photo wall.

Another way to display photographs is to mount them onto cubes or other three-dimensional forms. This provides several interesting advantages over conventional methods. First of all, no wall is needed to hang the pictures. The photo cube can rest on a table shelf or even the floor. Secondly, as many as six images can be placed on each unit, thereby expanding in a limited space the number of images displayed.

Mounting Methods

Dry Mounting. At room temperature, the typical dry-mounting material looks like a piece of tissue paper, but it contains a thermal adhesive that melts at an 85–90 C (180–200 F) temperature range to form a permanent bond between the print and the mount. You need a thermostatically controlled electric iron for mounting prints by this method. For occasional use, an ordinary household-type iron works well if you set it at "Silk."

To mount a print with a hand iron, follow these simple steps:

1. Attach the tissue to the back of the print by touching the tissue quickly with the tip of the hot iron.
2. Trim the print and tissue to the required size.
3. Iron the mount to remove any moisture, which normally exists on porous material.
4. Protect the emulsion surface with brown paper.
5. Iron the print onto the mount.

When tacking a sheet of dry-mounting tissue to the reverse side of the print, start from the center and work out toward the corners. A tacking iron is the ideal implement. Then, trim the edges of the print so that the borders of the print will coincide exactly with the dimensions of the mounting tissue. Work on a flat surface, position the print as desired on the mount, and tack it in place; then, with a double overlay of wrapping paper or a thin sheet of cardboard to protect the print emulsion, mount the print. (The paper or cardboard should first be dried out in the press or else it will stick to the print.) If you use a dry-mounting press, apply the pressure to the mounted print for about 30 seconds and then release it. Allow enough time for the heat to penetrate the overlay, print, and tissue to effect a proper seal. If you use a thick cardboard for the cover sheet, heat for at least 45 seconds.

The temperature of the iron or press is important. If it is not hot enough, the adhesive will not melt; if the temperature is too high, the adhesion will be only temporary. Since excessive heat may also scorch the emulsion or melt resin-coated papers, test a household iron for approximate temperature by touching it lightly and quickly with a wet finger before beginning the mounting operation. If the moisture just sizzles, the temperature is about right.

When the mounted print is removed from the press, place it face down on a cool tabletop and allow it to cool in this position. This will minimize the usual tendency to curl.

Mounting with Cement. This material, such as Kodak rapid mounting cement, is made especially for mounting small prints rapidly and permanently to any clean, dry surface. The cement should be colorless, moisture-resistant, and nonstaining to prints, album pages, or mounts.

To mount pictures in an album, arrange the prints on the album page in their desired order. Take the first print and lay it face down on a clean sheet of paper. Squeeze the tube of cement gently and touch the nozzle to the back of the print, drawing a

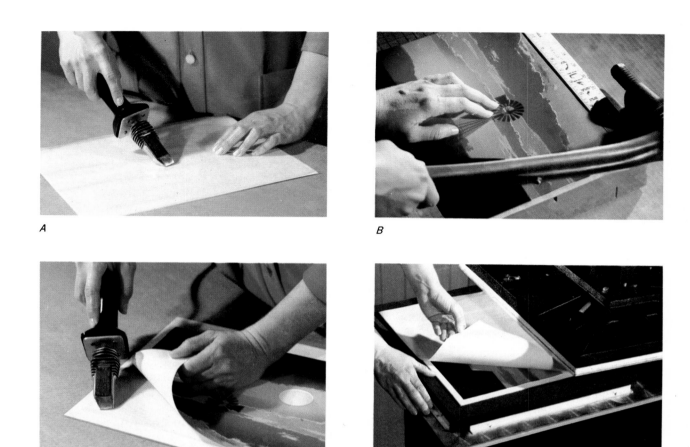

Dry mounting technique. (A) Tack the tissue to the reverse side of the print. (B) Trim the excess tissue together with the print border. (C) Position the print on the mount board and tack the tissue to the mount at the four corners. (D) Use an overlay of paper or thin cardboard to protect the print surface; preheat and dry the overlay in the press to prevent sticking.

line of cement around all four sides. Keep the line about ⅛ inch in from the edge of the print so that the cement will not squeeze out when you mount the print. Now, put a single drop in the center of the print and let it set for a few minutes. While you are waiting, you can be applying cement to the next print.

After the cement has set slightly, mount the print in the desired place by positioning it and applying moderate pressure. Rub the print from the center outward to avoid wrinkles. If excess cement should ooze from the edge of the print, remove it by wiping with ordinary cleansing tissue.

If necessary, you may be able to remove prints mounted in this way without damaging them. To do this, place a sheet of clean, heavy paper or cardboard over the print and heat with a warm (not hot!) electric iron for 10 or 15 seconds. Then, remove the cardboard and the print as quickly as possible. If too hot, an iron might scorch the print; if too cool, it will not melt the cement.

Mounting Water-Resistant Paper Prints. Prints made on water-resistant, resin-coated papers can be mounted on mounting board, tempered hardboard, or plywood with adhesives that have good adhesion properties, have no deleterious effect on image stability, and have resistance to blistering and wrinkling. There are many adhesives available. Among them are the following:

1. Cascorez GRC-7, Borden Chemical Company.
2. Special #67 GV Padding Compound, Harad Chemical Company.
3. Elmer's Glue-All, Borden Chemical Company.
4. Lamin-All, McDonald Photo Products Inc.
5. Glue-Fast, Glue-Fast Equipment Company Inc.
6. Kodak Rapid Mounting Cement, Eastman Kodak Company.
7. 3M Mounting Adhesive Sheets, 3M Company.

Rubber cement is also satisfactory for applications where easy removal of prints may be required. However, rubber cement will eventually stain fiber-base prints.

Adhesives that depend on solvent evaporation do not work well when resin-coated paper prints are mounted on nonporous surfaces. It is necessary to use a contact adhesive or double-faced adhesive tape. An alternative is to use a thermo-setting adhesive, which depends upon heat to set the adhesive that provides the final bond. Such an adhesive is Lamin-All (McDonald Photo Products Inc).

It is advisable to make tests and evaluate an adhesive according to a particular application.

Although it has been common practice to mount large, regular paper base prints by soaking them in water to facilitate handling, wet-mounting procedures are not applicable to water-resistant paper prints. Soaked resin-coated paper prints retain essentially the same stiffness as dry prints.

Special Mounting Situations

Mounting Prints onto Wood. Mounting prints onto wood is an unusual way to display them, as wood makes a sturdy, rich-looking mount. There is a great variety of wood finishes and shapes that are suitable for mounting pictures. For example, a picture mounted on distressed wood fits in well with an Early American décor. Driftwood and weather-beaten boards make good mounts.

If the wood you have selected has a smooth mounting surface, you can mount the print directly on the wood with a white glue, such as Elmer's Glue-All. Use a damp sponge or a paint roller to apply an even coating of adhesive to the back of the

Mounting prints on wood. (A) Peel resin coating from print. (B) Clip image face to cardboard; coat back and wood plaque with Lamin-All. (C) Plaque should be dry and back of print tacky when joined. (D) Remove cardboard; cover print surface with neoprene pad. (E) Clamp assembly between plywood; dry two hours.

A

B

C

D

E

Prints, Mounting

print. With a dry roller or a soft cloth, press the print to the mount. Work from the center of the print toward the edges to remove any air bubbles.

Mounting on Canvas. You can mount resin-coated prints—both color and black-and-white—onto canvas or even raised-grain pieces of planking. To do this successfully and so that the texture of the mount material is actually impressed into the print emulsion, a special procedure is necessary. The emulsion, the resin coating directly underneath the emulsion, and the paper base must be stripped off the bottom resin-coated layer.

It is easier to do this than it might sound: Use a sharp knife or razor blade and split one corner of the print down about 6 mm (¼ inch)—just enough so that you can get hold of the two portions with your fingers. Now, lay the print *emulsion-side down* on a clean table surface. Hold down the bottom split layer and carefully peel off the top layers. You must peel the uppermost part nearly 180 degrees back on itself—*do not pull it straight upwards or you'll tear it.* You will also tear the picture if you try to separate the layers with the emulsion side uppermost. There should be no problem with this operation; just don't rush it. Call for another pair of helping hands if you think you will need them for a large-size print. An especially good procedure for a large print is to pull the bottom layer of the print back about 51 mm (2 inches). Tape the top edge of the print face down on a table. Tape the resin film to a mailing tube and simply wind up the mailing tube, rolling and peeling the film straight back.

The back of the stripped image is then coated with a thermo-setting adhesive, such as Lamin-All, and mounted with a dry-mounting press. (Complete instructions on using Lamin-All to produce "instant ancestors" is available in the Lamin-All Canvas Kit available from photographic dealers.) The press should be fitted with a Teflon-coated neoprene pad to provide adequate mounting pressure over the irregular mount surface and to achieve the transfer of the mount texture to the face of the print.

• *See also:* ARCHIVAL PROCESSING; DECORATING WITH PHOTOGRAPHS; DRYING FILMS AND PRINTS; LAMINATING; LARGE COLOR PRINTS AND TRANSPARENCIES; MURALS; PAPERS, PHOTOGRAPHIC; PRINT FINISHING; RESIN-COATED PAPERS; RETOUCHING; SPOTTING PRINTS; WRITING ON FILMS AND PAPERS.

  Prisms

An optical prism is a solid block of transparent material (glass or plastic) used to modify the path of light by refraction, reflection, or dispersion. The surfaces of a prism are smooth planes. The operational planes—those that intercept the path of light—are not parallel to one another, but the sides or ends of a prism may be parallel. The simplest and most common prism is a triangular block of material.

The operational planes of refractive and dispersive prisms are completely transparent so that light can pass freely. One or more planes of a reflective prism may have a reflective coating, such as silver, or an opaque coating to prevent the entrance of light from an unwanted direction. If a light path within a given prism is greater than a certain critical angle, total reflection can occur from a completely transparent, uncoated surface.

Like plane mirrors, reflective prisms cannot form images, but they can change the path of image-forming light rays. By far the widest use of prisms in photography is to turn an image path through a right angle—for example, in an eye-level viewfinder—or to reverse an image laterally (left-right) or vertically.

Advantages

Although these same effects can be achieved with mirrors, prisms have a number of advantages.

Identical Alignment. The solid form of a prism insures that the planes will be held in precise relationships with a single mounting. In addition, identical prisms can be manufactured in great numbers with no significant variations. Mirrors must be individually mounted. Alignment depends on the original precision of the mountings and their security through long periods of use. Although identical mirrors can be manufactured with ease, the chances for identical alignment are reduced in geometric proportion to the number of surfaces and mountings required in a given piece of equipment.

No Double Images. Common rear-surface mirrors produce double images because reflection occurs at the front glass or plastic surface, as well as at the rear reflective-coated surface. This effect is especially noticeable at close optical distances,

Principles of Prisms

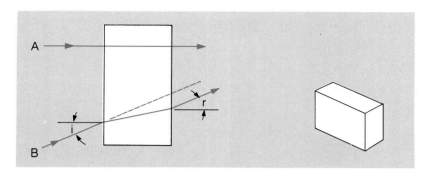

An optical flat is a transparent solid in which the plane surfaces are parallel. (A) A ray incident along the normal (the perpendicular) at a surface point passes straight through. (B) A ray incident at an angle to the normal is refracted as it enters and again as it leaves. The exit path is parallel to the straight-line projection of the entrance path, because the angle of incidence (i) at the first surface and the angle of refraction (r) at the second surface are equal. The angles are measured to the normal at the respective boundary points.

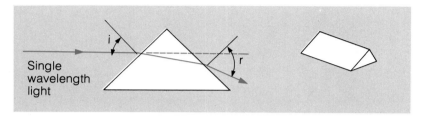

Single wavelength light

A prism is a transparent solid in which the planes intercepting the light rays are not parallel.

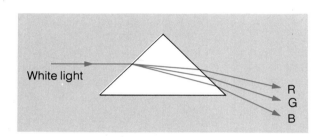

White light

R
G
B

(Left) Refraction in a prism differs with wavelength; it becomes continuously greater as the wavelength grows shorter. Thus, a ray of multiple-wavelength energy, such as white light, is dispersed into a spectrum of its constituent wavelengths. This effect is the basis of many wavelength-analysis devices, such as the spectrograph. Prisms made to disperse light into spectrums are usually made of flint glass, which provides a high degree of dispersion. (Left below) Although prism surfaces are transparent, some internal reflection occurs as a light ray passes from the more dense medium (prism) to the less dense medium (air). When the angle of incidence is less than a certain critical value, light is both transmitted and reflected internally. As the angle increases, progressively less light is transmitted and more is reflected. (Left bottom) At the critical angle and greater angles of internal incidence, reflection is total; no light is transmitted even though the surface does not have a reflective coating. The value of the critical angle depends upon the refractive index of the glass. The effect of total reflection from an uncoated surface holds true for single rays, as illustrated, and for narrow beam widths (up to about a 30-degree spread); therefore, such prisms can be used in conjunction with some long-focal-length lenses. Note that the angles of incidence and reflection are equal for any particular ray, as is the case with all smooth reflecting surfaces.

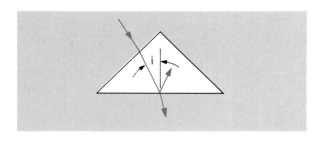

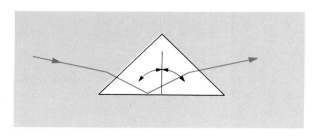

Principles of Prisms (continued)

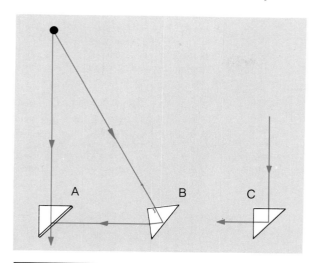

A basic optical rangefinder uses a prism with a semi-transparent ("one-way mirror") coating (A) to combine the directly viewed image with that reflected from the prism, with a totally reflective coating (B). This second prism pivots to aim at subjects at various distances; it is usually coupled to a camera-focusing mechanism or to a distance scale. When the two images coincide, the lens is focused on the subject, so the distance can be determined accurately. Long-distance rangefinders may use a movable prism oriented as at (C).

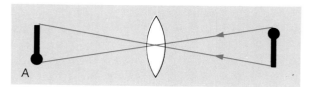

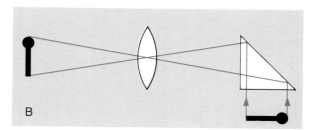

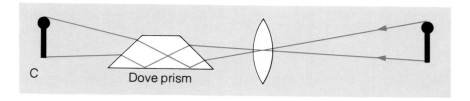

Dove prism

Reversing prisms are widely used in process cameras, copiers, and similar equipment to achieve lateral (left-right) reversal or vertical inversion of images. This is often necessary in graphic-arts applications to obtain intermediate images that can be photographed or contact-printed from the emulsion side. Although image orientation could be reversed by photographing or printing through the film base, sharpness would be reduced. (A) The lens forms a reversed/inverted image. (B) The prism, oriented for right-angle use in front of the lens, produces a mirror reversal, which the lens then restores to right-reading orientation. This arrangement is often used in copiers for compactness. A mirror used in this application would require a much larger reflecting surface. (C) The in-line prism behind the lens restores the image orientation while allowing the camera to be aimed directly at the subject. If internal angles of incidence for all rays in the image-forming beam from the lens do not exceed the critical angle, the reflective surface of the prism need not be coated. Such prisms are called dove prisms, and for geometric reasons, require light that diverges and converges only slightly; hence they can only be used with long-focal-length, narrow-angle lenses. In either arrangement, the prism can be oriented for lateral or vertical reversal, but not for both.

Principles of Prisms (continued)

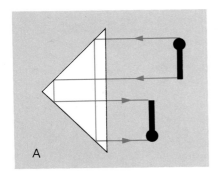

(A) The double reflection from the silvered right-angle surfaces of a Porro prism returns an inverted or reversed image in the direction of the subject. (B) Paired Porro prisms are used to achieve correctly oriented images in monoculars and binoculars.

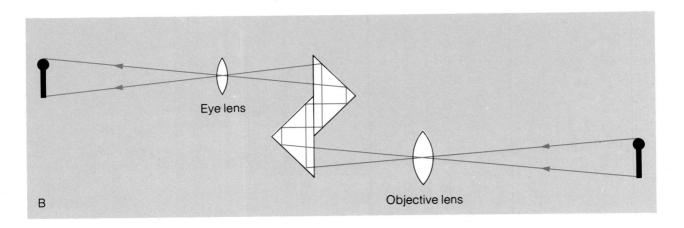

Eye lens

Objective lens

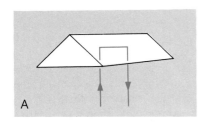

(A) The roof prism is named for its configuration and use above an image plane. Reflective surfaces are at 90-degree angles to one another to provide lateral reversal. (B) When placed at a 45-degree angle in a viewfinder above a reflex mirror and viewing/focusing screen, a roof prism provides a laterally correct, upside-down image.

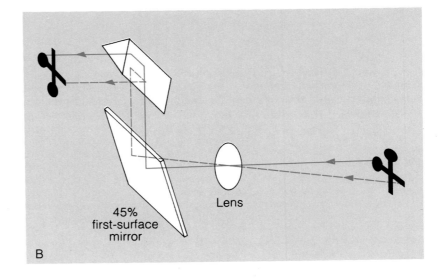

45% first-surface mirror

Lens

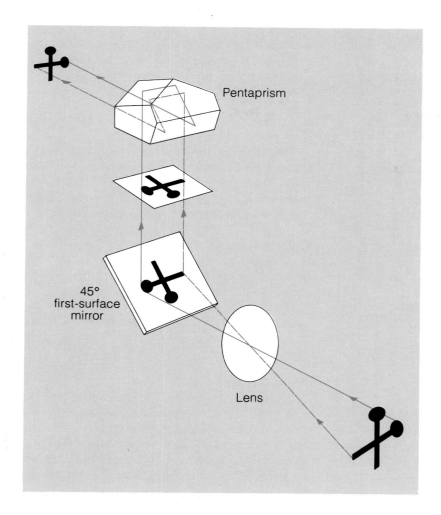

Pentaprism

45° first-surface mirror

Lens

Small-format, single-lens reflex cameras commonly use a pentaprism that triple-reflects the image to provide lateral correction while maintaining the uprightness of the image on the viewing/ focusing screen. Although shown separated here, the prism usually rests directly on the screen, which may be composed of microprisms for focusing. Only the lateral ray paths from the subject are shown for clarity.

which are common in photographic equipment. Prisms do not exhibit double-image reflection because no two operational surfaces are parallel (any first-surface reflection is in a non-interfering direction), and because the surfaces are much more widely separated than those of a mirror.

Protected Surface. Metallic and front-surface glass or plastic mirrors do not exhibit double reflection, but their delicate reflective surfaces are essentially unprotected. Many reflective prisms do not require surface coatings. However, when coatings are required, they are protected from the front by the whole thickness of the prism material, and can be given whatever protection is required from the rear without interfering with the prism's operation.

Space-Saver. Prisms usually occupy less space than mirrors that produce the same reflections of the same size light beam. For example, a simple 45-degree mirror that is used in front of a camera lens to provide a lateral reversal protrudes farther from the front of a camera and is wider than a prism that accomplishes the same function.

Disadvantages

The primary disadvantage of prisms, as compared with mirrors, is weight. A prism adds more to the weight of equipment, and the greater weight limits prisms to stationary functions or those that require only slight movement, such as the rotation required in a rangefinder. This is because the weight of a prism gives it considerable inertia. It is not practical, for example, to substitute a prism for the instant-return mirror of a single-lens reflex camera.

The accompanying illustrations explain the principles and the primary photographic applications of prisms. There are many other specialized prisms and prism applications:

1. A Nicol prism of calcite crystals polarizes light.
2. A rotating prism is used as a shutter in certain very high-speed motion-picture cameras.
3. Various stereoscopic devices use prisms to maintain separate image paths and correct image orientation.

• *See also:* BEAM SPLITTER; DIFFRACTION; DISPERSION; HIGH-SPEED PHOTOGRAPHY; MIRRORS; RANGEFINDER; WEDGE SPECTROGRAM.

Process Camera

Process cameras are special cameras used specifically for reproduction work in the graphic arts. Basically, they are heavy, rigid cameras with sufficient bellows extension for at least 1:1 reproduction with a standard lens; usually some additional extension is available for a moderate degree of enlargement.

Some smaller types of process cameras are made to operate in a vertical position, in order to take up less floor space. These are generally used in small offset shops, and have a limited range of enlargement or reduction.

Large horizontal process cameras are used in photoengraving, offset, map reproduction, and other work, and may be made as large as 20″ × 24″, and occasionally even larger. They fall into two classes: the gallery camera and the darkroom camera.

Gallery Camera

The gallery camera is self-contained and is used in a fully lighted room; it has a back that accepts sheet film or plate holders of various types, which can be loaded in the darkroom and carried out to the camera for use. The film holders have dark slides, similar to those used in sheet-film holders for view cameras.

Darkroom Camera

A darkroom process camera is built into the wall between the darkroom and the adjacent exposure room. All controls are at the rear, so the camera can be focused and operated from inside the darkroom. Such cameras have two hinged backs. One is the ground-glass back, usually hinged on the left side

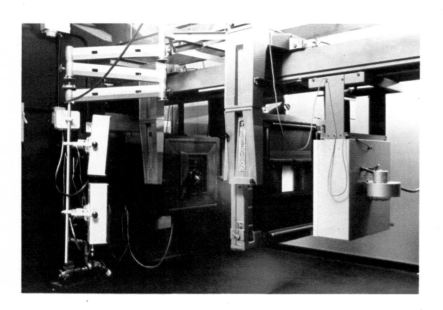

Process cameras are specialized cameras used in photoengraving, lithography, and map-making. Copy negatives from this type of camera are remarkably accurate in size and shape of the image. Process cameras resemble a view camera that is extremely large and lacks the view camera's system of swings and tilts.

of the camera back. The vacuum, film-holding back is hinged to the bottom of the camera back. After the camera is focused, the ground-glass back is swung out of the way, the film is loaded on the vacuum back, and the back is swung into position for the exposure. The film is then removed from the camera and processed in the same room. If tray development is being used, there may be a processing sink in the room with the camera back; for machine processing, the input end of the machine is in the darkroom and it delivers the finished film into the adjacent, fully lighted room if desired. For black-and-white work, red safelights are used in the darkroom, but for color processing the operator must work in the dark.

Process Lenses

Process cameras must be fitted with process lenses; generally these are of long focal length for covering the large-size films. For 8″ × 10″ film, the lens may have a focal length as long as 15 inches, and for 11″ × 14″ film, the usual focal length is 19 inches.

• *See also:* GRAPHIC ARTS PHOTOGRAPHY; PROCESS LENS.

Process Colors

Process colors are the basic ink colors used in photomechanical-reproduction processes to produce full-color images. They are the same subtractive colors—cyan, magenta, and yellow—that are used in the dye layers of photographic color films and papers; but common usage from the earliest days of color reproduction has established inaccurate names for two of them:

Common Ink Name	Actual Color
Process red	Magenta
Process blue	Cyan
Process yellow	Yellow
Black	Black

The preferred modern usage identifies the inks by their actual color names. These colors are used for four-color reproduction, the method by which the vast majority of full-color images are printed.

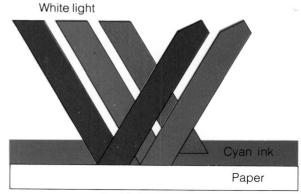

Cyan ink absorbs the red part of white light. Where cyan ink is printed, only green and blue light can reach the paper and be reflected from it, visually creating cyan.

Red light absorbed

(Above) If cyan ink were a perfect absorber, it would absorb only red light, and the paper would reflect blue and green light. But, cyan ink also absorbs some green and blue light. It acts as if it were contaminated with inks that absorb green and blue light (magenta and yellow ink, respectively).

(Below) This diagram represents the proportion of blue, green, and red light reflected by white paper on which cyan ink has been printed.

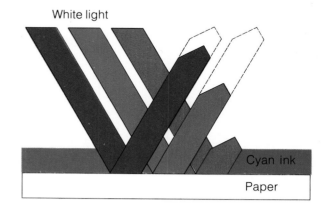

Because its major deficiency is to act as though it contains magenta ink, the correction for cyan ink is to reduce the magenta printer in those areas where cyan is also printing.

Magenta ink absorbs the green part of white light. Where magenta ink is printed, only red and blue light can reach the paper and be reflected from it, visually creating magenta.

Yellow ink absorbs the blue part of white light. Where yellow is printed, only red and green light can reach the paper and be reflected from it, visually creating yellow.

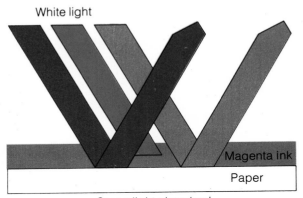

Green light absorbed

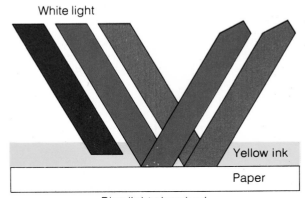

Blue light absorbed

(Above) If magenta ink were a perfect absorber, it would absorb only green light, and the paper would reflect blue and red light. But, magenta ink also absorbs some blue and red light. It acts as if it were contaminated with inks that absorb blue light (yellow ink) and red light (cyan ink).

(Above) If yellow ink were a perfect absorber, it would absorb only blue light and would reflect red and green light. But, it does absorb a small amount of green light, and therefore acts as if it were contaminated with a trace of the green-absorbing (magenta) ink.

(Below) This diagram represents the proportion of blue, green, and red light reflected by white paper on which magenta ink has been printed.

(Below) This diagram represents the proportion of blue, green, and red light reflected by white paper on which yellow ink has been printed.

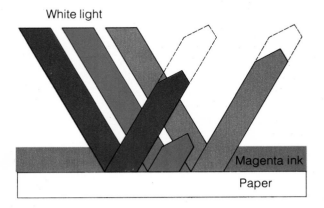

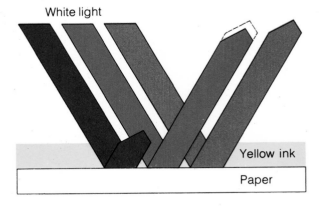

Because its major deficiency is to act as though it contains some yellow ink, the correction for magenta is to reduce the yellow printer in those areas where magenta ink is printing as well.

The correction for yellow is to reduce the magenta printer slightly in those areas where yellow ink is also printing. Often little or no yellow correction is required in full-color halftone reproduction.

Process Colors

Note that while photographic materials require only magenta, cyan, and yellow dyes, printing methods usually also require a black ink to increase shadow density and overall contrast in the image because of inherent deficiencies in the inks. In some cases, more than four inks may be used when extremely delicate or unusual color effects are desired, but the expense and the difficulties of precise control make this feasible only for very special applications. Excellent results are obtainable by the four-color method, as the illustrations in any high-quality magazine or book demonstrate.

Printing

Process color inks are printed in halftone dots to create a color mosaic. The eye cannot distinguish the dots at normal viewing distances and so blends their color effects. Since the inks act subtractively on white light, the effects are the same as in color photography:

Cyan + Yellow = Green
Cyan + Magenta = Blue
Magenta + Yellow = Red

Intermediate colors are produced by printing larger dots and thus more of one process color than another. Tints are produced by printing small color dots so that the white paper is also seen and blended into the total effect. Shades are produced by printing large color dots plus black dots to cover the white paper. Although the combination of all three process colors produces a dark brownish-gray, black ink produces a stronger, "cleaner" effect where pure black is required.

Each ink is printed from a separate halftone plate, prepared by means of color-separation photography. The methods are explained more fully in other articles listed in the cross-references. As the accompanying illustrations show, certain corrections must usually be made in the printing plates, because process color inks do not have perfect absorption-reflection characteristics.

• *See also:* Color Films; Color Separation Photography; Color Theory; Graphic Arts Photography; Halftone; Photomechanical Reproduction Preparing Photographs for; Screened Negatives and Prints.

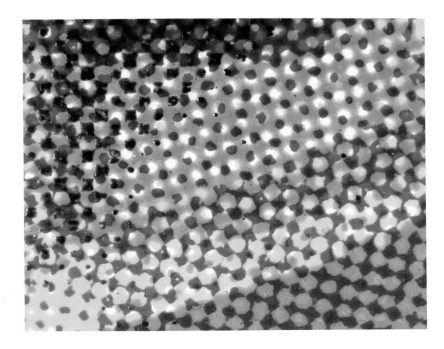

As this magnified detail shows, a full-color halftone reproduction is actually a mosaic of colored dots. Cyan, magenta, yellow, and black inks are printed from separate plates. Dot size determines how much of each ink is printed in a given area. The subtractive color effects of adjacent dots are blended by the eye; the relative dot sizes determine what composite color is actually seen.

Process Control

Process control describes the methods for preparing process chemicals, testing their activity, monitoring their current condition, and diagnosing and correcting variations. Problems can be prevented before they occur by carefully following recommendations given for mixing and storing chemicals and by adhering closely to recommended process specifications. Processing solutions can be tested to evaluate their effectiveness and to determine when they should be replaced. Daily records, continuously kept, help locate processing troubles when they occur and help determine process replenishment rates. Process control strips monitor developer activity when they are run with regular work, and the densities are measured, plotted, and compared with standard references.

Preventing Troubles Before They Occur

Chemical Mixing. One of the most important requirements in preventing unsatisfactory results during processing is the careful and correct mixing of the photographic chemicals used in the process. It is often difficult to diagnose the cause of poor-quality work when improper mixing is to blame, and the discarding of incorrectly mixed solutions increases chemical costs and cuts down on production.

Mixing, storage, and processing equipment should be made of proper materials. Any equipment that comes in contact with processing solutions must be made of glass, hard rubber, polyethylene, hard PVC, enameled steel, stainless steel, or other chemically inert materials. This includes not-so-obvious equipment such as plumbing, mixing impellers, and even the cores of filter cartridges. Do not allow tin, copper, iron, brass, or their alloys to come in contact with developers or developer replenishers. These materials can cause chemical fog, rapid oxidation, or contamination of the solution. Also, do not allow aluminum, zinc, or galvanized iron to come in contact with developers or fixers.

NOTE: During the mixing and use of photographic processing chemicals, be sure to observe all precautionary information on chemical containers and in instructions.

Storage of Solutions. Follow storage and capacity recommendations packaged with chemicals. Do not use chemicals that have been stored longer than recommended. Discard unreplenished solutions when their recommended capacity has been reached.

Do not store solutions at extremely high or low temperatures. All solutions should be stored at close-to-normal room temperature, between 18 and 27 C (65 and 80 F). Storing solutions, particularly developer, at elevated temperatures can produce rapid oxidation, resulting in loss of activity and a tendency to cause stains on the film. Storage at too low a temperature can cause some solutions to crystallize, and the crystals may not redissolve, even with heating and stirring.

Following Processing Recommendations. During the manufacture of films and papers, sophisticated control procedures are used for monitoring production and for establishing processing recommendations. These recommended process conditions should be followed closely to produce negatives having optimum photographic and physical characteristics, including proper densities, contrast (density differences), and speed, and having satisfactory keeping characteristics after processing.

Testing of Processing Solutions

Developer. The main function of the developer is to convert exposed silver halide crystals in the film emulsion into a silver image or a color dye image. Developer activity is usually "tested" by processing and evaluating film control strips, as described later in this article.

Black-and-White Processes. Black-and-white processing is relatively simple, and the stop and fixing baths can be monitored with comparatively easy tests. To be effective, the stop bath should have an acidity value between pH 4.0 and 5.0 (except for a freshly made bath, which will have a value of approximately 3.0). The pH can be tested with commercially available test papers. Testing solutions are also available to determine the amount of hypo left in films after washing.

Color Processes. Color processes are more complex, usually involving more steps and processing solutions. Large processing facilities with chemical labs analyze tank and replenisher solutions at regular intervals to monitor mixing and replenishment. Even small labs can use basic analytical tools to check mixing and working solution conditions. Specific-gravity measurement using a hydrometer is a quick way of checking the mixing procedure when packaged mixes are used. Measurement of the pH of tank solutions not only tells their condition, but permits a remedy for partially used developer. Often, the efficiency of developer can be restored by adjusting the pH to the normal value. Details of mechanical and chemical specifications and adjustments are usually available from the manufacturer of the film or chemical.

Physical Examination. If physical examination of the films after washing shows dirt or scum that was not present before washing, the wash tanks should be drained and cleaned. Drain wash tanks whenever they are not being used (overnight, weekends, or longer).

Some processes recommend the use of a wetting agent to promote uniform draining of the film after washing and to minimize drying marks. If scum and dirt are found on the film, replace the wetting solution more often than usual, taking care to dilute it according to package directions.

Keeping Daily Records of Process Conditions

An accurate daily record should be kept of conditions affecting the process, including developer temperature, amount of film processed, volume of replenisher added, and identification numbers of control strips processed at particular times.

Use of commercially available forms will help you establish and maintain correct replenishment rates, in addition to providing a continuous check of the process so that conditions that influence processing quality can be recorded. When control strips indicate that the process is out of control, several potential causes can be eliminated by checking the form, helping you to diagnose the real source of trouble more quickly. In addition, the use of record forms helps to remind production workers of the need for process control and provides an incentive to follow recommended procedures carefully.

Monitoring the Process with Control Strips

Development is the most critical stage of the photographic process. While control strips may serve as indicators of certain problems in other solu-

tions, their primary function is to monitor the activity of the developer. Other processing solutions must be tested according to manufacturers' directions.

Control Strips. Process control strips consist of precisely controlled exposures made on strips cut from a uniform piece of sensitized material. Although they vary in format, control strips usually have a series of gray patches differing in density by a fixed amount. These patches are called "steps," and they are usually identified by numbers. Process monitoring relies primarily on the measurement of densities of the gray patches. These gray patches represent the subject tones in pictures. It has been found that if key tones are controlled by monitoring, the process can be adequately controlled.

Since the details of the monitoring procedure change somewhat with each of the many processes, the manufacturer's instructions are needed. Monitoring manuals describe the process, the specific control strip to be used, the steps to be read, the calculation of reference values and control values, specific plot patterns, and plot pattern interpretation.

Reference Strips. A few control strips from each batch are processed by the manufacturer in a near-standard process, and one of the processed strips is included with each package of exposed but unprocessed control strips. The processed strips, called reference strips, convey to the processor a description of the result considered acceptable by the manufacturer for the process in question. To convey this message accurately, it would be necessary to have sensitized material, exposing conditions, and a process, all without variability. This is a practical impossibility, but as long as the sources and significances of the variables are known and understood, perfection is not necessary. In order to adjust for known, small variations in some processes, the relationship of each process used for processing reference strips to the desired standard level is measured. The deviations from the desired level are supplied as correction factors with each batch of control strips. The processing laboratory adjusts its density readings of the reference strip by using the correction factors, thus obtaining initial reference values for a package of control strips.

Processing Control Strips in Various Equipment. Control strips should be processed under the same conditions as regular work, using consistent

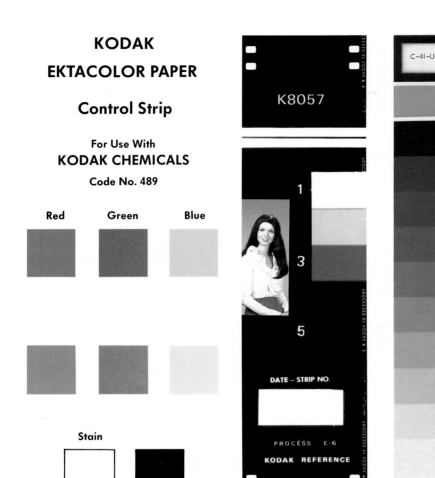

KODAK EKTACOLOR PAPER

Control Strip

For Use With
KODAK CHEMICALS
Code No. 489

Red   Green   Blue

Stain

K8057

1

3

5

DATE – STRIP NO.

PROCESS   E-6

KODAK REFERENCE

C-41-U-7097

Control strips from each batch are processed by the manufacturer in a near-standard process and included with each package of control strips. (Left) Ektacolor paper control strip. (Center) Standard negative with graduated gray patches or "steps." (Right) Reference positive for reversal transparencies.

handling and processing procedures so that all control strips receive the same treatment. For instance, when processing racks or hangers are used, every control strip should be processed in the same position on the rack or hanger.

Frequency of Processing Control Strips. When starting up the process, or after an extended period of time without processing, process and evaluate a control strip before processing any production work. Process and evaluate one strip at the beginning, one at the middle, and one at the end of a long work period. By processing a strip near the end of the work period and immediately making any required corrections to the process, you can avoid delays in processing regular work at the beginning of the next work period. Process and evaluate a control strip

whenever you suspect trouble in the process, after any correction or change has been made to the process, and when any fresh solution is put into the process.

Identification of Control Strips. Control strips should be numbered consecutively for identification. If more than one process is being monitored, control strips used for monitoring one process can be identified starting with A-1 and A-2, and strips used for a second process can be identified B-1, B-2, and so forth.

Immediately after each control strip has been processed and dried, it should be identified with the date and hour of processing and with the control strip identification number. Pressure-sensitive labels are useful for identifying control strips. Be sure to place the label near the end of the control strip, not in the area to be used for density readings.

• *See also:* ARCHIVAL PROCESSING; DENSITOMETRY; DEVELOPERS AND DEVELOPING; DEVELOPMENT; MIXING PHOTOGRAPHIC SOLUTIONS; REPLENISHMENT; STORAGE OF SENSITIZED MATERIALS AND PROCESSING SOLUTIONS; TESTING.

Processing for Permanence

The degree of permanence that a photographic image should possess depends on its intended use. A picture for immediate test or identification purposes, or one for the paste-up from which magazine or newspaper printing plates are made, is a temporary, discardable image. It can be processed for short life by activation-stabilization or similar procedures. However, most photographs must be processed for moderate to long-term permanence—from 5 to 50 years.

The greatest degree of permanence is generally known as archival permanence, although the ANSI standards do not use this term. An archival image is generally considered to be one in which the quality of the image remains unchanged for as long as the physical life of the base material; in any case at least 100 years, if it is stored and displayed properly. Historical documents, works of art, portraits, and many other kinds of photographs should be made for archival permanence. In many cases the negative is the most important image to preserve because prints can be taken from it as required. But with an interpretive print that is valued as a work of art, or with older prints for which negatives no longer exist, it is the print image that must be preserved.

When photographic permanence is required, there are three factors to be considered:

1. Choice of material that can be made to be permanent.
2. Processing—probably the major factor in permanence.
3. Subsequent storage and handling of the processed image.

Materials

Some black-and white photographic materials can be made archivally permanent in terms of the definition given earlier; at the present time, most color materials cannot be made permanent. Although the images in the emulsion are most susceptible to damage and deterioration, the base material must be considered with regard to black-and-white negatives and prints.

Black-and-White Materials. Glass and metal are free of contamination, are nonabsorptive, and possess maximum dimensional stability. However, the fragility of glass and the need to protect metal from corrosion are drawbacks, as is the weight of these materials and, in some applications, their inflexibility. Consequently, glass and metal are commonly used as base materials only for specialized scientific and industrial purposes.

The most common, modern plastic film-base materials offer light weight and flexibility—distinct necessities for roll-film cameras. However, these materials can be crimped, gouged, scratched, or torn by improper handling. It is obvious that gelatin emulsions are even more susceptible to this kind of damage than the bases they are coated on. Polyester and similar plastic-base materials are physically superior to cellulose triacetate, in terms of dimensional stability, low absorption, and resistance to physical damage; however, with proper handling and storage, both types of film base can be considered permanent.

Fiber-base paper-print materials can be washed clean of chemical contamination, if processing has not been improperly prolonged and if fresh solutions have been used; however, they are highly absorptive and thus open to contamination at all times. They are also subject to dimensional change both during processing and thereafter, in response to variations in humidity. In fact, they can become permanently distorted under the worst conditions. They are also easily bent, folded, cracked, and torn. In spite of these deficiencies, there are thousands upon thousands of paper prints that have been preserved in perfect condition without unreasonable effort.

Papers with water-resistant or resin coatings absorb virtually no moisture (except at the very edges); they have relatively high dimensional stability and resistance to tearing. However, their long-term keeping characteristics are unknown; some materials have deteriorated rapidly under ultraviolet radiation (as from sunlight), others have shown little or no change.

At the present time, it is not known whether it is possible to obtain archival permanence with these materials; moderate-term permanence varies among different products. It is believed that prints made on water-resistant paper base may last as long as prints made on conventional paper base, if given proper dark storage.

Color Materials. The same considerations of base-material characteristics apply to color materials, but they are of secondary importance. The primary cause of impermanence in color materials is the nature of the dyes that form the image. All dyes are subject to fading at unequal and variable rates. Some color images have lasted 40 or more years with little or no perceptible change; others have faded noticeably in less than 2 years, even when stored in darkness under optimum temperature and humidity conditions. It is generally agreed that the only way a color image can be made archivally permanent is by means of color separation negatives made on black-and-white materials that can be made archivally permanent, and that can be used to make a new image on fresh color materials whenever required. (*See:* COLOR SEPARATION PHOTOGRAPHY.) Color negatives can be expected to last for years if they are sealed in waterproof containers and stored in a freezer at −18 C (0 F), or lower.

Processing

Proper processing is essential for photographic permanence. The best-quality materials and perfect storage conditions are worthless if the image carries the cause of its eventual destruction within itself. Images are primarily destroyed by chemical attack. In processing, all light-sensitive substances must either be reduced to an insensitive state (silver) or removed, and all traces of processing chemicals must be removed as well. Thus, fixation and washing are the most critical processing procedures.

Solutions must be properly prepared so that unwanted chemical compounds that would affect the image are not formed, and so that the desired compounds are at the proper strength to do their jobs effectively. Improper fixation is probably the single most important cause of the eventual deterioration of photographic prints; too little fixing leaves light-sensitive compounds in the emulsion; using exhausted fixer leaves compounds in the paper base that cannot be washed out.

The processed silver image of negatives and prints is also susceptible to attack by atmospheric contaminants at any time. Treating the image in a dilute selenium toner, or a gold chloride protective solution, increases protection by coating the silver with a more nearly inert metal or metallic salt. The procedures for achieving optimum permanence of silver images are given in the article ARCHIVAL PROCESSING.

Storage and Handling

Processed images must be protected from attack by:

> Contaminants in the storage materials (sleeves, envelopes, cabinets, and so forth).
> Atmospheric pollutants.
> Excessive temperature and humidity.

The effects of such attacks are: fading, staining or discoloration, spotting, and growth of fungus. (*See:* FILING AND STORING NEGATIVES, PRINTS, AND TRANSPARENCIES; FUNGUS ON FILMS.)

Anyone concerned with the permanence of photographs should, as a matter of course, handle them with extreme care to prevent damage by dust, dirt, grease, moisture, and physical carelessness. It is also necessary to establish strict handling standards for those who are less informed about the problems and probable consequences.

Two important additional factors that can significantly affect permanence are the display and viewing of photographs. Displayed materials must be protected from excessive exposure to the ultraviolet content and the heat of direct and reflected sunlight; projected materials must be protected from the heat and infrared radiation of the light source. Color images are rapidly affected by these factors. The general rule for slides or transparencies is that they should be projected as infrequently as possible, and then for no more than 15 seconds at a time. Although color images cannot be considered permanent, their useful lives can be significantly extended by careful handling and viewing.

• *See also:* ARCHIVAL PROCESSING; COLOR SEPARATION PHOTOGRAPHY; FILING AND STORING NEGATIVES, PRINTS, AND TRANSPARENCIES; FIXERS AND FIXING; FUNGUS ON FILM; STORAGE OF SENSITIZED MATERIALS AND PROCESSING SOLUTIONS; WASHING.

Processing Long Rolls

Long rolls of negative films (black-and-white and color) of various widths can be processed in special spiral reels, such as the Honeywell Nikor reel or the Kindermann reel. An assortment of reel-and-tank combinations, film loaders, and other accessories is available for processing.

Loading

Extreme care must be exercised in loading the reel. As with standard reels for roll films of normal length, it is advisable to become familiar with the loading technique by using old film in full room light before attempting to load good exposure film in the dark. The manufacturer's recommendations for loading should be read carefully. Sometimes undue pressure on the film in the loading chute may cause plus or minus density streaks or lines on the film. Watch for these effects when viewing the results on a trial process. Secure the end of the film with a clip, a rubber band, or waterproof tape to prevent the film from unwinding during processing.

Agitation Procedure

Manual agitation, rather than nitrogen agitation, is recommended for tank processing of roll films in spiral reels. Too little agitation during development will cause mottle and uneven development. Too much pumping of the reel in and out of the developer can produce streaks across the film at the reel spokes or film sprockets. The following agitation procedure provides a compromise that minimizes these undesirable effects.

1. Lower the reel into the developer, giving it a vigorous turning motion sufficient to cause the reel to rotate one-half to one revolution in the developer.
2. Raise and lower the reel approximately ½ inch (keeping the reel in the solution) for the first 15 seconds of the development time, tapping it against the bottom of the tank to release air bubbles from the film.
3. Agitate once each minute by lifting the reel out of the solution, tilting it 30 de-

grees to drain for 5 to 10 seconds, and immersing it again with a vigorous turning motion sufficient to cause the reel to rotate one-half to one revolution in the developer. Alternate the direction of rotation each minute.
4. Just before the end of the development time, drain the reel for 15 seconds and proceed to the next step.

Agitation in the other processing solutions should be done in the same manner.

Processing

Develop black-and-white films for the times given in the film instruction sheets for the particular developer-and-temperature combination. For color films, follow the procedure given in the instruction sheet for the processing chemicals.

Drying

Treat black-and-white film in a solution of wetting agent, such as Kodak Photo-Flo, after washing.

NOTE: Most color-film processes finish with a stabilizer that contains a wetting agent. In such cases, no wetting agent is recommended. The drying operation should be carried out in a dust-free place. In most cases, the film can be dried on the reel.

A drying motor attachment is available from Honeywell Photographic. The motor will rotate the reel on the loading stand while an electric fan provides circulation of air around the reel. Dryers can also be constructed from heating coils and blower units. The temperature of the drying air that strikes the film should not exceed 35 C (95 F).

Cleaning Processing Reels

The processing reels should be cleaned periodically to remove dried gelatin:

1. Place the reels in a clean porcelain, glass, plastic, or hard-rubber container.
2. Fill the container with a 5 percent solution of sodium hypochlorite (household bleach).
3. Soak the reels in this solution for 15 to 20 minutes at room temperature with

periodic agitation. Brush lightly with a bristle brush if gelatin particles adhere to the reels.

4. Wash the reels thoroughly with water and allow them to dry.

Processing Black-and-White Long Rolls in Roller-Transport Processors

Black-and-white film in long rolls can be conveniently processed in roller-transport-type processors such as the Kodak Versamat film processor, model 11C-M. This method provides consistent, uniform processing of all portions of the long rolls, freedom from bonding, and freedom from significant density and contrast variations from the ends of the rolls to the center.

Kodak Versaflo chemicals, or similar chemicals produced by other manufacturers, are used for normal-contrast, continuous-tone negative materials. Special spindles are available to feed the film automatically into the processor and to take up the dry film on a roll as it leaves the processor.

The roller-transport method is generally used when the quantity of long rolls is considerable.

Processing Color Long Rolls in Continuous Processors

Most color film is processed in continuous processors. Short camera-length rolls are spliced together to make long rolls that feed through the various tanks on rollers. If long rolls are to be processed, they are run through the processor in the same way.

Water jackets with thermostatically controlled water keep the solutions at the required temperature. Solutions are automatically replenished from replenisher tanks placed higher than the solution levels in processing tanks. Quality is monitored by running process control strips at regular intervals, measuring the color densities on the processed strips, and plotting the values on continuous graphs.
See: COLOR FILM PROCESSING; PROCESSORS.

Reel-to-Reel Processing with Rewind Equipment

Long rolls of black-and-white aerial film are sometimes processed in rewind equipment. The film rolls on itself as it is wound on a flanged reel. A rewind tank holds the supply reel, solutions, and a take-up reel.

This rapid color processor is designed to process prints of up to 30″ × 40″ and film as large as 20″ × 24″. While equipment that handles material of this size should suffice in most commercial darkrooms, larger processors are also available for longer rolls.

The film is prewet by putting water in the tank and winding the film from the supply reel to the take-up reel through the water. The supply reel is kept dry while the film is being fed from it to the take-up reel.

After the film is all on the take-up reel, both reels are placed underwater, and the film is rewound onto the supply reel through the water. In other words, the film makes two passes through the water.

The reels are then removed from the tank and drained. The water is replaced with developer. The film goes back and forth between the reels during development. The normal stop and fix steps use the same procedure. For the wash step, the water is run through the tank while the film is run through the wash water from reel to reel. The film is then removed from the reels for drying.

• *See also:* DEVELOPERS AND DEVELOPING; DRYING FILMS AND PRINTS.

Process Lens

A process lens is a lens made for reproduction work usually in a process camera, although process lenses are sometimes used in enlargers for critical work.

The essential attributes of process lenses are a very flat field, a very low degree of distortion, high resolution, and apochromatic color correction. Especially if they are to be used for color separation work, lenses must produce images through red, green, and blue filters that are exactly the same size, otherwise it will be impossible to register the printing plates for the three colors.

Because a symmetrical lens is inherently free from distortion and lateral chromatic aberration when used at small ratios in the vicinity of 1:1, most process lenses are of symmetrical or near symmetrical construction. For critical correction of astigmatism (necessary for high resolving power) and for a perfectly flat field, these lenses are made of very modest apertures; they are seldom faster than $f/9$, and are usually stopped down to the $f/22$ to $f/64$ range in use.

The high degree of correction for lateral and longitudinal aberration is necessary. Ordinary achromats are not good enough for reproduction work; they bring two of the three primary colors to a single focus, but the third is noticeably out of focus. Apochromatic lenses are always used for color process work. These may be specifically corrected for three colors by the use of three different types of glass, or they may be corrected in the normal way by the use of special glass pairs that eliminate the secondary spectrum in other ways. Such lenses, whichever type of correction is used, are distinguished by the use of the word "Apo" in the name, such as Apo-Artar, Apo-Ektar, and Apo-Tessar.

The diaphragms and diaphragm markings are special on process lenses because they are used just for close-distance photography. Older style process lenses used waterhouse stops for diaphragms—these were inserted in a slot in the side of the lens barrel. In addition to round apertures, specially shaped apertures were made for certain halftone screen processes. Most modern process lenses have many-leaved diaphragms that make nearly perfectly circular aperture openings. Since f-numbers are accurate only for normal and long-distance photography, process lenses have special markings. The markings may indicate the effective numerical diameter of the aperture in millimetres, or in fractions or decimals of an inch. Many are marked in aperture ratios, which give the equivalent setting for an f-number for each magnification (a percent size) the lens is likely to be used.

Flare is a problem in making graphic arts reproductions; the process lens surfaces are coated to minimize lens surface reflections. The lens surfaces must be kept clean, and the light from the copy lights must not be allowed to fall directly on the lens. Special filter adapters are usually attached to the front of a process lens to hold the special square PM gelatin filters used to make masks and separation negatives for color reproduction.

• *See also:* GRAPHIC ARTS PHOTOGRAPHY; PROCESS CAMERA.

Processors

Photographic processors are either machines or automatic systems used in place of manual processing in order to handle a greater volume of material in less time and with more consistent results. Processors suitable for small darkrooms or low-volume applications are usually drums, tubes, or roller-transport devices such as stabilization processors.

More sophisticated processors can be used to achieve both efficiency and economy wherever high-volume output is required or large-sized materials are handled. These include:

Film processing and printing labs;
Busy illustrative and portrait photo studios;
Industrial and corporate photo departments;
Reprographic concerns handling architectural or engineering drawings and similar originals;
Surveying, mapping, and reconnaissance-surveillance organizations;
Public-relations and other concerns with a need to produce or distribute multiple copies of photographs.

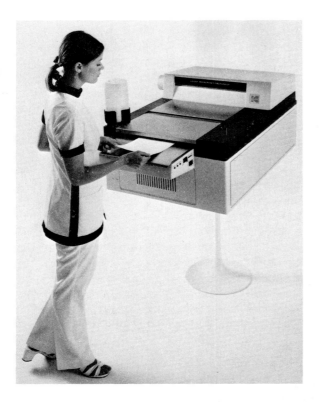

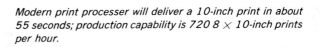

Modern print processer will deliver a 10-inch print in about 55 seconds; production capability is 720 8 × 10-inch prints per hour.

Processor Operation

High-volume processors automatically control temperature, timing, and cycling throughout the process. The most modern and complex processors are computer-controlled by stored programs; other control methods include magnetic tape, punched card, disk or tape, and electromechanical timer-thermostat devices.

The primary task of an operator is to start and stop the processor, feed material in, and remove the finished results. Operating personnel may also monitor results by making periodic checks and tests at various processing stages, and perhaps adjust processor operation accordingly. (*See:* PROCESS CONTROL.)

Some relatively low-volume, moderate-speed processors operate by holding the material stationary and changing solutions around it, either by repeatedly filling and emptying the processing chamber, or by spraying or flowing the solutions over the material. Increased volume and speed are achieved by moving the material from solution to solution. Print processors that handle sheet materials com-

monly use either roller-transport systems or baskets connected to belts or chains; mesh dividers keep prints separated in each basket. Sheet-film processors may use roller transport; or films may be secured by spring clips in holders that are moved in batches in a supporting rack. Even short roll films may be handled in this manner.

Speed and Efficiency

By far the greatest speed and efficiency is achieved by processing materials in continuous lengths. Commercial labs utilize print paper in rolls up to several hundred feet long; short rolls may be spliced together to form greater lengths. Similarly, roll and cartridge-load films are spliced into continuous lengths. Motion-picture film is handled in the same way. A leader strip is used to pull the material through the various solution chambers and washing and drying stations. The material is moved at a constant speed; the size of a chamber and the length of the path through it—which is established by multiple series of support rollers—determine how long the material remains in each solution. As the dry processed material emerges from the processor and moves past an inspection station, associated equipment may automatically trim, mount, sort, and even package the results.

Since the function of a processor is to give efficient, uniform processing, material must be properly exposed for optimum results. Some color-film processors permit adjusting the first development time to compensate for films exposed at greater than normal speed ratings. (*See:* PUSH PROCESSING.) However, most materials that require special treatment must be separated out for manual processing.

The economies in staff, materials, and time that may result from using a processor are not always readily apparent. Consultation with a manufacturer's technical or sales representative can be extremely valuable in deciding whether—or when—to invest in automatic processing equipment.

• *See also:* DRUM AND TUBE PROCESSING; PROCESS CONTROL; PUSH PROCESSING; RAPID PROCESSING; STABILIZATION PROCESS.

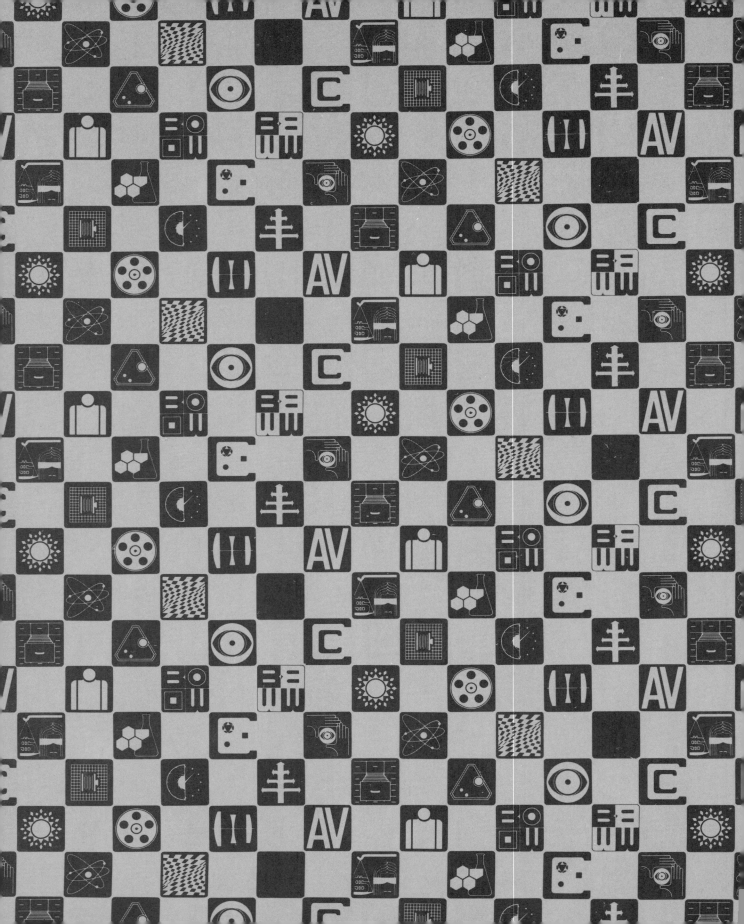